Israel: Utopia Incorporated

Uri Davis

To my mentor Stanley Diamond
and my patrons
Anthony Wilson
Adam Curle
and my mother Blanka.

Israel: Utopia Incorporated

A study of Class, State, and corporate kin control.

Uri Davis

Zed Press Ltd., 57 Caledonian Road, London N1 9DN.

Israel: Utopia Incorporated was first published
by Zed Press, 57 Caledonian Road, London, N.1.
in September 1977.

ISBN Hb 0 905 762 126
     Pb 0 905 762 134

Printed by Wheaton & Co., Exeter

Typeset by Lyn Caldwell

Designed by An Dekker, Graphic Workshop

CONTENTS

I am grateful to the Institute of World Order (New York), the Richardson Institute for Conflict and Peace Research and the Gillett Fund (London) for making available to me grants which enabled me to devote portions of 1973 to preliminary writing of this study; to Professor Adam Curle and the School of Peace Studies at the University of Bradford for generously offering departmental facilities and secretarial assistance to aid me in the completion of this work.

I am indebted to Stanley Diamond for insights into the historicity of primitive customary stateless societies, and into the reality of the East European Jewish Shtetle, to Israel Shahak for insights into the Orthodox Jewish *Halachic* law, and to Roger van Zwanenberg, my publisher, for his editorial comments.

The re-editing of the work for publication has been carried out in the framework of my two year leave of absence from the School of Peace Studies to undertake research work in Israel. My thanks to the University of Bradford and the Cadbury Trust for the research grant they have generously made available to me.

Uri Davis
Kefar Shmaryahu
Winter, 1976

INTRODUCTION

The purpose of this small book is to introduce the reader to aspects of Zionism and its colonial efforts in Palestine and of the subsequent emergence and consolidation of the state of Israel as a Jewish state which are not readily available in historical and political analyses published hitherto.

This is largely an anthropological study. It is therefore primarily concerned with the problem of origins. It aims to give an insight into the origins of the Zionist endeavour as an attempted solution to the Jewish problem. Key institutions (e.g., the Israeli-Jewish kibbutz) and key chapters in Zionist and Israeli history (e.g., the status of the Middle Eastern and North African Oriental-Jew within the Israeli-Jewish society) can only be misunderstood unless related to the original impulse of the Zionist movement. It is to the Zionist aspiration of putting forward a solution, *the* solution, to the Jewish problem and to the original Zionist response to the destruction of the customary traditional Jewish way of life in Central and East Europe (the Jewish Shtetle) that our attention will, therefore, be initially directed.

All parties of the Zionist movement — labour Zionism, Religious Zionism and Revisionism — share, above and beyond very real differences of policy and political ideology, a common goal which links them all as members, often conflicting members, of the movement. This goal is the solution of the Jewish problem by way of establishing and consolidating in Palestine a Jewish state *for* Jewish people. This formulation is in no way arbitrary. Not only did it reflect the reality of the Jewish situation and of the Zionist movement as a harassed minority movement within the world Jewish context at the turn of the century, but it equally reflects the reality of the Zionist endeavour throughout the past seventy years.

It was evident both to the veteran Zionist generations, as well as to their successors, that if a Jewish state as a solution to the Jewish problem was feasible at all, it could only be forged by a dedicated minority establishing the civil administration, state machinery and political sovereignty *for* the Jewish masses. Thus Jewish communities outside Israel would by virtue of the demonstrated success of the effort on the one hand, and by the validity of the Zionist analysis and prediction that Jewish communities have no lasting place within non-Jewish societies on the other, be moved to seek refuge and salvation in the state designated specifically for this particular purpose.

As we shall see below, this has resulted, and unavoidably so, in the monopolization of the state power and the state machinery once established and internationally recognized, by the East European veteran generation, who had literally established the state *ex nihilo*.

Over a period of less than 45 years (1905-1948) the administrative underpinnings for a Jewish state were laid out following patterns that have been rather standard in all colonial ventures. There was one major difference however which has coloured the Zionist endeavour and which makes it in many respects unique. The Zionist movement did not originally predicate its efforts on colonization of the native land by way of exploitation, but rather, systematically followed the pattern of colonization by way of dispossession.

It is in this context that the power strongholds of the incipient Jewish state were established, namely: Jewish metropolitan centres along the seaboard, the network of collective kibbutzim along the frontiers of the Zionist colonized areas, the Jewish Agency, particularly its Jewish labour administration, the Histadrut which served as a political administrative bureaucracy and the *Haganah*, its military arm.

As noted above, the specific pattern of the Zionist colonial initiative in Palestine and its success in establishing the Jewish state of Israel as an attempted solution to the Jewish problem *ex nihilo* has resulted in the monopolization of state power and the state machinery by the East European veteran generation. This led to the emergence, within the span of a single generation, of a number of dominant lineages out of whose corporate and interlocking kin and pseudo-kin network the Israeli-Jewish ruling elite is almost invariably recruited.

In examining the Israeli-Jewish ruling elite and the utilization of corporate kinship and kinship metaphor as a criterion of recruitment into this elite we shall focus on a number of key families. By tracing the political, economic and military history of their individual members, we hope to offer a concrete insight into the history of the Zionist movement and the state of Israel.

Raphael Rosenzweig and Georges Tamarin in 1969/70 examined the personal histories of about 140 members of today's Israeli power elite. The profile for the core leadership of Israel: cabinet ministers, MPs, parliamentary committee chairmen, supreme court judges, party leaders, members of the Histadrut Central Committee and decision makers of economic units with an annual budget exceeding IL 100 million emerges as follows:

> ' 'X' originated from somewhere within a circle of about 600 kilometers around Pinsk. The actual dispersion is even smaller than that but is concentrated around two centers — one in the Ukraine and one in central Galicia. Some large Jewish centers are conspicuous in their absence, such as Lithuania. He was born prior to 1910. (Obviously this characteristic changes with time but it is still true of

more than 80 per cent of our list in outgoing 1969.) He came to Israel prior to 1930 and had no more than a secondary education, usually less . . . These characteristics of leadership are not of equal significance in determining their attitudes. *The most important from the evidence we collected seems to be the birthplace; the "Staedtl psychology" remains the key factor.* It gives rise to over-compensations and reaction formations such as the kibbutz society, which often tends to appear like a Red painted ghetto, the derision heaped on Diasporah Jews, the official atheism in early left wing Zionist movements and so forth . . . Common Staedtl origin (not only East European background, since city born people tended to be different) formed the socio-psychological background common to the members of the "inner-in-group", or *Unsere Menschen* in the leaders language. *Unsere Menschen* are people whose relationships are well known, who have an understandable background and who, therefore talk the same language, even if their opinions might differ. That is why left opposition labour leaders such as M. Yaari and M. Tabenkin were always much closer to Levi Eshkol, the (later) conservative former Prime Minister, than members of his own party such as the British-educated Abba Eban or A. Ruppin, a German-educated sociologist active in Zionist settlement activities. If the birthplace or at least the father's birthplace is "right", some of the other attributes can be missing. This probably unconscious attitude might explain, for instance, the fact that the Canadian-born Samuel Dubiner, who tried to make millions by introducing cardboard containers for citrus exports failed to get the cooperation of Pinhas Sapir, then Minister of Commerce, while Efraim Ilin, in a much less promising industrial activity (automobile manufacture) was backed beyond all rhyme or reason.' (1) (emphasis added)

Written kin history is enlightening in many ways. It offers us the best available literate instrument for the de-mystification of the so-called paramountcy of 'objective historical forces' over human vision, aspiration and concerted action. Human history as state history attended to through the political biographies of existing or aspiring state ruling elites has a profoundly healing effect in exposing the origins of the established political, social and economic reality as a *constituted* reality sustained by an ongoing intentional human interpretive effort.

Aproaching human history through this vein has an additional merit: it is fascinating. It appeals to, and recreates an original human passion which is socially instituted in all human societies, though its significance and portent is rarely recognized by the schooled social sciences, namely gossip.

The peak of historical achievement is that which combines a passion for the uncovering of underlying structures with an equal taste for gossip and anecdote. This we shall now attempt to do, hopefully with a reasonable measure of success.

The Hebrew speaking student of history is privileged and fortunate to have access to a unique primary source of material, David Tidhar's *Encyclopaedia of the Pioneers of the Yishuv and Its Founders.* Tidhar's work is unique in many ways. It is the only source that provides information pertaining to family affiliations sustained among the persons who in his opinion have merited inclusion. However limited the information provided, his is the only source available for systematic research into the subject. There are no other primary source materials in existence which could compensate for and supplement the limited information he provides. An amateur historian and a renowned private detective, he had a passion for family gossip and family trees thus far not replicated among Zionist historians. As a detective he knew how to appreciate their social and political significance. As an amateur historian he is the only one who sensed their historical relevance. Also the individual entries are a unique historical record in that they authentically betray the spirit of the Zionist effort in a manner otherwise accessible only in individual biographical records. And so in following the kin affiliations of the pioneers of the *yishuv* and its founders through cross reference of the 19 volumes of his *Encyclopaedia*, one gets a taste of the Zionist effort otherwise lost.

This study traces the process through which a dominant class, whose nucleus is composed of interlocking familial and quasi-familial associations, crystalizes at a particular moment in the history of the Zionist movement and the state of Israel, constituting itself as the executive arm of the Jewish state. The kinship associations maintained by that nucleus remain, of course, first and foremost, political. They are directed and utilized to meet the requirements of executive, civil and military state domination. The traditional content and meaning of kin relationship could not but be a casualty to the process of state formation. These false pseudo-morphs of kin affiliation can be contrasted, on the one hand, with the authentic extended family in the traditional *Shtetle*, which was the mediator of the whole JewishDiasporatradition in Europe, and, on the other, with family fragmentation which is found among the proletariat, where surrogate kin relationships are established for political and economic purposes, and function in an egalitarian way. (E.g., the factory shop, where decisions are taken by consensus among the workers acting as heads of families; trades unions and clubs; trades councils; craft guilds; benefit clubs; provident and friendly societies etc.). The cohesion of the ruling class, on the other hand, is based on the consolidation of class power and the utilization of formal kinship or kin metaphor as a principle of recruitment to positions of exercise of power.

This book traces the making of the Israeli-Jewish labour-Zionist ruling class as it emerged during the past one hundred years and articulated in the specific historical context of the Zionist movement and its various agencies: the World Zionist Federation, the Jewish Agency, the Jewish National Fund, the General Federation of Labour (the Histadrut) etc. It further attempts to outline the various specific implications of the fact that its formation was largely shaped in relation to the requirements of a praxis predicated upon the colonization of a native land, Palestine, and aiming towards the establishment of a Jewish state as a solution to the Jewish problem. Under such circumstances it could hardly demonstrate much regard to the native Palestinian-Arab population. The specific forms of the destruction of the Palestinian-Arab society by the Zionist colonial effort in Palestine are traced and outlined against the context of the consolidation of the pre- and post-1948 formations of the state of Israel.

As one could imagine, a project as ambitious as that of establishing a Jewish state in Palestine from nothing could hardly be successfully achieved without western capitalist support. It is this fact above all else, which has determined the character of labour-Zionist ideology, and of all Zionist institutions, not the least of which being the utopian Israeli-Jewish kibbutz. The study details in some length the economic structures of key labour-Zionist economic foundations, e.g., the General Federation of Labour (Histadrut) and its holding company, the Workers' Company (*Hevrat Ovdim*), as well as the ownership structures of key labour-Zionist industries, including kibbutz industries. It is through the examination of this domain and through the analysis of interlocking directorships within the labour-Zionist economic sector that key ruling lineages of the Israeli-Jewish ruling class were identified.

The book is offered as a case study in support of the conquest theory of state formation, and as a contribution to a critique of western civilisation, whose essential features are spelled out in particular prominence and lucidity in the history and structures of the periphery of its colonial extensions.

THE MORAL DILEMMA

Israeli-born Jews (sabras) of the author's generation were born into the state of Israel. And that is no innocent statement. It means that a conceptual, perceptual and temperamental barrier exists between this generation and those who were born into the pre-state situation and witnessed the state come into being as a result of sustained effort and unrelenting struggle. When the effort turned out to be a success, it gave the founding veteran generation a sense of happiness and pride that always goes with having achieved something and pulled it through the difficulties involved. We who were born into the state have, of course, been divorced from the experience, and necessarily so.

One consequence of this success has been the ability of the original ruling elite to sustain and consolidate their domination and control of the state by reinterpreting their success as if it was historically inevitable and necessary. They have attempted to hide as effectively as possible the origins of the struggle as human endeavour; they have avoided the ambiguity of the struggle which was that they could have failed in creating the state of Israel. This human aspect of the original struggle is now hidden from the founding generation itself so that the history of the origin of the Israeli state is rooted in abstract and reified forces of eternity, historical necessity and human nature.

I, for one, am very wary of ideologies which root their descriptive and prescriptive argumentation in historical necessity, so-called. They are invariably attempts to systematically justify totalitarian policies. History, being humanly constituted, is rooted in the ambivalence of human intention and human effort. It is anything but a random process however. It is highly structured and predictable. And yet, to predict the future of instituted human projects is possible in the first place only because any human project is an intended project, sustained by the continuous effort of people acting in concert. This effort is not necessarily significant. It is significant if and only if it is continually supported by concerted human action. Its meaning, strengths, weaknesses, contradictions, failings and potentialities can be understood only in terms of the biographies of the people involved, their hopes, aspirations and perceptions of what constitutes a worthwhile, meaningful life. Accounting for human achievement in its concrete historical context is always challenging. The ambiguity thus revealed at the root of every human instituted effort is an invitation for critical judgment: Were the aspirations correct in the first place? Was the motivation justifiable? Were the original perceptions of what constitutes good life worthwhile? Does the instituted achievement fulfil the original criteria set by its founders as their normative frame of reference? If not — at what junctures did the business go wrong? Why and in response to what needs?

All such questions are, of course, irrelevant in a historical necessity frame of reference. In such a frame of reference, people obviously do not make mistakes, and everything is justifiable *ex post facto* in the name of the objectively necessary march of human history.

It is in the effort to disguise the concrete context of the emergence of the Zionist movement that the Israeli-Jewish obsession with archeology, a desperate attempt to legitimize the endeavour in terms of ruins 2000 years old, is rooted. Similarly, the consistant avoidance of dealing with the era of the crusades; the compulsion to obliterate all physical remains of the dispossessed Palestinian-Arab native peasant population (1) (385 Arab villages have been destroyed and razed to the ground within pre-1967 Israel proper); the reification of anti-semitic racism as an objective immutable, inherent characteristic of non-Jewish human nature; the militarization of the old testament, and finally, the elimination by fiat of 2000 years of the country's history and the seeking of justification not in terms of its concrete reality but in the genocidal conquest of the land by a Hebrew criminal, elevated to the position of national hero: Joshua son of Nun. How else could the Zionist endeavour be justified in terms of the concrete reality of Palestine, a country under Ottoman occupation with a native peasantry living under conditions of feudal tenancy and serfdom.

The Zionist colonial pioneers intended anything but sharing the country equally with the native population, joining hands in common struggle against their common exploitation and oppression. Rather, they came intending to solve the Jewish problem in terms of establishing in Palestine-Eretz-Israel an a priori privileged position and state monopoly for Jews, which necessarily meant the dispossession of the native population and its expulsion.

'The idea which I have developed in this pamphlet', wrote Herzl, 'is an ancient one: it is the establishment of a Jewish state. The whole plan is in its essence very simple, as it must necessarily be if it is to come within the comprehension of all. Let sovereignty be granted us over a portion of the earth's surface, large enough to satisfy our rightful requirements as a nation . . . The poorest will go first to cultivate the soil. In accordance with preconceived plans they will construct roads, bridges, railways and telegraph installations, regulate rivers and build their own dwellings. Their labour will bring trademarkets, and markets will attract settlers. . . The Jewish Company is partly modelled on the lines of a great acquisition company, but it cannot exercise sovereign power and has no other than purely colonial tasks.' (2)

Attempting to achieve the dream *in situ* the Zionist colonial pioneers translated the vision into such concrete terms as the *Ha-Poel ha-Tzair* (The Young Worker) second *aliya/*programme 'The necessary condition for the realization of Zionism is the conquest of all branches of labour in Eretz-Israel by Jews.'

The successful accomplishment of the Jewish colonial task and the establishment of the Jewish state of Israel followed rather standard patterns of colonial dispossession. Sensing clearly and correctly that the task required first and foremost the consolidation of monopoly over the land resources of the country, the Jews felt that their allies could not possibly be the impoverished, dominated local peasantry, divested of all legal rights, and transformed under the Ottoman imperial rule into tenants and serfs. Their allies could only be the big absentee feudal land owners who were thirsty for cash in order to enter into the capitalist market economy, introduced into the area by the European imperial powers and into agro-industrial business, specifically oranges. They willingly sold their poorer lands and swamp lands to accumulate the capital investment required for mass orange production on their better lands. However, it is well to remember that by 1947 only 8% of Mandatory Palestine was under Jewish ownership. Approximately half of this 8% was under the public Jewish control of the Jewish Agency, and specifically the Jewish National Fund (JNF).

It is not incidental that Jewish colonization originally aimed to achieve as extensive a Jewish monopoly over lands in Palestine as possible. The physiocrats are basically correct in arguing that commerce, like industry, is merely a branch of agriculture and that all wealth originates from the land.

The Palestinian-Arab feudal landlords have few qualms about selling large tracts of land to the Jewish Company (The Jewish National Fund) for good hard cash, and backing the deal with the bayonettes of the Ottoman standing army and police. They saw to it that the native peasantry who had, under Ottoman law, no legal rights to the land they cultivated, were driven away and the land turned over to monopolized Jewish use. It is in this context that Dr. A. Ruppin, the architect of the Zionist colonization endeavour in the 'twenties and 'thirties made it clear that 'on every site where we purchase land and where we settle people, the present cultivators will inevitably be dispossessed'. (3)

Under these circumstances one realizes why the effort could not possibly be justified in concrete historical terms. Why the origins of Jewish colonization had to be hidden the moment it was successfully consolidated. Why it was imperative to present the venture in terms of the just struggle as soon as it became a successful eventuality.

But for us, the generation born into the state, the Jewish state of Israel was our ahistorical point of departure. It was only after 1967 that some of us recaptured the history of Jewish colonization, that we protested against massive destruction of Palestinian-Arab villages, expropriation of

urban and rural property, massive dispossession and population transfer.
Israel Galili, Premier Golda Meir's top advisor, (Golda's Guru) and
Minister without Portfolio, responded with incredulity and arrogance
when faced with demonstrations against the expulsion of 6000 Palestinians from the Gaza strip in the spring of 1972. Their houses and wells had
been destroyed and 10,000 acres were fenced off for the purposes of the
establishment of a cluster of Jewish settlements. Israel Galili argued at this
time that 'Our right on Gaza' is 'exactly like our right on Tel-Aviv. We are
colonizing Gaza exactly in the same manner in which we colonized Jaffa.
Those who doubt our right on Gaza should doubt our right on Tel-Aviv as
well.' And when he says 'right' what he has in mind is obvious: an a priori
privileged position and Jewish monopolistic control over available resources.
Who should know better than Israel Galili that Gaza is being colonized in
the same manner as Jaffa was colonized; after all he was one of the leading
veteran architects of the original colonization effort.

After participating in the protest, which he helped to organize, the
leading Israeli columnist Amos Kenan wrote that if 'one who believes that
he has no right to Gaza must also doubt his right to Tel-Aviv,' then he,
Amos Kenan, 'would begin to doubt if indeed I have a right to Tel-Aviv
— at least to Tel-Aviv as it now is; a Jewish city, in a Jewish state with a
million Arabs deprived of rights.' (4)

The traumatic effect of Israel Galili's statements cannot be fully apprec-
iated unless one realizes that thereby the founding leadership tampered
with the supposed moral basis of the original colonization as a whole. The
Zionist effort rooted its morality in a number of new fictions: the a-hist-
oricity of anti-semitism as an inherent feature of Gentile nature, the
definition of Palestine as an empty land: a land without people for a people
without land, and after the 1948 war, in the fiction that the native
Palestinian-Arab population had voluntarily withdrawn from their villages
and towns of residence at the explicit call of their leaders in order to return
as conquerors. The question of how it came about that a state without
people had on the day of its declaration of independence (May 14, 1948)
some 750,000 Arabs living there for many generations in villages and
towns of great renown such as Jerusalem, Hebron, Haifa, Acre and Tiberias,
was dealt with quite effectively in Orwellian doublethink terms. Like all
fictions of their kind they collapse under scrutiny. For instance the fiction
that the 1948 Palestinian-Arab exodus was carried out by evacuation orders
from the Arab leadership has been conclusively examined, as early as 1961
by Erskine Childers:

> 'Examining every official Israeli statement about the Arab exodus I
> was struck by the fact that no primary evidence of evacuation orders
> was ever produced . . . There had allegedly been Arab radio broad-
> casts ordering evacuation . . . I next decided to test the undocumen-
> ted charge . . . — which could be done thoroughly because the BBC
> monitored all Middle Eastern broadcasts through 1948. The records,
> and companion ones by US monitoring unit can be seen at the
> British Museum. There was not a single order, or appeal, or suggestion

about evacuation from Palestine from any Arab radio station inside or outside Palestine in 1948. There is repeated monitored record of Arab appeals, even flat orders, to the civilians of Palestine to stay put.' (5)

The key question is why, after 1967, did the founding leaders of the Zionist movement and the state of Israel find it necessary to tamper with the fictive foundation of Zionist morality. They could not but know and be aware that they did so at their own cost. The answer is not difficult to discover. After the 1967 war unabashed nationalism spread throughout Israel. Moderate labour Zionism with its 'socialist' programme and humanitarian principles was no longer appropriate as the ideology of a victorious nation. Reality undermined established fictive morality and Zionism had to reconstitute its moral justification, this time in terms more compatible with the truth. Since the programme of the state was now explicitly the judaisation of conquered territory by military means, it could safely be pointed out that this had always been Zionist policy and that therefore anyone who opposed it was at odds with the very idea of the Jewish state in Palestine. It is in the light of this new morality, which the authorities admit to inside Israel but not in the outside world, that this history of Zionism is written. We can now go back over the whole Zionist project, from its origins in Eastern Europe, through the pioneer kibbutz colonisation and the establishment of the state apparatus, and on to the consolidation of a class society based on a considerable degree of racism.

THE ORIGIN OF ZIONISM

It was clear to the founding veteran generation of the Zionist movement, which was predominantly of East European origin, that for the Zionist venture to succeed, the customary communal underpinnings of traditional East-European life must be destroyed. The motivating vision of the new Jew, the Jew freed from Diasporah pathology by virtue of transforming himself into an upperdog citizen of a nation-state, was predicated upon the destruction of traditional Diasporah Jewish life, and specifically of the customary underpinnings of East-European Jewish life: the *shtetle*. This was no secret. Both opponents and supporters of the Zionist effort had quite a clear notion of what was involved as well as of the nature of the requirements in question. Supporters and opponents hardly differ on the matter. (1) The Zionist movement clearly considered itself to be a spearhead of the assault. It was fully conscious of the fact that there was no chance for the requirements of the Jewish state to be adequately met so long as the prospective pool of immediate recruits, members of the customary Diasporah *shtetle* communities of East Europe, remained bound to traditional Diasporah Jewish life. The only circumstance which could conceivably release the people in question and render them susceptible recruits would have to involve the destruction of the traditional Diasporah community, which the Zionist movement was far too weak to undertake on its own initiative.

ZIONISM AND ANTI-SEMITISM

Jacob Klatzkin, the chief Zionist ideologue of pre-war Germany proudly stated in 1925:

> 'Instead of establishing societies for defence against the anti-Semites, who want to reduce our rights, we should establish societies for defence against our friends who desire to defend our rights.' (2)

and Rabbi Joachim Prinz, Deputy Chairman of the World Jewish Congress could say:

> 'The significance of the German revolution (1933) for the German people will ultimately be revealed only to those who have undertaken to achieve it and have themselves shaped its form. Its significance for us (Jews) will be stated here: The liberal option has been lost for

ever, (liberalism) the only political way of life which Jewish assimilationism was prepared to promote has sunk away for good. How long it will survive in disparate individual countries only prophets can venture to determine. But the dispassionate, cool observer of world affaris can determine the following facts: everywhere throughout the world symptoms develop which spell doom to the cornerstone values of liberalism. Parliament and democracy are increasingly shattered. The exaggerated harmful emphasis on the value of the individual is recognized to be mistaken; the concept and reality of the nation and the people is gaining, to our happiness, more and more ground. The last and most powerful and sublime formulation of national rights and the rejection of internationalism is found in the demands of socialism that it be founded exclusively on the unique character of every nation and the special demands of every nation, namely national socialism.

The collapse of the Jewish anonymity is now clear to everyone. Jews are now torn away from the last hiding place: their aspirations for conversion to Christianity and mixed marriages. Thereby some of us have been made despondant (but) we consider this necessity an opportunity for a courageous and unequivocal statement in favour of standing amongst our own alone. We also see the fulfilment of our most sublime aspirations. In vain did *we* struggle against mimicry, conversion and mixed marriages. And now more powerful forces came to our aid and have redeemed us. The time has now come to draw the conclusions and not to destroy our lives in miserable indecision and spiritual sorrow over the destruction of something good. The theory of assimilation has been destroyed. There is no longer any hiding place for us under the negation which protected it. We want to posit instead of assimilation something new: *undertaking the yoke of joining the Jewish people and the Jewish race.* Only a state based on the principle of the purity of the nation and the race can possibly endow dignity and honour on (and only on) those Jews who themselves subscribe to this principle. The state cannot desire any other Jews except those who subscribe to this principle amongst their own people. It cannot desire to have sycophantic Jews. It must demand from us recognition of our absolute uniqueness and qualities, since only those who give full honour to their own uniqueness, their own blood, could gain the respect and honour which is bestowed by similarly inspired nations subscribing to the same principle. (3)

Thirty years later the same line of thinking is typically presented and re-affirmed in an article by Uri Harari 'Our Responsibility Towards the Jews in the Arab Countries'

'When we hear of riots, pogroms or hanging (of Jews) we seethe with anger, and justly so. We mobilize public opinion and we raise our warning. We try to do everything within our capacity to help the persecuted Jews. Then we ask ourselves "Where were they all these years?", "Why did they not immigrate to the country (Israel) in time?" . . . Still later, and deep in our heart there is also a tiny flicker of vicious joy: "Serves them right!"; "We warned them!"; "We told them so!". It is, of course, not customary for us to talk about it in public, but many of us felt a tiny bit of joy at another's calamity when we read in the papers reports about the swastika epidemic in Europe in 1960 or about the (pro-Nazi) Takuara movement in Argentina. And even today we have very mixed feelings when we read of De Gaul's anti-Semitic hints or about the intensification of anti-Jewish feelings among black leaders in the United States. Despite all the anger and the shock and the insult, these phenomena fit into our world view, because Zionism said then as it says today that this is the state of affairs, and that such it *must be* so long as Jews live among Gentile nations. In our great enthusiasm for the achievement of Israeli independence and sovereignty we sometimes forget the negative aspect of Zionism — its cruel world view . . . (Zionism) assumes the eternal hatred of the Jew by the Gentile, irrespective of how liberal the Gentile may be . . . Concerning one answer there is no discussion: of course we must do everything in order to enable every Jew who so desires to immigrate to the country and establish his life here. We have to save the Jews from Arab countries, to act with all our might to get the gates of East European countries opened. We must create in this country possibilities for the absorption of (Jewish) immigrants from western countries. So far this is all agreed. But does the state of Israel have duties towards Jews who can immigrate to the country and do not wish to do so? Furthermore, do we have the right to tell them: "We know better than you what is good *for you*, and we shall therefore act to get you to immigrate to the country; we might even act in order to facilitate the deterioration of your situation (in the Diaspora) so that you should have no other choice but to immigrate to Israel!". One should note that this last question is not imaginary. We have already had to face this question in very concrete situations, and we may have to face it again in the future.' (4)

In the obvious sense of the passages quote above Zionism was a grand exercise in bad faith.

The Zionist movement accepted uncritically the racist anti-semitic characterization of the Diaspora Jew and Jewish Life. Moreover, the effort was further predicated upon a curiously twisted acceptance of the anti-semite contention that Jews have no place in non-Jewish societies. The solution it therefore posited for the Jewish problem was: global concentration of Jews in Palestine-Eretz-Israel as proud and healthy citizens of a Jewish nation-state. Little surprise that the movement developed not only distaste and antipathy, but rather rabid hatred of Diaspora Jewish life, which again was not unlike racist anti-semitic hatred in its intensity and fervour. Today given the critical dependence of the Zionist movement, and the state of Israel on Diaspora Jewish financial support, the contempt, arrogance and hatred are much more subtle, subdued and veiled. Today one is not likely to find an Israeli-Jewish Zionist leader who would refer in public to Diaspora Jews as human dust. Yet, this was precisely the term of reference the late Israeli Premier, David Ben-Gurion, threw at his hosts when in the US on a fund-raising tour in the late 1950s.

Zionism appeared on the political Jewish scene at the stage where the traditional customary East-European Jewish community was in process of advanced collapse. It came as a response to the disintegration of the Jewish *shtetle*, and constituted, in fact, a minority response. The mainstream response of East-European Jewry at the turn of the century to the collapse of its traditional customary environment was emigration. It was in the late eighteen hundreds through 1914 that the mass migration of East-European Jewry to virtually all corners of the western hemisphere, primarily to the US, took place. Abraham Leon quotes the following table:

1830 - 1870	—	4,000 to	5,000
1871 - 1880	—	8,000 to	10,000
1881 - 1900	—	50,000 to	60,000
1901 - 1914	—	150,000 to	160,000

(Note that the first Zionist *aliya* experiment in Palestine involving 2-3 scores of people — the *Bilu* — dates 1882-4)

It is against this background that the Zionist idea was introduced as a solution to the Jewish problem. The only solution, it was claimed, was the transformation of world Jewry into citizens of a Jewish state in Palestine. To understand this one must grasp the intricate relatedness of the Zionist movement to its own destroyed customary underpinnings.

THE SEED-BED OF ISRAEL

The East European Jewish *shtetle* was — to borrow the term (and insight) from Stanley Diamond — a captive pyramid within the overall class-stratified pyramid of the mediaeval Gentile society. Throughout the Middle Ages up to the 19th century the Jewish *shtetle* had traditionally been the rural, mercantile and financial agent of the feudal landed nobility and grande bourgeoisie of Central and Eastern Europe. Indeed, like the Armenians in Asia and Asia minor and the Copts in Egypt, the Chinese in South East Asia, the Arabs and the Indians in Eastern Africa, it was an entrepreneural caste, closely knit by shared custom, tradition and the web of kinship whose economic underpinnings were circumscribed by the feudal aranda monopoly farming (lease) system. A people-class, to use the term coined by Abraham Leon, although this would be only technically correct. The class-stratification of mediaeval Europe, predominantly a peasant society, was so deeply embedded in an overwhelming customary peasant context that the area of domination of the central administration, including its financial dealings, was very circumscribed. Being subject to the requirements of customary (natural) economy it could provide, at most, for the emergence of ruling and middle castes as distinct from ruling and middle classes. It was only with the invention of modern locomotion and industrial machinery (The Industrial Revolution) that the traditional European mediaeval ruling caste acquired the necessary instrumentation to embark upon the age of mercantilism, colonialism and imperialism, and simultaneously destroy its customary peasant underpinnings, by way of transforming European native peasantry into industrial wage labour on the one hand, and subjecting its overseas colonies to industrial tyranny and economic exploitation on the other.

Obviously the destruction of the native European peasantry for the purpose of meeting the manpower requirements of a factory industrial economy spelled the doom of the Jewish *shtetle* and aranda farming system. With the transition from a state economy based on the collection of taxation in kind from a tenured peasantry, village industry (e.g. liquor brewing) and luxury item trade, to an economy based on market oriented cash crop agriculture, factory production and commodity trade, the middle financial agent caste was doomed to elimination. The peasant pogroms inflicted on the Jewish *shtetle* communities of Central and East Europe throughout the 18th and 19th centuries must be understood in this context. It was against the middle agent class that the peasant population, subject to policies of systematic destruction, directed its wrath. The industrialization of Europe on the one hand and the rise of the native bourgeoisie crushed the *shtetle* and completely shattered its economic base. During the 19th century we witness massive Jewish migration to the new industrial metropolitan centres of Europe, where a certain section was incorporated into the European bourgeois classes, although the slot was definitely not large enough to incorporate them all. Hence the massive overseas migration.

The Jewish *shtetle* was a captive pyramid within the overall stratified pyramid of the non-Jewish society, restricted in its social and geographical mobility and set apart by religion, culture, custom, in-group marriage, etc. The base of the *shtetle* pyramid consisted of self-employed artisans, exclusively confined to trades designated to meet the consumption requirements of the merchant and the landed nobility: gold and silversmiths (who always had a privileged position in this context), tailors, cobblers, itinerant peddlars, etc. The peasantry is traditionally self-sufficient, and does not critically depend on the product of the industrial worker or the pre-capitalist artisan. Where the peasant base of society remains relatively intact, the peasantry can quite easily dispense with such products, even where they have become habitual, by reviving village industries. The only artisan the peasantry has traditionally depended upon and employed on the basis of payment in kind has been the blacksmith, and it is in no way incidental that precisely this trade has been the one from which the Jewish *shtetle* community was excluded by virtue of its socio-political position as an agent caste for the ruling landed nobility and grande bourgeoisie. The middle ranks of the *shtetle* consisted of family owned and family run small shops, small sub-lease liquor farmers, etc. Its apex hosted the richer merchants, big aranda leasees, tax farmers of large estates, liquor and salt monopolies, as well as the traditional Talmudic intelligensia, the latter usually dependent on the former. The *shtetle* had no peasant membership, nor did it have an industrial proletariat. The hierarchy did not extend outside what could technically be called the petit bourgeois range of the Gentile society, and what would properly be called the entrepreneur middle caste.

Competition for wealth and prestige was a major factor in the *shtetle* life, yet the reality of the *shtetle* situation had to be structured so as to make impossible the formation of rigid class distinctions. Being sealed off from society at large by anti-semitism and internal caste restrictions and being subject to the arbitrary fluctuations of the speculative market, the apex of the pyramid could not constitute itself as a rigid upper class since merchants were often obliged to rely on the help of relatives and friends as a result of arbitrary impoverishment and market collapse. Consequently, the *shtetle*, though stratified by rank and prestige distinctions, was closely held together by a shared tradition and custom supported by a tightly knit web of kinship. The structure, in other words, provided for circular mobility in that wealth was re-distributed both along the lines of communal charity support, as well as through arranged marriage between the prestigeous poor scholar and the rich merchant (*gvir*). It was standard custom for the rich not only to marry their daughters to the prestigeous scholar (*iluy*), however poor, but to support scholars at their table, donate heavily to the community synagogue, which usually housed the community school (*Beit Midrash*) and fill the coffers of the general charity support system. Conversely, however, the rich merchant quite often found himself impoverished overnight and had to fall back on kin and community support. The *shtetle* quite plainly guaranteed food, shelter and clothing to each of its members by way of re-distribution of wealth along interlocking extended family lines and public charity. The *shtetle*, like the pre-industrial capitalist society in which it was embedded, was shaped internally predominantly by the order of custom. (5)

In this context the rise of the Zionist movement was in no way arbitrary. Herzl was profoundly marked by the chain of bloody pogroms in Central and Eastern Europe during the second half of the 19th century. The background was the rise of the European nation state, and he was very much a man of his time in thinking that the solution to the Jewish problem lay in transforming Jewish populations throughout the world into the citizenry of their own Jewish state.

THE MISSIONARY VISION

Though Zionist history in Palestine begins in 1881-2 with the immigration to the country of the first Bilu *aliya*, it was the second Zionist *aliya* (1905-1914) which in effect laid the basis for the post World War I pragmatic bureaucracy to coordinate the systematic Zionist colonization of the land. By the end of the 19th century twenty one Jewish agricultural settlements were established in Palestine following the initiative of the first Bilu settlers, with about 4,500 inhabitants, of whom some two thirds were employed in agriculture. There is little doubt that the Bilu initiative would not have survived, let alone grown, without the philanthropic intervention of Baron Edmond de Rothschild and his support to the estimated tune of the round sum of $5 million during the 1880s. These settlements soon became completely dependent on Baron de Rothschild's philanthropic administration in Palestine. Yet, after the initial decades of costly trials and setbacks they achieved a measure of material affluence and evolved into viable commercial ventures. Within three decades not much was left of the original Bilu pioneering spirit and by 1910 the settlers established themselves as owners of plantations, employing mainly cheap Arab labour and sending their children to be educated in France.

The real concrete practical foundations of the Zionist effort in Palestine were laid out by a different stock, the East-European labour Zionists, and more specifically, the second Zionist *aliya*. It was there that the visionary impulse of the original Zionist endeavour was located — a visionary impulse which immediately speaks to the western mind precisely because it harks back to the original visionary underpinnings of the mainstream tradition of western civilization. Consequently, its glory notwithstanding, it was bound to be likewise predicated on racism and to follow the well-trodden road of western progressivism, namely conquest, occupation, corruption and crime.

It is the problematics of the second Zionist wave of immigration (the second *aliya*, 1903-1914) which are the most portentous in this context and contain in embryo the logic of Zionist practice to be followed thereafter.

The second aliya: 80% left shortly after their arrival, 12% of the remaining committed suicide, 10% were killed, 15% died of disease, hunger and malaria.

'The second Zionist *aliya*, a handful of people reduced by 1909 to a
mere one hundred and sixty five. Clustered in small communities,
primarily in Galilee, torn apart in and among themselves, generating
tension that often led to suicide and haunted by a blinding vision
which led many to sheer desperation and utter withdrawal. They were,
quite clearly, persecuted by the 50,000-strong old *yishuv*, which was
relatively well established as urban middle class and farmers (not
peasants) and which they, in turn, utterly despised. Petah Tikvah,
hallowed as the Mother of Jewish (agricultural) settlements, was often
referred to by them as a *shmutzige* (dirty) *shtetle*, worthy of nothing
other than contempt, the embodiment of Jewish life which they were
determined to end, a replica of precisely that which they committed
themselves to abolish. They were committed to establish in Palestine
the complete and radical antithesis of the despicable traditional
Jewish Diaspora existence. They quite clearly perceived themselves
to be the vanguard of the radical world-wide Jewish transformation
and liberation. The heat of their vision was plainly fed by their utter
rejection and hatred of Diasporah Jewish existence and culture. They,
the committed few, would pull the people they so despised out of
their 2000 year-long inferior humanity and pathological degradation
into the light of redemption and the march of liberation and
progress.' (1)

The impulse is hardly unique. That kind of dehumanization of those
earmarked for redemption into the community of the civilized faithful is
shared by all missionaries and mission institutions operating under the
tacit consent or explicit active support of the colonial administration and
the imperial state. Missions operating in such contexts hardly ever directly
engage in the destruction of the community earmarked for transformation,
and quite explicitly rely on the colonial administration and the imperial
state bureaucracy to do the job. The Zionist movement has a notorious
history in that respect. It has consistently refrained from active opposition
to the destruction of Diasporah Jewish communities, the World War II
Nazi holocaust included.

Christopher Sykes is absolutely correct in his descriptive analysis of the
Zionist position vis-a-vis the 1938 Evian Conference, concerned under
public pressure on western governments to open the gates for Jewish
refugees and suspend their quota systems. 100 Jewish organizations were
represented, but the biggest and most influential — The World Zionist
Organization — abstained:

'The Zionists, who played no part in the conference, were not
worried by its failure. They seem to have expected no great result
from it, and gave no expression of embitterment when the results
turned out to be negative. From the start they regarded the whole
enterprise with hostile indifference. Zionist writers scarcely mention
it. The fact is that what was attempted at Evian was in no sense
congenial to the spirit of Zionism. The reason is not obscure. If the
thirty one nations had done their duty and shown hospitality to
those in dire need, the the pressure on the National Home and

heightened enthusiasm of Zionism within Palestine, would both have been relaxed. This was the last thing that the Zionists wished for . . . Even in the more terrible days ahead they made no secret of the fact even when talking to Gentiles, that they did not want Jewish settlements outside Palestine to be successful.' (2)

Similarly, Ben-Gurion in his letter written to the Zionist Executive on December 17th, 1938, just a few weeks after the first Nazi pogroms, said:

'The Jewish problem is not what it used to be. The fate of Jews in Germany is not an end but a beginning. Other anti-semitic states will learn from Hitler. Millions of Jews face annihilation, the refugee problem has assumed world wide proportion, and urgency. Britain is trying to separate the issue of the refugees from that of Palestine, it is assisted by anti-Zionist Jews. The dimensions of the refugee problem demand an immediate, territorial solution; if Palestine will not absorb them, another territory will. Zionism is endangered. All other territorial solutions, certain to fail, will demand enormous sums of money. If Jews will have to choose between the refugees, saving Jews from concentration camps, and assisting a national museum in Palestine, mercy will have the upper hand and the whole energy of the people will be channelled into saving Jews from various countries. Zionism will be struck off the agenda not only in world public opinion, in Britain and the USA, but elsewhere in Jewish public opinion. If we allow a separation between the refugee problem and the Palestine problem, we are risking the existence of Zionism. (3)

And Yitzhak Greenbaum, Director of the Rescue Committee of the Jewish Agency announced in Tel Aviv in 1943:

'And when I was asked: but you could donate from the resources of the Foundation Fund to the rescue of the Jews in the Diaspora, I said: no. And I say again: no. I know that people wonder why I found it necessary to say that. Friends tell me that even if these things are true, one should not reveal them in public at a moment of such sorrow and anxiety. I cannot agree. In my opinion one has to combat this wave, which relegates Zionist activity to a secondary priority.

And because of that I was called anti-Semitic and was judged to be responsible for the fact that we do not absorb ourselves completely in the rescue activity.' (4)

From the Zionist point of view, the worse the Jewish condition in the Diasporah becomes, the better chance there is for the Zionist effort to come to full fruition, even though whenever Diasporah Jewish communities responded to adverse conditions in terms of mass migration, it was never more than a trickle that worked its way into Palestine-Eretz-Israel. The only *exception* are the Jewish communities in Asia and Africa. (see below).

It was the second *aliya* which sustained the visionary underpinnings of Zionism in general and laid out the basis for the post-World War I large-scale, pragmatic bureaucracy which co-ordinated the systematic Zionist colonization of the land. The second *aliya* generated not only the visionary leadership of the Zionist endeavour, but also, correlatively, its real political leadership which translated the blinding, labour Zionist, utopian vision into the instituted political reality of a class-stratified, exclusively Jewish-state. It could, of course, be argued that there are no necessary connections, that the vision of human liberation of the second *aliya* did not necessarily determine the actual terms of its political institution as a class-stratified, exclusive Jewish nation-state predicated upon massive dispossession of the native Palestinian Arab population, that the true labour Zionism was not fulfilled, but rather . . . betrayed.

Was it? Labour Zionism, we have already noted, so immediately speaks to the western mind, because it harks back, both in its visionary as well as in its real political aspects, to the mainstream tradition of western civilization. It is sustained by a very specific and clearly identifiable western utopian tradition, which in turn has its roots in the original foundations of western civilization: the Greek polis and its ideological correlate, Platonic philosophy.

Plato's Republic . . . a utopian paradigm of western civilization. The beacon of reason and light sustained by a hierarchical, class-stratified state ruled by a corporate class of philosopher-kings; Plato's Republic . . . a western paradigm of state domination, so fundamentally and deeply rooted in western, racist, civilized ethnocentricity, yet acclaimed as the institutionalization of nothing other than human enlightenment and progress. The amazingly repressive edifice of human domination that the 'Republic' would represent has its origin in a fascinating vision of human liberation. The Republic *is* the instituted reality of the vision of liberation so forcefully articulated in the Parable of the Cave.

The Parable of the Cave, like labour Zionism, is predicated on missionary elitism that would redeem the ignorant, chained, and inferior masses, submerged in darkness and terrorized by shadows. The original vision of liberation from the darkness of the cave into the blinding glow of goodness can only be politically institutionalized in terms of a highly bureaucratic class-stratified Republic. David Ben-Gurion's well-known preoccupation with Plato was not spurious or idiosyncratic. He, for one, fully realized that to the extent that labour Zionism perceived itself to be a vanguard committed to liberating the Jewish people chained to the caves of 2000 years of Diaspora existence, the effort could only be instituted in Platonic Republican terms: a Jewish state. His was a vision of a Jewish state that would not only carry the beacon of enlightenment and progress — the standard western, civilized justification for conquest, domination and exploitation — into the barbaric hinterland of the Near East, but most ambitiously, betraying the chosen people's ethnocentricity, would posit a paradigm of enlightenment and liberation for the western world at large. The leading executive of the Jewish state had both his feet right in the mainstream of western civilization.

THE KIBBUTZIM

The immediate response of the Zionist *aliya* intending the establishment of Jewish state monopoly in Palestine-Eretz-Israel populated by native Palestinian-Arab peasantry under highly exploitative Ottoman rule was collectivization. The first kibbutz, Dagania, was established in 1909. One must remember that the people in question recognized themselves as the frontline elite of the endeavour, which indeed they were. They generated the political and military elite of the pre-state *yishuv*, and to this day, though barely 3% of the total Israeli-Jewish population, people of kibbutz origin contribute approximately 25% of Israeli cabinet members (5), 22% if not higher, of the Israeli middle and high military command (6), and constitute the overwhelming majority of air-force pilots, the elite unit of the Israeli army (7).

The reality of the kibbutz cannot be understood unless it is realized that the kibbutz collective (Hebrew has a different term to designate community, namely *kehilah*) identified itself quite correctly as being entrusted with the execution and consolidation of the future state's front line interests. To use the Platonic Republic's class-stratification terminology, it should properly be seen and analysed in terms of being the base for both the ruling philosopher-king class and the soldier class of the future Jewish state.

A lot of effort originally went into the destruction of inner kibbutz family ties, primarily the children parent link. Children were separated from adult life and parental company, raised collectively in the children's house under the care-giver and allowed a set number of hours a day to spend with their parents. One must understand that this was not arbitrary; that parental preoccupation with raising children was identified as a burden diverting effort from the really important business, rather than an integral aspect of adult life. It was sensed, and correctly, that maintaining the integrity of parent-child relations was incompatible with the basic frontier requirements of the venture. Now, the original endeavour having been successfully achieved, the necessity is not acute and kibbutz family life is falling back upon standard atomized middle-class nuclear family structure. (8) On the other hand as Diamond pointedly notes (9) the kibbutz never severed its kinship links with the outside metropolitan Jewish society.

The kibbutzniks collectivized, and they collectivized in a colonial context, on land gained initially by legal dispossession of the native peasant population. Let us however, examine the collectivization in question in some detail. They did not own the property. Kibbutz property is owned by the Zionist movement: The Jewish National Fund, The Foundation Fund or the Kibbutz Federation. The kibbutz runs and manages it. What they created were not workers collectives; from the very start they were management collectives. As Hagar Enosh correctly points out, the kibbutzniks were originally given management wages by the Jewish National Fund, and in turn employed hired labour which was far less well paid. Obviously, initially, until sufficient capital accumulated they had to rely on self-labour and, not surprisingly, reified the necessity into abstract dogma. The advantage of abstract dogmas is that they are never binding. With the accumulation of capital assets in agro-industry, and shortly afterwards with the development of a pre-dominantly consumption industry, the kibbutz immediately resorted to hired wage labour on a very large scale, 59 per cent in kibbutz industry as a whole in 1966 (Kanovsky, 1966), kibbutz members monopolize managerial positions. Someone with superficial acquaintance of kibbutz collective ideology and dynamics, would have expected the kibbutz to share its revenues equally among all workers, kibbutz and non-kibbutz members, which the kibbutz has never done and could never do (see Chapter 6 below).

If indeed it is correct to submit that the western Platonic concept of human liberation — the now worn-out western, ideological justification for colonial conquest and imperial domination — can only be instituted in terms of a class-stratified hierarchy controlled by a corporate ruling class, then the emergence of the kibbutz network as the first institutional underpinnings towards the consolidation of a Jewish nation-state in Palestine-Eretz-Israel becomes quite rational. The kibbutz has undoubtedly been the locus of the original managerial elite of the labour Zionist effort in Palestine. One should not underestimate the effort nor its underlying vision. It was this elite, instituting itself in the network of kibbutzim along the frontiers of the Zionist colonization effort, which undertook to establish the Jewish nation-state *for* the Jewish people and to liberate the entire Jewish Diaspora by transforming it into citizenry of an exclusively Jewish state; should we be surprised to find it at the front line of the post-1967 colonization effort in the Golan Heights, the West Bank, the Gaza Strip and the Sinai?

The kibbutz was itself the major instrument of the Zionist movement and the state of Israel in their drive to establish and consolidate monopolistic control of the land in Palestine. Kibbutzim were, and are, always established at the frontier-line of Jewish colonization in the country. As Alex Bein correctly notes they can be

> 'easily transformed into a military camp for the defence of the settlement and the surrounding area. Logically, therefore, this form of settlement was preferred in the first stages of the new colonization period; most of the military strongholds (*mishlatim*) in the first year after the foundation of the state were kibbutzim'. (10)

Many of those created after 1948 were, in fact, initially established as *Nahal* outposts. To paraphrase the *Encyclopaedia Judaica* again, *Nahal*, an abbreviation for *Noar Halutzi Lohem* (Fighting Pioneer Youth), is a regular unit of the Israeli army, whose soldiers are organized in *garinim* (nuclei) of pioneer youth movements in Israel and Zionist youth movements in the Diaspora. Since these movements are politically affiliated to one of the various Zionist parties the political affiliation of the prospective settlement is determined according to the relative power of the parties in the Israeli parliament and in the world Zionist movement. A *Nahal* nucleus recruited from the *Betar* youth movement (affiliated to the right wing *Herut* party) will not be sent to supplement a settlement manned by people recruited from *Hatenua Hameuhedet* (affiliated to *Ahdut Haavoda*, now a faction within the ruling Labour Party). The relative number of *Nahal* outposts manned by recruits from *Betar* will not exceed the relative strength of *Herut* in the Israeli parliament and the world Zionist movement. *Nahal* has two aims: to produce first class soldiers and to prepare *gar'inim* for establishing new settlements (or joining existing settlements). Training consists of an initial basic military training at the *Nahal* army camp which is combined with ideological and social activities. There is then a period of combined agricultural and military training in a kibbutz or *Nahal* outpost. Advanced military training in paratroop, tank, artillery or other units follows for men, while women live in their own settlement where they are later joined by the men. A *Nahal* outpost is a typical army camp with military ranks and discipline. *Nahal* is sometimes employed in special projects; for example in 1949 it built the road to Ein Gedi on the western bank of the Dead Sea, and in the early 1950s it organized large scale vegetable production.

In 1970, out of a total of 231 kibbutzim, 149 had been established prior to 1948 and 82 in the period following. Kibbutzim are distinguished by collectivization and collective forms of social organization, of the kind useful whenever and wherever the state has to carry out an unusually exerting and extended or sustained effort. The original kibbutz collectivity, like military collectivity was Spartan; it required destruction of kinship and family ties and the abolition not only of private property but of individuated possession as well. Rarely, however, is the activity of the kibbutz assessed in terms of its concrete context. Sabri Jiryis correctly points out that

'The best evidence of the great extent of the areas of land acquired (by Israelis from Arabs) at this period — the period of the Arab-Jewish war of 1948 — is the existence within Israel of the ruins of more than 250 Arab villages demolished after the expulsion of their inhabitants. In addition, of course, there are the lands of the Arabs who were expelled or fled from the larger towns.' (11)

And Dr. Israel Shahak basing his report on the excellent work of the late Palestinian historian Arif al-Arif, documents the destruction of 385 villages in Israel *before 1967*.

Contrary to the misconception that the kibbutzim are the basic agricultural unit in Israel, the network of kibbutzim were never the major supplier of agricultural products. In the pre-state period the bulk of agricultural products came from the Palestinian-Arab peasantry, and with its dispossession (almost 1,000,000 Palestinian refugees were created on the one hand and massive confiscation of refugee and non-refugee Palestinian property by the state took place on the other) the country felt an acute and drastic shortage in agricultural products. The shortage lasted well into the late 1950s, a period known in Israel as *Tzena* (austerity) and involved strict rationing, which was terminated through the transformation of much former Arab lands into *moshavim* of Oriental Jewish farmers, whose production enabled the gradual meeting of the overall needs of the state at large (269 of the 346 *moshavim* existing in 1970 were founded after the establishment of the state).

Correlatively the kibbutzim underwent a process of industrialization, not shared by the *moshavim*. Today some of the major industries are located in the kibbutz network, and the overall kibbutz production, according to the *Encyclopaedia Judaica*, is 12 per cent of the country's G.N.P. This has been sustained only by extensive reliance upon hired labour. The hired labour employed is usually Oriental Jewish and Arab.

THE MOSHAVIM

The *moshav* agricultural structure was established early in the history of Zionist colonization efforts in Palestine. The first *moshav*, Nahallal (1921), was founded twelve years after the establishment of the first kibbutz, Deganiya (1909). It was started by a group headed by, among others, Defense Minister Moshe Dayan's father (Shmuel Dayan), which left Deganiya dissatisfied with its internal collective arrangements (such as the destruction of family ties) and founded Nahallal in the Jezreel Valley as a smallholder's co-operative agricultural settlement, where nuclear family structures were retained and equal plots of land were allotted to each family, meaning that production and consumption were not collectivized.

The *moshav* co-operative structures are restricted to marketing, wholesale purchase and investments in the *moshav* as a whole. The establishment of Nahallal was identified by the labour Zionist groups spearheading the colonization of the land as defection from the frontier line. The veteran (pre-state) *moshav* provided an outfit for those labour Zionist colonial pioneers who preferred to partake in the colonization endeavour in agricultural terms somewhat less taxing than those required on the frontier. That the situation in Palestine did not make this option widely available is clearly indicated by the fact that up until 1948, in contrast to 149 kibbutzim only 77 *moshavim* were established, all of which were predominantly of Ashkenazi Jewish origin, as was the 650,000 strong Jewish population as a whole. By 1970, however, 346 *moshavim* had been founded, a total of 269 having been established since the creation of the state. The *moshavim* population was 124.563 as against 77.152 population of the kibbutzim. (12)

The substantial rise of the *moshav* agricultural co-operative begins in the early 1950s, and is intimately related to the acute need, after the consolidation of the 1949 borders of the state, to provide as we have already noted for Jewish farming which replaced the dispossessed Palestinian-Arab peasantry. As Alex Bein correctly notes:

'As a result, a peculiar situation arose; large stretches of fertile land remained uncultivated, while at the same time (1948-1952) the growth in population was accompanied by shortage of the agricultural produce required to feed it. The conquests of the Israeli army after the end of the first cease-fire and the mass flight of the Arabs from their villages made the foundation of new settlements more urgent. These extensive areas of land abandoned by their former cultivators, uncultivated and unsettled, could not be left untended. This would be dangerous for the security of the country and damaging to its economy. Here the interests of both security and colonization pointed in the same direction and required the foundation of new settlements.

Without any clear plan to begin with, immigrants were therefore taken out of the camps and housed in abandoned Arab villages, where the dwellings had been repaired for the purpose. But this work of creating immigrants' villages (*kefarei avoda*) only solved the housing question for a limited number of them. The chief problem remained unsolved — how to effect the closest possible settlement of our frontiers with a chain of almost continuous settlements; how to revive the extensive areas which had been abandoned and whose produce was needed to support the population growing by leaps and bounds; how to divert the current of immigration from streaming into the main towns and to arouse in the immigrants the desire and ability to take possession of the soil and develop it.' (13)

And as Alex Weingrod points out:

'During the period of heavy immigration, agricultural produce was in short supply, and the villages were an important factor in meeting the nation's basic food requirements. In addition, the investment required for establishing the villages was presumed to be less than the capital demanded by urban-industrial development.

The program was also viewed as a means of dispersing the population throughout the country, thereby counteracting the tendency to concentrate in a small number of urban centers. The villages also served military functions, particularly in areas such as the Jerusalem corridor, where they were established along the border. Finally, rural life was highly valued in the pre-state Jewish community, and the planning authorities saw the program as having positive social as well as economic results.

The type of village established, and the organizational framework of the settlement system, were adopted for two principal reasons: the villagers were non-selected immigrants, and in most instances they had no previous experience in farming. Unlike the pre-state period, when many immigrants were self-selected and of a 'pioneering type', the post-1948 immigration was primarily a population transfer, including broad segments of European and Middle Eastern Jewish communities. In order to minimize the immigrants' crises of adaptation, the settlement authorities directed them to a type of village known as the *moshav;* in relation to the immigrants' background and preparation the *moshav* demanded the least amount of overt, revolutionary change. While other factors were involved in this choice — mainly political ones — the belief that the *moshav* provided a suitable format for immigrant absorption was the determining reason.' (14)

Similarly; the 1961 *Census* says of the geographical distribution of Oriental Jews:

'There are very considerable differences from region to region concerning the percentage of population born in Africa and Asia. In some regions the population of this origin constitutes the greater majority of the total population born abroad. Out of the 36 natural regions there are 5 (the Plain of Judea, Hatzor, Lower Western Galilee, Gerar and Besor — U.D.) in which the percentage of Jews born in Asia and Africa exceeds 80 per cent and on the other hand, there are two (Harod Valley and Kokhav Heights — U.D.) in which their percentage does not even reach 20 per cent. The highest percentage of persons born in Asia and Africa is located in the northern and southern part of the country. This is mainly as a result of the fact that a very high percentage of the immigrants from Asia and Africa came to the country after the establishment of the state, and that those new immigrants settled to a large extent in the lesser populated development areas, which are removed from the centres of the country.' (15)

It is also important to note, however, that the distinctions which set the kibbutz and the moshav radically apart (see below) have been blurred and do not apply to the Zionist colonial effort in the post-1967 occupied territories. Here the role of the kibbutz and the role of the *moshav* cannot be distinguished. Nor does the pre-1967 ethnic distinction between the kibbutz and the *moshav* apply here. *Both* the kibbutz and the *moshav* established *in the post-1967 occupied* territories are predominantly populated by Israeli-Ashkenazi (western) Jews. Out of a total of 224 kibbutzim in 1961, 61 had up to 4.9 per cent of persons born in the main countries of birth in Asia and Africa who immigrated since 1948; 79 had 5.0-14.9 per cent; 44 had 15.0-24.9 per cent; 21 had 25.0-34.9 per cent; 7 had 35.0-44.9 per cent; 4 had 45.0-54.9 per cent; 4 had 55.0-64.9 per cent; 4 had 65.0-74-9 per cent; none had above 75 per cent. In contrast, the population of foreign origin of the post-1948 new *moshavim* is predominantly Oriental-Jewish of Asian and African origin. 71 per cent of all foreign born of the post-1948 *moshavim* population were born in Asia and Africa.

Israel's Oriental-Jews do not participate in the Zionist colonial effort in the post-1967 occupied territories. In fact, when suggestions were made to the effect that their terrible housing conditions could be at least somewhat relieved in the settlements and townships established in the post-1967 occupied territories, they flatly refused the offer and demanded rehabilitation in the areas of their present residence, often the slum belt of the major metropolitan centres of the country.

THE ORIENTAL JEWS

THE FEAR OF 'LEVANTIZATION'

Against official school textbook history and its concomitant morality the need for a critical radical history aiming to expose the lie, reveal the truth and reconstitute social morality is paramount. The true history of the Oriental-Jewish society in Israel is a case in point. One cannot possibly gain a meaningful insight into this chapter of Israeli social and political history through official textbooks. Much can be gleaned by critical reading of straightforward scholarly studies. Often, however, an insight into the true history of a given society can only be gained through the traditional oral history conveyed from generation to generation. Thus it is the narratives based on oral history, which are still alive within the Oriental-Jewish communities, that offer the best insight into the totality of their experience in Israel.

It is not incidental that the study of oral Oriental-Jewish history has not been systematically and professionally pursued in Israel. The history of the internally colonized Oriental-Jewish society, much as the history of the externally colonized Palestinian-Arab society, is under systematic official onslaught.

For a political order predicated upon conquest and colonization the destruction of the authentic history of the colonized is an imperative of the first order. Such political systems must therefore attempt a double lie: they must hide from themselves their own original contingency and ambivalence under the guise of pre-determined and historically necessary success, and they must simultaniously attempt to rob the colonized of their own authentic history, presenting the conquest and the destruction it carries in its wake as the pre-determined objectively necessary advancement of progress and enlightenment.

As we shall see below, Oriental-Jewish participation in the Zionist effort in Palestine is characterized by built-in passivity. They do not share the Zionist vision in its classical sense. They cannot. The political and educational system and the social values in the Jewish state of Israel reflect the cultural mores of its European founding pioneer ruling elite, who saw and intended Israel to become a modern, technological and above all, western solution to the Jewish problem. Their worst nightmare and greatest concern has always been to keep the Orientalization of the Jewish state, which is after all situated in the Middle East, at bay. Abba Eban, in his capacity as Israel's Foreign Minister, pinpointed the issue at hand accurately and succinctly:

> 'So, far from regarding our immigrants from Oriental countries as a bridge towards our integration with the Arab-speaking world, our object should be to infuse them with an Occidental spirit rather than allow them to drag us into an unnatural Orientalism'. (1)

The same reality, cultural and political, is described, though in terms of opposite value notations, by Kokhavi Shemesh, one of the leading members of the radical fringe of the Israeli Black Panther Organization:

> 'Ever since I came to consciousness, people tried to convince me that there is a big difference between me and the Arabs, that is, they have tried to instil into me that Jews are better than Arabs and that we, the Jews, are a chosen people. Reality shows, at least to me, that there is no difference between the Arabs and me. The only difference is the religious origins. Those who claim that it is the religious origin which determines national affiliation must concede then that the Catholic Arab and the Catholic French, for instance, belong to the same nation.' (2)

The term 'Oriental-Jew' was coined in Israel to categorize and identify the post-1948 massive Jewish immigration from Asia and Africa. It is an ideologically motivated term of reference, coined in an attempt to hide away a critical contradiction underpinning the social and political reality of the newly established state. The majority of Israel's post-1948 Jewish population, (approx. 60 per cent) is culturally Arab, and yet divorced from its Arab heritage and affiliation through being situated in Israel as second-class citizens of a western extension, a settler colonial polity, based on the distinction between Jew and Arab and on the exclusion and dispossession of the latter in the process of transforming Palestine into Israel. Being thus situated Israel's Oriental-Jewish citizens face a set of key problems. The specific terms of their determination has far-reaching implications on the eventual destiny of the Jewish state of Israel.

THE ARRIVAL OF THE IMMIGRANTS

Israel, thus, has a dual history. One which dates back to the first Zionist Congress (1897), and the other dating back to Israel's declaration of independence (1948). This latter history is the history of the majority of Israel's Jewish citizens: those who have not participated in the creation of the Jewish state *ex nihilo*, but who were brought, came or were forced to immigrate to the already established state in massive waves between 1948 and 1956, largely from Middle Eastern and North African countries, to replace the native Palestinian-Arab on his land and fill the vacuum created by the massive dispossession of the Palestinian-Arab people through the 1948 war. The Jewish communities in the Middle East and North Africa were the only Diasporah Jewish communities that could possibly be considered as candidates to replace the Palestinian-Arab peasantry. Euro-American Jewry, which was well-integrated into the post-World War II western nation-states' affluent middle-classes, could best be lured to immigrate and join the Israeli ruling bureaucracy and privileged classes by way of generous tax exemptions, privileged housing conditions and secure administrative (both academic and bureaucratic) jobs. The only pool of labour that could be considered was the customary traditional Jewish communities in Asia and Africa, most of which were situated in analogous socio-political positions to that of the 19th century East European Jewish *shtetle*. This time, however, their destruction was not left to the workings of external agents. The needs were too acute, the requirements too pressing and the opportunity far too tempting.

The Zionist movement had some previous limited experience in this field before 1948. As early as the first decade of the 1900s, notes Alex Bein, it was clear that

> 'The Ashkenazi (East European) Jews of the old *yishuv* had already settled in the towns and would probably not be suitable for other than urban occupations; but the Oriental Jews, particularly those belonging to the Yemenite and Persian communities, could enter agriculture. As their needs were few, they could compete against the Arabs. Already Yemenite Jews were being employed for seasonal work at several Jewish settlements. If they could be transferred permanently to the settlements, there would be employment for them, while their women-folk could work as domestic servants in the settlers' homes instead of Arab women.
>
> The success achieved in settling the Yemenite Jews who arrived in 1908 and 1909, together with news of the serious plight of the Jews in Yemen, moved the Palestine office, in conjunction with *Hapo'el Hatza'ir* to undertake the necessary steps to receive further immigrants from that country. In 1910 an emissary was sent out there. The result of his mission was that in 1912 several hundred families immigrated — more than had been anticipated. Indeed it was found necessary to send word back to Yemen that no further immigration should take place until notice was given; for Palestine was not yet ready to absorb so many newcomers at a time. Gradually, however, work was found for the majority — with the assistance of *Hapo'el Hatza'ir* — in the larger villages and the Zionist organization's settlements. But their living conditions were deplorable. Disease made serious inroads upon them, and the need for help became most pressing. A special housing campaign launched by the JNF netted £11.200 by the end of 1913.' (3)

Speaking of the general campaign by the Jewish National Fund to improve housing conditions, Bein writes:

> 'The houses — *larger for workers of East European origin, and smaller for the Yemenites* — were built in part by the JNF itself, and after 18 years, with the termination of the instalments, transferred to the ownership of their tenants. In part they were built by the tenants themselves, who received longterm loans or financial

> building grants. As it was found that the Yemenites adapt better to
> life when living together in their own environments, special quarters
> were built for them at the outskirts of the settlements. The land was
> usually donated by the settlements to the JNF, and in individual
> cases purchased by it.' (4) (emphasis added)

After 1949, the task was of a qualitatively different order. Until 1948
only 10.4 per cent of the Jewish immigration to Palestine was of Middle
Eastern or North African origin. After 1948 54.6 per cent of the Jewish
immigration to Israel originated from Asia and Africa. Between 1948 and
1959 the Jewish population of the country grew from 758.701 to
1.858.841 of which 945,261 were immigrants. The table overleaf gives
the total and the breakdown of post-1948 immigration to Israel from Asia
and Africa.

The patterns that determined the destiny of the limited Yemenite
immigration in the early 1900's, were replicated on a vast scale generating
immeasurable human suffering and destruction. Housing shortage was the
obvious glaring difficulty. The mass of the new Oriental-Jewish immigrants
were housed on arrival in Maabarot- transit camps — some, it soon trans-
pired, doomed to live there for no less than a decade.

> 'We went to register for immigration and never imagined that the
> emissaries were cheating us. They told us that there are houses
> waiting for us; (prefabricated) houses which can be erected within
> 24 hours; that each of us has a job waiting for him; that in Israel
> everyone is honest and one does not even have to keep the door
> of one's house locked (which, as it transpired, was ironically true,
> since who can lock the door of a tent?). Why could the emissaries
> not tell us the truth? It would have been so much easier had we
> been aware of what to expect. But we continued without knowing
> what was awaiting us. We actually forced out way into the lorries
> that would take us to the wonderful place promised to us by the
> emissaries.The lorries stopped suddenly in the middle of a field
> of thorns, and we were told: "That's it. Now take these (tarpaulin)
> sheets and erect your tents." And then the screaming, and children
> crying, and the scorpions, and the tents collapsing over our heads
> or being washed away in the rains, and the violence — all this is now
> well known. Only years later did I recover from the experience, in
> fact, only in 1959, when I married.' (5)

CULTURAL HOSTILITIES

Who were they, these refugees, who were later to populate the Moshs-
avim of the agricultural hinterland and the slum belts of the big cities?
Until 1949 the major body of the Jewish communities in Asia and Africa
lived in the largely pre-industrial commercial urban centres of their
respective countries. Like Central and East European *shtetle* and urban
Jewish ghetto communities, they had for the most part no history of
farming and peasantry. Their livelihood depended on commerce, trade

ORIENTAL JEWISH IMMIGRATION TO ISRAEL 1948-1972

	Total	'48-'51	'52-'54	'55-'57	'58-'60	'61-'64	'65-'68	'69-'71	'72
Asia	333,868	237,704	13,581	9,988	13,551	19,899	15,528	20,256	3,360
Africa	400,113	92,616	27,344	101,847	13,520	115,668	27,448	17,986	3,685
Total	733,981	330,320	40,925	111,835	27,071	135,567	42,976	38,242	7,045

Source: The Statistical Abstracts of Israel, 1973, Table V/2 pp.126-7

retail and craftsmanship.

'Regarding Iraqi Jewry, the picture is very clear. This was a community of some 150,000 people who had been living in Iraq for 2,500 years. All its members were educated, and a very high percentage had completed secondary school and higher education. Among the Iraqi Jews who immigrated to Israel in 1950-51 (over 110,000 people in a single year), the proportion of physicians was *four times higher* than among the (pre-1948) Jewish Yishuv in Eretz Israel (which in turn could boast one of the highest ratios of physicians per 1,000 people anywhere in the world).

36.5 per cent of Jewish immigrants from Iraq were members of the free professions. Iraqi Jews in fact administered the Iraqi state and the Iraqi economy. They were directors of the railway service, specialists, senior government officials, bank managers, rich merchants, lawyers, doctors and accountants. There were, of course, also poor Jews among them, but proportionately much fewer than among the Polish Jews, for example.

Iraqi Jews received an excellent Jewish and general education. In Jewish gymnasia (grammar schools) in Iraq, English and French were taught as foreign languages, and thus the Jewish intelligentsia tended to serve as a bridgehead between modern western culture and the stagnant culture of fanatically religious Iraqi society. To give an example, Iraqi Jews were among the pioneers of modern Iraqi poetry.)

Morroccan Jews tended to be the capitalists in that largely agrarian state. They were big, medium and small merchants, but also craftsmen such as gold, copper and silversmiths and carpenters. They made money by trading in the local Muslim produce and mediated between the French regime and the population at large, as well as between the local rulers and their subjects. They had a long and proud cultural tradition — Jews had resided in Morocco already in the days of Bar Kochva (132-135 A.D.)

Equally, Morroccan Jews played an important role in the modern nationalist movement in Morrocco. After Morocco became independent, its first cabinet had a Jewish Minister, Dr. Ben Zaken. Many had also been involved in the Jewish renaissance movement in the 1830's. Long before the arrival of the first Bilu Pioneers, Morroccan Jews were immigrating to Israel . . .

Jews emigrated from Morrocco in the pre-state illegal immigrant ships and were detained by the British Mandate's authorities in camps in Cyprus. In 1948, several thousand Morrocan Jewish youth rushed to Israel and fought the Egyptian army, participating in the hardest battles in the south of the country, especially on those fronts where our soldiers had failed so far (f.i. against the Egyptian Hulayqat fortifications). Many of those youths were killed and many more were injured, yet after the war their achievements were forgotten. They had come without their families and had no relatives in the country, so they demonstrated in the streets for some sort of state assistance. They were nicknamed "knifing Morroccans". Most of them went back to Morocco and returned only years later with the mass wave of imigration from Morrocco. Today there are 380,000 Morroccan Jews in Israel who are invariably described as having come from either terrible urban Ghettos or mountain caves.' (6)

Many of the Jews from Asia and Africa were in fact part of the cultural elite of their countries — but when they emigrated to Israel they were

confronted by the racism implicit in the fear of 'Orientalization' which
so animated the Ashkenazi veteran establishment who controlled the state.
When the doctors, lawyers, merchants and administrators arrived from Iraq
they were crowded into transit camps and offered only manual jobs. A
general image was built up of them as primitive and backward, as people
with no culture. This attitude still prevails and in some ways the Iraqi
Jewish community has never recovered from the social dislocation and
cultural humiliation they suffered upon their arrival in Israel.

The fear and contempt for the culturally Arab Oriental Jewish population is still manifest in Zionist culture. A fifth form school textbook,
for instance, was the subject of a recent scandal over the way it presented
the history of the Jews in Arab countries.

'The Jew was forbidden to give his children any sort of general
education. The children's learning was limited to religious studies,
which also were only permitted in the framework of the Jewish
Talmud Torah (religious) schools. Jewish girls, like their Muslim
counterparts, were married at six to nine years of age and boys at
the age of thirteen. The fate of the Jews in Syria and Iraq was a
similar one (to that of their Morroccan brethren). . .'

'The general atmosphere in Muslim countries affected Jewish life
as well. There was little spiritual activity during that period (19th
and 20th century — Baruch Nadel), and the economic situation of
the Jews was dominated by poverty and hardship. . .'

'The Jews lived in Ghetto-like quarters in poor housing that did
not meet hygienic requirements. They suffered from various illnessess
and plagues. In Morrocco and Persia these Ghettos were known as
'Millah' and in Tunisia as 'Hara'. They earned their livelihood by
primitive craftsmanship and very small-scale retail trading.' (7)

A DIVIDED SOCIETY

This assault on the cultural identity of Oriental Jews is in fact only one
aspect of the split in Israeli Jewish society, where class divisions and ethnic
divisions overlap. A brief examination of some official statistics will confirm
this, see tables on following pages.

The interesting and important point in the Income Table is the absence
of any indication of a trend towards the narrowing of the ethnic/class gap.
Differences do occur from year to year, but no continuous diminishing
trend can be discerned. Housing is also an important indicator of standard
of living and class stratification. The ethnic/class gap emerges clearly from
the table below. Even in terms of absolute figures the situation is bad.
Only about half of the Oriental-Jewish families in Israeli live less than
two people per room. It should be noted that families living in crowded
conditions are usually the larger families, therefore the percentage of
individuals living under such conditions will be still higher than the figures
given by family. The category of Israeli-born is both deceptive and useless.

INCOME

Monthly income per family, equality measures, 1956/7-1969

	1956/7	1957/8	1963/4	1965	1966	1967	1968	1969
All the population	268	266	553	648	725	781	799	875
Asia-Africa	219	172	402	515	563	562	638	692
Europe-America	300	304	640	719	825	923	909	1000
Measure of equality	73	57	63	72	68	61	70	69

Based on the study of Sarouka and Peres (1972)

HOUSING

Jewish families by number of persons per room and continent of birth of head of family

	Europe-America		Asia-Africa		Israeli born	
	1961	1969	1961	1969	1961	1969
Less than 2 per room	66.9	85.6	32.6	52.9	68.1	75.3
2 persons — less than 4	30.9	13.5	48.9	40.1	27.8	19.5
4 persons and over	2.2	0.9	18.5	7.0	4.1	5.2

Source: *Statistical Abstracts of Israel, 1970, p.181*

9 out of 10 large nuclear families are Oriental-Jewish families.
According to the data compiled by Dr. Jacon Habib 280,000 children
live in conditions that are under the poverty line or under the
poverty line threshold (according to the 1969 data)
30% of the children of Asian and African origin are raised in poor
families, as compared with 4% of children of Western (European and
American) origin and 8% of the children of Israeli born parents.
the per capita food consumption of essential staples like meat, milk
and milk products of large nuclear families (6 persons or more) is
only 2/3 of that of a small nuclear family (3 persons).' (10)

As Sami Smooha put plainly:

'Briefly, the major divisions in Israeli society are along lines of
nationality, culture and religious observance. They make up the
following dichotomies: Jews vs Arabs, Ashkenazim vs Orientals and
non-observant Jews vs observant Jews. While Ashkenazim constitute
a numerical minority (45 per cent of the Jewish population, but only
39 per cent of the total population) they are in fact a dominant
minority with all the distinguishing features of a majority. The
general distribution of resources (such as income, education, or
occupation) between Ashkenazim and Orientals is roughly two to
one. Disparity of power is much more considerable and discrete.
Ashkenazim are in full control of the three power centers in the state
— the state Government, the Histadrut and the Jewish Agency — as
well as the public and the private sectors of the economy. In the
intermediate power echelons Ashkenazim are several times over-
represented compared to Orientals. The ratio is five to one respectively. Only in the local power positions is there a roughly proportional
representation (short of equality) of each group. The Ashkenazi
group is also the dominant cultural group in a culturally diversified
society. Aside from a few token examples like the *humus* and *tahini*
dishes and the Yemenite traditional crafts, the Ashkenazi or western
values and practices predominate. History texts used in Jewish schools
hardly mention Oriental Jewry of the last 500 years. Literature is
exclusively Ashkenazi. Music follows suit. The prevailing social
ideals are completely Ashkenazi — a small middle-class urban family,
a kibbutz member, the *sabra*, the socialist society. The Oriental-Jew
cannot recognize himself in such image of Israel.' (11)

The specific terms of the Zionist colonial effort in Palestine as formulated in the aspiration of the Zionist colonial labour pioneers aimed to
establish in Palestine a Jewish state — modern, western and socialist — as
a solution to the Jewish problem and a refuge for Jews from persecution
and harassment. Given the cultural imperialism which always underlies
efforts of this kind, it became clear from the very early beginning of the
venture that the Oriental-Jewish citizens of the newly founded state are
doomed, to the extent that the existing Zionist structures of the state of
Israel are to remain unaltered, to what can be euphemistically termed
'transformative absorption through passive participation', and what should be
properly termed 'internal colonialism'. This is, of course, congruent with,
and necessarily follows from the colonial premises underlying the Zionist
effort from its initial conception. Sami Smooha recognizes this — to a

point — when he says:

> 'The conservative solution to Israel's ethnic dilemma is to allocate more resources to help the Orientals. A radical alternative is to make Israel a non-Jewish state and thus reduce the tension among Orientals and Ashkenazim, observant and non-observant Jews and Arabs and Jews. Since the second definition is incompatible with whatever Israel today stands for it is understandably avoided. But why is the first, extremely narrow definition of the problem not challenged?' (12)

To my mind, at least, there are specific conclusions to be drawn from the above analysis. These will be elaborated in another chapter, where the role and potential of the Palestine resistance movement as it relates to the internal settler-colonial contradiction underlying the class stratification of the Israeli-Jewish society will be examined in further detail.

KINSHIP AS HISTORY

'If one wants to grant to Marxist thought its full complexity, one would have to say that man in a period of exploitation is at once both the product of his own product and a historical agent who can under no circumstances be taken as a product. This contradiction is not fixed; it must be grasped in the very movement of praxis. Then it will clarify Engels's statement that men make their history on the basis of real, prior conditions (among which we would include acquired characteristics, distortions imposed by the mode of work and of life, alienation, etc.), but it is the men who make it and not the prior conditions. Otherwise men would be merely the vehicles of inhuman forces which through them would govern the social world.'
J.P. Sartre, *The Problem of Method*, London 1963
....

No, I'd say: I'd swear
that men have always lounged in myths
as Tall Stories,

that their real earnest
has been to grant excuses
for ritual actions.

Only in rites
can we renounce our oddities
and be truly entired.

Not that all rites
should be equally fonded:
some are abominable.

There's nothing the crucified
would like less
than butchery to appease Him.

CODA
From Archeology
one moral, at least, may be drawn
to wit, that all

our school text-books lie.
What they call History
is nothing to vaunt of,
being made, as it is,
by the criminal in us:
goodness is timeless.

W.H. Auden, 'Archaeology', *Thank You Fog*, London 1974

'UNSERE MENSCHEN'

In this chapter we shall pursue our critical presentation of Zionist history, aiming to recapture the original contingency and ambivalence underlying the original efforts of the Zionist colonizer. This we shall do through following the available political-biographical records of dominant Zionist lineages, which have emerged from the pioneering second *aliya* labour Zionist colonizing spearhead and have subsequently come to constitute the core of the Israeli-Jewish ruling elite. Written kin histories offer themselves in many ways as a revolutionary point of departure. They offer a historical narrative, which unlike official ('Royal' — to use Plato's Republican terminology) textbook history, is the least conducive to the mystification of the so-called paramountcy of 'objective historical forces' over human vision, aspiration and concrete action. State history critically attended to through the political biographies of existing or aspiring ruling elites has a profoundly healing effect. It betrays and exposes the origins of the established political, social and economic reality as constituted reality sustained by ongoing intentional human interpretive effort.

We have already noted in our Introduction that the Hebrew speaking student of Zionism and Israeli political history is fortunate to have access to the nineteen volumes of a unique repository of primary source material, namely, David Tidhar's *Encyclopaedia of the Pioneers of the Yishuv and Its Founders*. This is the only historical record that provides systematic information pertaining to family affiliations among those men and women who in Tidhar's opinion merited inclusion. The next in order of importance is E. Salpeter and Y. Elitzur's *Who Runs Israel*. Salpeter and Elitzur are two leading Israeli-Jewish journalists. Their volume is essentially anecdotal (which is not said disparagingly, since the anecdote belongs to the nature of such tasks) and constitutes to my knowledge the best supplementary source material to Tidhar's *Encyclopaedia*.

We shall take their lead and begin our study in this chapter with the man they have characterized as 'the most related person in Israel' (meaning the most significantly related man within the Israeli labour Zionist ruling elite), namely David ha-Cohen — a classical proto-type of a labour Zionist leader and member of the innermost circle of 'Unsere Menschen' ('our people') which has governed Israeli politics since the 1930s. We shall thereby be immediately introduced to the core cluster of the dominant lineages of the Israeli-Jewish labour Zionist ruling elite (or 'tribes' as they are popularly — and properly — called in Israel). These, we shall see, are inter-related through kin and corporate pseudo-kin relations that can be systematically traced through cross references in Tidhar's nineteen volume *Encyclopaedia*. Thus we shall be introduced not only to the original workings of the labour Zionist effort in Palestine, but also, to the important links and relations of mutual dependancy entertained by the labour Zionist pioneering, and subsequently ruling, elite with Zionist big business interests and with public (Histadrut) corporate interests, which in turn are linked to western international corporate monopolies, and with the Israeli military establishment.

We shall, in other words, thereby be afforded a concrete insight into the Zionist totality. And given the above analysis, we should at this point not be surprised that the insight is afforded to us through the venu of kinship as incorporated, transformed and utilized in the process of conquest and state-building. In other words, through the venu of corporate kinship.

THE HA-COHENS

Mordechai

David ha-Cohen was born in Homel, Russia, on the 10th October, 1897, to his father Mordechai Ben Hillel ha-Cohen (1856-1936) and his mother Shifrah, daughter of Nathan Pevzner. His grandfather (Hillel ha-Cohen) was a wealthy Russian merchant, learned traditional scholar and a descendant of Rabbi Yehiel from Paris. His grandmother, Rivkah (nee Warhaftig) is related to the Warhaftig House, and thus to e.g. Zerah Wahaftig, Israeli Minister of Religious Affairs for many years.

His father, Mordechai Ben Hillel, received traditional religious education in his native town of Mogilev, but in addition was privately tutored in Hebrew and secular studies. He also showed talents for writing and already at the age of 17 published in the Hebrew-Russian papers of *Ha-Levanon* (The Lebanon) *Ha-Shahar* (The Dawn) as well as in the Russian-Jewish papers of *Razsvet* (Dawn) and *Russki Yevrey* (The Russian Jew). He joined his father (Hillel ha-Cohen) in Petersburg in 1878, where the family business was centred, and became the secretary of the *Razsvet* Editorial Board, where he came into close contact with the foremost Jewish writers of the time: Buki Ben Yogli, A.A. Harkabi, Peretz Smolenskin and others. He withdrew from his public and literary commitments completely for four years (1884 - 1888), which he dedicated to the expansion of his business ventures. During that period he also married Shifrah, daughter of Abraham Nathan Neta Posner, a public figure and a merchant from Homel (Russia) and a founding member of the *Hovevei Zion* (The Lovers of Zion) movement. He then moved to Homel, where his in-law's large timber trading business was based and returned to public activity and writing. He became a leading member of *Hovevei Zion*. His business commitments required extensive travelling to Kiev, Odessa, Minsk and Vilna, and thus he was able to maintain regular contacts with other leading Jewish writers and public figures of the time: Lilienblum, Ahad ha-Am, Levinsky and others.

He first toured Palestine in 1889. His critical articles and reports about the nature of the Jewish settlement in Palestine as well as his regular contributions to all current Hebrew, Yiddish and Russian-Jewish papers raised him into prominence. He became the director of the Homel Mutual Credit Bank, Chairman of the Trade Association and a prominent member in various committees in the province and in the capital.

In 1907 the family immigrated to Palestine and settled in Jaffa. He became the Director of the Leon Stein Metal Works and Cast Iron Factory, was one of the 60 founding members of Tel-Aviv's first Jewish residential quarter, *Ahuzat Bayit*, and drafted its first Constitution. He became a member of the Board of Directors of the *Herzliyyah* Hebrew Gymnasia, one of the single most important institutions generating pre- and post-state Zionist urban elite leadership up until the mid 1950s, and other public committees; President of the Hebrew High Court of Peace; Founder of the *Halva'ah ve Hisakhon* (Loan and Saving) Cooperative Bank in Jerusalem; Founder of the *Zerubavel* Bank, Honorary Citizen of Tel-Aviv, etc. His prolific writings are collected in a number of anthologies. He died in Haifa in 1936.

His children were the late Shmuel ha-Cohen, a prominent public figure in Haifa; Hannah, who married Dr. Arthur Ruppin, the Chief Architect of the Zionist colonial efforts in the 1930s and 1940s; Shoshanah (Rosa), an advocate married to Shlomo Ginsberg (Ginosar), Ahad ha-Am's son (Hebrew University administration and Israeli diplomatic service); Dinah Broche, an MD living permanently in Paris; David (ha-Cohen) (see below); and Shimon (ha-Cohen), a farmer in Binyaminah.

David and his kin

David ha-Cohen came to Palestine with his family at the age of 10. He graduated from the *Herzliyyah* Hebrew Gymnasium and with the outbreak of World War I joined the Turkish Army with other *Herzliyyah* graduates. In 1919 he left for Britain where he studied political economy for four years at the London School of Economics under Clement Attlee and Dr. Edward (later Baron) Dalton, leading members of the British Labour Party. During that period he studied and shared an apartment with Moshe Sharett (Shertok) (see below), who was to become Israeli Foreign and then Prime Minister. He returned to Palestine in 1923 and was appointed Director of the Office of Public Works and Construction of the Histadrut which under his and Dov Hos's leadership (see below) developed into the largest corporation in Israel (*Sollel Boneh*). Due to his close contacts with the top British military administration in Mandatory Palestine (he was the *Haganah* liaison officer to the British army during World War II) he secured for *Sollel Boneh* the major public works contracts (e.g. construction of the chain of Tegrat fortresses along the northern borders, construction of roads, army camps, an air field, British oil construction works in Iran, etc. In 1930 he married Ruth, daughter of Yehezkel Kravatzov (died 1945) and then the writer Brachah Habas, daughter of Rabbi Israel Habas (see below). His third wife is Tziporah Arbel (Idelnant), who, through her grandfather is linked to the veteran Zionist Abuhab Tel-Aviv family and through her mother (Meirovitz) to the now legendary nucleus of first *Bilu* Jewish immigration to Palestine.

David ha-Cohen's corporate kin links cement not only his labour Zionist affiliation; through his second wife Brachah Habas he is again linked to the founding generation of the Zionist National Religious Party. Her father, Israel Habas, is related to a prominent Rabbinical line (Ha-Yesod, Hebrew initials of Yehudah Safrah ve-Danyah), and was a wealthy merchant in Lithuania. Her mother is related to the Rabbinical line of Volozhin. Israel Habas spent his youth in Rabbinical schools, and after his marriage he devoted himself to successful commerce and Zionist national religious activity and was one of the prominent founding members of *Ha-Mizrahi*, the precursor of the National Religious Party. He immigrated to Palestine in 1907 where he established the largest leather and tannery business (Israel Habas & Sons) and entered into large real estate ventures (the family owns large sections of the city of Benei Berak, both buildings and orange groves. Benei Berak itself is today one of the ten towns which form the metropolitan area of Tel-Aviv. It was established in 1924 on the lands of the Arab village Ibn Ibraq by a group of Orthodox families from Poland and has remained under Orthodox Israeli political control. The value of its real estate properties have of course rocketed sky high with the urbanization of the Tel-Aviv area and the establishment of important industrial parks in the city's outer belt (diamond polishing, light industries, etc.).

But the story does not end here. David ha-Cohen's children (all from his first wife) are Esther, Adah and Yehezkel. Adah ha-Cohen is married to Aharon Yadlin, former Secretary of the Labour Party and now Minister of Education. Aharon Yadlin's cousin, Asher, became the Director of the Histadrut Health Insurance scheme (the largest in the country) and the Chairman of the Board of Directors of the Workers Company, the holding corporation of all of the Histadrut's giant business interests. He in turn is married to Daliyah Golomb of the Golomb-Hos-Sharett 'tribe', which again constitutes a major pool for recruitment into the Israeli ruling establishment. (see charts below).

Through David ha-Cohen we are introduced to the two major economic pillars of the Zionist establishment: the Histadrut, its holding corporation The Workers' Company,and specifically Sollel Boneh, on the one hand, and the key economic pillar of revisionist (*Likud*) Zionism: The Meridor maritime empire.

The Histadrut

The Histadrut (The Federation) was established in 1920 as the General Federation of Hebrew Workers in Eretz Israel, in an effort by the two rival major labour Zionist parties, *Ahdut ha-Avodah* and *Ha-Poel ha-Tzair* to coordinate Jewish labour matters. Until 1948 the Histadrut was the administrative backbone of the Jewish *yishuv* in Palestine, controlling its colonization effort, economic production and marketing, labour employment and defense (the *Haganah*).

The Histadrut is an economic empire controlling a good portion of Israel's economy: holding corporations, companies, banks, industrial concerns, agro-industries, etc. Its union activities constitute a fraction of its interests, concentrated in one of its numerous specialized departments, the Department for Labour Unions.

According to the *Encyclopaedia Judaica* the Histadrut controlled industries employ 23.3 per cent of Israel's total labour force and produce 20.8 per cent of Israel's GNP (figures for 1968/69). As the second largest employer in the country (second to state employment) it controls the national wage policies together with the Government and the private sector organized in the (national) Association of Industrialists. The Histadrut has virtual monopoly over health insurance services (there is no national health insurance in Israel) and operates mutual aid funds and pension funds for its members. (75% of the total Israeli work force are members of the Histadrut). The availability of these funds, however, is controlled by the Histadrut hierarchy in that, for instance, mutual aid funds are released only to Histadrut authorized strikes, and these, as one can imagine, are very rare indeed.

The other major Histadrut departments and institutions are:
1. The Central Tax Department
2. The Department of Tourism and Excursions
3. The Department for Religious Needs
4. The Arab Department
5. The Political Department
6. The Department of Organization
7. The Department of Culture and Education
8. The Employment Fund
9. The Department of Absorption and Development
10. The Pensions Department
11. The Mutual Aid Department
12. The Department for the Academic Employee
13. The Secretariat of the Workers' Company
14. The Histadrut Legal Department
15. The Histadrut Central Auditing Committee
16. The Histadrut Supreme Court.

In order to illustrate the concrete implications of the above, let us have a closer look at one of the Histadrut's key economic institutions, a central pillar of the *yishuv's* pre-state economy co-founded and for many years directed by David ha-Cohen, namely *Sollel Boneh*.

Sollel Boneh

Sollel Boneh Ltd. is the major executive arm of the Histadrut in the
field of construction and related industries. The scope of its activity and
the number of its employees place it at the top of the list of the large
Israeli companies. In 1972 it employed 35,000 people and its turnover
reached 1.6 milliard Israeli Pounds. The early beginnings of *Sollel Boneh*
date to the early 1920s when under the initiative of the Histadrut an
Office for Construction and Building was established as a small workers'
owned contracting venture. During the period of the Mandate, especially
during World War II, the company specialized in constructions of fortifications, air fields, public and government buildings — all this in addition
to its regular activities as a contractor and builder. Since the establishment
of the state in 1948 the company had the key position in all branches of
construction and public works in the country. After the 1948 war *Sollel
Boneh* directed most of its efforts into the most urgent area of the period:
home construction for the absorption of waves of new immigrants. In that
context *Sollel Boneh* built new towns, industrial constructions, educational
institutions, and created urban centres where public services were concentrated. During 1949-1958 *Sollel Boneh* contributed to the industrialization
of the country by establishing, among others, a pipe line factory in Acre,
the *Harsa* ceramic works in Beer Sheba, the *Nesher* cement factory in
Ramleh, the *Shimshon* cement factory in Har Tuv and the tyre factory
Alliance in Haderah. It enlarged the Haifa deep water port, constructed
the Kishon port, constructed the earthworks involved with the draining
of the Hulah valley, constructed most of the hospitals built in the country
during this period, built the university campuses in Haifa and Jerusalem,
the steel mills in Acre, the sugar refinery in Afulah, Reading 2 electricity
power station in Tel-Aviv, the new potassium factory at the Dead Sea, the
Timhah copper mines and many others. No wonder therefore that during
the first decade of the Israeli state the turnover of *Sollel Boneh* increased
from IL 6 million in 1948 to IL 140 million in 1957, and the number of
its employees grew from 800 to 14,000.

The first reorganisation of the company was undertaken after the first
decade of the state. The company became a complex corporation with
holdings both in Israel and abroad. The Histadrut holding company, the
Workers' Company, of which *Sollel Boneh* was a subsidiary decided to
split the complex into specialized independent corporations. Thus the
company's industrial interests were organized into a separate corporation
(Koor), and the company's interests and commitments abroad were
organized in the Overseas and Harbour Works Company, which was later
re-incorporated into its mother company. A number of subsidiaries
remained affiliated to *Sollel Boneh* such as the Lime and Stone Production
Co. Ltd. (the state's main supplier of aggregates (70%) and lime (90%) as
well as gypsum, marble, etc.), *Herut* Ltd. (installation, air conditioning,

heating, lifts, refrigerating, etc.), *Hemar* Ltd. (Mosaics, tiles, building blocks, etc.). In general the company is active in the following fields:
1.   Public works, town-planning and town building, hotels and power stations.
2.   Roads and air fields.
3.   Timber industries, metal industries, mechanical industries, as well as auxilliary industries in cement and asphalt.
A special rural department in *Sollel Boneh* concentrates on rural construction in villages, kibbutzim and *moshavim*. In recent years *Sollel Boneh* was the major company involved in construction of emergency shelters, especially in the Jordan Valley and in the north; the Bar-Lev line, the Elat-Sharm el-Sheikh road, the supersonic air strip in Lydda airport, the new central station in Tel-Aviv, the Judaization of East (Arab) Jerusalem, the Elat-Ashkelon oil pipe-line, etc.

  The second reorganization involving the transformation of the company and its subsidiaries into a business concern was carried out in 1971. Accordingly it was organized in seven specialized sections:
1.   Building Division — undertakes construction of residential dwellings including prefabricated housing, industrial complexes, public buildings, hospitals, hotels, defence works etc. It operates through 17 branch offices located from the Golan Heights to Eilat. Turnover totals about IL 750 million in 1972.
2.   Road and Earth Moving Division — undertakes all phases of road construction and public works projects, including clearing areas for agriculture and building, laying road foundations, paving roads, laying pipelines and building airfields. The division operates the largest fleet of mechanical equipment in Israel. It supplies its own requirements of concrete and asphalt. About 25% to 30% of Israel's road construction is performed by this division.
3.   Manufacturing Division — includes industrial plants producing metal products, furniture, building components such as building blocks, floor tiles and pipes, repair shops, and sundry services required by the other divisions of Sollel Boneh, as well as by outside clients.
4.   Herouth Ltd. — acts as contractor in all branches of mechanical and electrical engineering, sanitary installations, plumbing, air conditioning, central heating and elevators. The company owns auxiliary enterprises producing and marketing water boilers, electrical heating units, water purification units, centrifugal concrete pipes and other industrial products.
5.   Quarries — Lime and Stone Production Co. Ltd. is the largest producer and supplier of aggregates (70%) and lime (90%) in Israel. It operates 12 stone quarries, 5 marble quarries, 5 lime kilns, 2 marble and building stone plants, 1 gypsum quarry and plant and 8 ready-mix concrete plants. Its products are aggregates for building and road construction, concrete asphalt, lime, both burnt and hydrates, marble blocks and slabs, monuments, building stones, raw gypsum for the cement industry, plaster-

of-Paris and ready mix concrete.

6.   Sollel Boneh International Ltd. — specialists in large-scale projects
in developing countries, mostly in Africa, Asia and South America. It
operates through joint companies with the local governments or through
its own independent branches. Sollel Boneh personnel from Israel provide
the core of the administrative and professional staff for its world-wide
activities. The Company builds hotels, office building, public institutions
and factories, and also undertakes road, bridge and harbour construction.
It competes successfully with large international concerns and its turnover
for 1972 exceeds $50 million.

7.   Diyur B.P. Ltd. — This company plans and promotes the construction of apartments, offices and shops for sale to the general public. It
builds medium cost housing units in various parts of Israel. In addition a
number of smaller companies are affiliated to the concern and are under
its direct control.

The capital and trust assets of the concern amounted to IL 200 million
in 1972. The concern constantly modernizes both in management and
technology and has adopted the policy of relative independance to its
different sectors in order to encourage productivity and profitability. It
has offices in Britain (Soltrade Ltd.) and in the United States (Reynolds
Construction Co. Ltd.)

Maritime Fruit Carriers

It is evident from the above detailed description that *Sollel Boneh*
effectively operates in all relevant respects as a multi-national capitalist
corporation. After his retirement from *Sollel Boneh* in 1970 there were
therefore no difficulties for David ha-Cohen, its founding member and
long time Managing Director to seat himself comfortably in the Chairman's
seat of the Atalantic Fisheries Co. Ltd., one of the important subsidiaries
of Israel's largest privately owned maritime multi-national corporations,
Maritime Fruit Carriers Co. Ltd. There is, however, an aspect relating to
this Executive move that requires further elaboration.

The key members of the Board of Directors of Maritime Fruit Carriers
Co. Ltd. are intimately associated with right wing revisionist Zionism,
and since 1948 with the Herut Party (see Herut and I.Z.L. in Glossary),
the traditional political rival of labour Zionism and its challenger for
political hegemony in the World Zionist Federation and the state of Israel.
The Maritime Fruit Carriers Co. Ltd. is in fact its major pillar. We have
already noted that the rise of 'socialist' labour Zionism to a position of
political hegemony since the 1930s within the World Zionist Federation
and (since 1948) in the state of Israel did not go unchallenged. In fact,
the 1948 war, Israel's war of independence from British Mandatory rule,
brought the rivalry and the conflict between labour Zionism and revisionist Zionism almost to the point of civil war.

We shall not go into the details of the process of the strategic convergence of labour Zionist and revisionist Zionist positions since 1948. For our purpose it will suffice to point out that whereas the bitter conflict and important strategic differences between these two rival political Zionist parties was dramatically brought into sharp focus during the 1948 war in the 'Altalena Affair', when the Haganah elite units shelled and sank Altalena, the IZL (see Glossary) ammunition ship anchored opposite the shores of Tel Aviv, their gradual strategic and ideological convergence was similarly dramatically demonstrated in the formation of the 1967-1970 National Unity Government. This Government was formed on the first day of the 1967 war (5.6.1967) coopting Menachem Begin and Y. Sapir (Likkud, see Glossary) as Ministers without Portfolio and Moshe Dayan as Minister of Defense. It ran the administration of Israel and the post-1967 occupied territories for the three critical years following the war, during which the dynamics of the post-1967 Greater Israel were irreversibly set.

David ha-Cohen's move from a key position in the Histadrut owned *Sollel Boneh* giant corporation to a key position in the Maritime Fruit Carriers Co. Ltd. as the Chairman of its Atlantic Fisheries Co. Ltd. would have been inconcievable before 1967. Further such an executive move from a key position in one of the economic pillars of the ruling labour Zionist establishment to a key executive position in the economic pillar of its strongest historical political rival and challenger of its hegemony is of further particular significance since David ha-Cohen is by no means a member of the new professional 'non-political' Israeli Executive class, but a labour Zionist veteran leader of the first rank.

The amusing point in the story, however, is that in following David ha-Cohen political career into his new job with the Atlantic Fisheries Co. Ltd. one discovers that it could hardly be said that he stepped outside the boundaries of the 'proper family'. The Board of Directors of this maritime empire of which the Atlantic Fisheries Co. Ltd. is a subsidiary consists among others of Captain Milah Brener, the co-founder of the Company with Jacob Meridor. The latter was one of the central leaders of I.Z.L. the right-wing unofficial underground which together with the *Lehi* was responsible among others for the Deir Yasin Massacre (see Glossary). The former however, is the nephew of the leading early labour Zionist Hebrew writer Joseph Haim Brener and husband of Michal (nee Dunie), niece of Dr. Haim Weizmann, first President of the state of Israel. He is also the cousin-in-law of General (Reserve) Ezer Weizmann, former Commander of the Israeli Airforce, former Likkud (see Herut in Glossary) Minister of Transport in the 1967-1970 National Unity Government and another cousin of Dr. Haim Weizmann. Finally The Maritime Fruit Carriers Co. Ltd. corporate business ties are further clinched through the marriage of Jacob Meirdor's daughter Rachel to Joseph Krammermann, an IZL veteran and one of Israel's richest industrial magnates, who also serves as the Chairman of the Herut Party Financial Department.

Arthur Ruppin

We now return to the labour origins of David ha-Cohen. His sister Hannah married Arthur Ruppin who was, as we have noted, the architect of the Zionist colonial effort during the 1930s and 1940s.

Arthur Ruppin (1876-1943) was born in Rawitsch (Prussia) to Isaac Albert a wealthy merchant and Sicilia, daughter of Julius Burk from Posen who is related to the renown Rabbi Zvi Hirsch Kalischer family. He was educated in German universities (law and economics) and got his Ph.D. in 1902. Between 1891-98 he was an agent for a large grain trading company in Magdeburg and after he obtained his Ph.D. he served as a deputy judge and advocate in the same city. In 1903 he was appointed Director of the Bureau for Jewish Statistics and Demography founded by Alfred Nossing, and it was then that he began to take active interest in Zionism. There he first met his lifetime colleague Dr. Thon who became the long time Director of the Palestine Office of the Jewish Agency and with whom he worked in close collaboration. Ruppin himself was sceptical of Herzlian political Zionism, but was very much attracted to what was termed (in seeming contradiction) practical utopian Zionism, which was the underlying commitment of the first and second *Aliyot*, the original leadership of labour Zionism. They placed as first priority for the Zionist movement to embark upon the practical colonial effort of establishing agricultural colonies. Utopian — of course: these were intended to provide the means and the institutional tool for raising, nurturing and cultivating the New Jew, the consumation of the Zionist solution to the Jewish problem. This brought him close to the minority faction within the Zionist movement, which found itself in opposition to political Zionism. This position, which did not emphasize aspirations for political Jewish sovereignty formulated its vision in terms very close to those of Ahad Ha-Am: an autonomous renewed centre for Jewish cultural life. They maintained that the Jewish effort in Palestine need not necessarily involve a clash with the native Palestinian-Arab population. Out of these Jewish circles, centred mainly in Berlin (Bernard Feibel, David Treitsch, Martin Buber and others) stemmed the Brit Shalom of which he and some of his lifetime colleagues, Buber, Rabbi Binyamin (Radler Feldman), Haim Kalvarisky, Yehudah Magnes and others were founding members. However he soon came to realize that his Zionist commitments and his commitments to Arab-Jewish existence were in reality incompatible:

'it became clear how difficult it is to realise Zionism and still bring it continually into line with the demands of general ethics'.

And in 1936 he had to admit that it was not only 'difficult' but simply impossible.

'On every site where we purchase land and where we settle people, the present cultivators will inevitably be dispossessed.'

And he concluded:

'The Arabs do not agree to our venture. If we want to continue our work in Eretz Israel against their desires, there is no alternative but that lives should be lost. It is our destiny to be in a state of continual warfare with the Arabs. This situation may well be undesirable, but such is the reality.' (1)

Ruppin saw clearly that there could be no compromise between Zionist colonization and its victims. The choice — then, as now — was between Zionism and 'general ethics'. Being an ardent Zionist he opted for Zionism and the 'continual warfare' that it implied and still implies.

In 1905 he joined the Zionist Federation and in 1907 he was appointed by Professor Otto Warburg to conduct a detailed survey of the Jewish reality in Palestine. In 1908 he immigrated to Palestine and opened the Palestine Office in Jaffa. A German-Jew in a predominantly Russian-Jewish milieu, his acclimatization was long and painful. His first attempts failed. He attempted to prove that the Jewish colonial effort in Palestine was not only ideologically necessary, but also commercially profitable. The farms he established in Ben Sheman, Huldah and Kinneret proved to be a disaster in this respect. There were not only financial difficulties, but labour difficulties as well. The Jewish workers on the farms continually rebelled against their appointed managers. His breakthrough came when he decided to allocate to the most rebellious group in Kinneret the newly acquired lands of Umm Juni for collective management.

'Ruppin's improvised solution had miraculous results. The Kinneret farm was pacified, and out of Umm Juni emerged the first collective agricultural settlement (Deganiya, the forerunner of the Israeli-Jewish kibbutz).' (2)

His next breakthrough was in the successful implementation of a 'compromise' investment policy of private and public (Zionist Federation) capital. The company he subsequently established in 1909, Palestine Land Development Corporation — together with the President of the Zionist Federation Executive at the time, Dr. Otto Warburg and with Dr. Jacob Thon, his successor as Director of the Palestine Office — served as a real estate puchasing company both for the Jewish National Fund and private investors. The same pattern was adopted later (1934) in the establishment of Rassco, Rural and Surburban Settlement Company Ltd., which is one of the largest mixed (private and public ownership) contractors in Israel, servicing both the private and public sectors.

Whereas both the Jewish National Fund and Sollel Boneh established themselves as the major 'state-on-the-way' powerful agencies, acquiring Jewish monopoly over landholdings and construction respectively, the Palestine Land Development Corporation and Rassco respectively catered to the private middle and upper middle class business interests of Jewish immigrants in these fields. The Palestine Land Development Corporation concentrated on purchase both of urban and rural properties. The rural properties were generally, but not exclusively, leased to the Jewish National

Fund. The urban properties were developed by the Corporation itself or by private initiative. After the establishment of the state of Israel in 1948 the company concentrated on urban development projects. Its urban real estate holdings are large, and now of prime value. The company encourages other companies and private investors, local and foreign, to participate in dividend bearing investment projects. In recent years the company has entered into the tourism industry, and through subsidiary daughter companies controls the Sharon Hotel, the Eshel ha-Sharon Hotel, the Nigdal ha-Sharon service apartment hotel — all situated on the prime Herliyyah coast, the Galei Kineret Hotel in Tiberias, the Rimonim Hotel in Safad, and the Neptune Hotel in Elat. It established a subsidiary M.N.I. Resort Hotels in Israel (Management) Ltd. which contracts the management not only of the company's own hotels but others as well. The founding shares of the company are predominantly in national (public) hands: the Jewish National Fund and the Foundation Fund. They also have privileged voting rights. But they have no priority over ordinary shares in what pertains to profit distribution. The ordinary shares of the company are distributed among individuals in the country and abroad and are traded in the Tel-Aviv bourse. The turnover of the Corporation and its subsidiaries totals IL 100 million.

It is the introduction of this investment pattern which made Ruppin the key figure in the Zionist efforts. Combined to and following this pattern he successfully promoted the establishment of smallholder agricultural settlements, which when the land is privately owned are called *Kefar* (village) and when under the control of Zionist institutions are called *moshav* or *moshav shitufi* (collective *moshav*). He did this against enormous opposition from many sections in the labour Zionist movement who for a variety of ideological reasons insisted on the exclusivity of the collective kibbutz agricultural settlement and opposed the 'embourgeoisement' of the movement. He had the upper hand, and for reasons which very soon became obvious. For the Zionist colonization to survive in Palestine and develop into a state solution for the Jewish problem it had to align not only with the imperial interests predominant in the area but also with the elements of Jewish big business.

One must emphasize that the Zionist contempt of Diaspora Jewishness was directed against the destroyed poor *shtetle* Jew. The *Gvir*, the rich merchant, trader or banker always commanded respect. In most cases, one is almost tempted to say invariably as the evidence is simply overwhelming, the Zionist leadership itself came from the wealthier Jewish strata, as David ha-Cohen typically demonstrates. Although the Jewish collective settlement was to some extent motivated by socialist/Marxist aspirations, these had to be, and very soon were, compromised. As a matter of fact, the alliance with private Jewish capital could quite comfortably be accepted even by the more militant proponents of Marxist Zionism (Borochovism), since if the solution to the Jewish problem involves as first stage the proletarianization of the Jewish people, one must admit and align with Jewish industrial and commercial capital; how else could one expect a Jewish proletariat to be created *ex nihilo?*

Under Arthur Ruppin's leadership the Palestine Office of the Jewish Agency engaged in widespread purchase of lands. This activity generated local resistance and in 1917 brought him under increasing fire from the Ottoman administration. The Ottoman Governor of Palestine, Jamal Pasha, came under increasing pressure to curb the Zionist activity of the Palestine Office which ended up with Ruppin's expulsion to Constantinople. In 1919 he returned to the now British Mandatory Palestine and was nominated Director of the Department of Settlement of the Jewish Agency. In 1933 he became the Director of the Jewish Agency in Jerusalem.

His first wife was his cousin Shulamit, daughter of Raphael Lubeck (founder of the Shulamit Conservatory in Tel-Aviv under the management of Moshe Hupenk). He later married Hannah, daughter of Mordechai Ben Hillel ha-Cohen (David ha-Cohen's sister). From his first wife he had a daughter (Ruth), married to Dr. Peled (Fechtholtz) and from his second wife two daughters: Carmelah, who married General Yigael Yadin (Sukenik) (Israeli 2nd Chief of Staff and a renown archeologist), and Ayah, who married Dr. Zvi Dinstein. Through the Yadlin cousins we are led to the Sharett-Golomb-Hos connection, and with them we move from the predominantly economic labour Zionist domain into its military and political agencies.

THE FOUR BROTHERS-IN-LAW

Eliyahu Golomb (1893-1945) was born in 1893 in Volkovysk, Bielorussia. His family were large flour mill farmers and among the first Zionists to send their children for education in Palestine. Eliyahu was sent to Herzliyyah Gimnasiah in Tel Aviv in 1909 and his family sold their business and joined him in 1911. They settled in Jaffa where they opened a large scale flour mill enterprise. At the Herzliyyah Gimnasiah he organized a group of students who were too ardent pioneers to care about graduation and wanted to join the colonial effort immediately at the Ben Shemen farm. Under family pressure he graduated and after graduation (1913) he joined Daganiyah and Kinneret kibbutzim but returned shortly thereafter (1914) to Jaffa to run the family business following his father's death. When World War I broke out he found himself in opposition to many of his colleagues (among which his future-in-laws, Sharett and Hos) who joined the Ottoman army, not so much on ideological grounds as on the ground that the meagre forces of the *yishuv* must consolidate in Palestine. For a while he had to hide as a deserter.

The Golomb flour mills were the chief flour suppliers to the Ottoman army, and Golomb was given official passes to travel throughout the country including the battle zones. He utilized his pass in order to smuggle and transfer arms to the various Jewish settlements and his cart (Golomb's cart) became famous throughout the *yishuv*. Once the Chief Ottoman Military Governor, Hasan Bek, ordered him to work on the Sabbath, which he refused, and as a result he was badly flogged at the Military Governor's building. During the general deportation of non-Ottoman Jews from Jaffa there was a danger that deportation would extend to many agricultural settlements. He was among those who planned armed resistance against this eventuality.

When the British army occupied the southern regions of the country he was among the first (together with his in-law Dov Hos, Berl Katzenelson, a founding leader of *Mapai*, David Sverdlov and Shmuel Yavneeli) who initiated the campaign for Jewish draft to the British army. When the British-Jewish Legion was disbanded at the end of the War he rejoined his kibbutz (Kinneret) and then left with the founding group of En Harod, which split from Kinneret on ideological grounds. He married Adah Sharett in 1921 and when the Arab rebellion broke out in Jaffa he was called to come and organize the Jewish defence.

Golomb realized that Jewish defense was a matter for the Jewish population at large, and not the concern of an elite of fighters. He successfully propagated this idea among the leaders of the *yishuv*. From 1921 Golomb was a member of the Haganah Committee of the Histadrut and, in 1922, was sent abroad to purchase arms; he was arrested by the Vienna police in July of that year. He purchased arms and organized pioneering youth work in Europe until 1924. In 1931 he was one of the three representatives of the Histadrut in the parity National Command of the *Haganah*.

Golomb regarded the *Haganah* as the arm of the nation and of the Zionist Movement and thus brought it under the auspices of the national institutions, although these were unable to express their opinions on defense matters openly. In consequence, he was violently opposed to the dissident armed organizations, IZL (*Irqun Zeva'i Le'ummi*) and *Lehi* (Lohamei Herut Israel), but tried to avoid futile hatred and attempted to find ways of reuniting them with the main body. In 1939 and 1940 he and Berl Katznelson tried to reach an agreement with the Revisionists over the reunification of the Zionist movement and the formation of a single defense command.

During the Arab rebellion of 1936-39 Golomb was one of the initiators of the 'field units' that went out to confront Arab commanders in combat. He thus supported active defense and the punishment of what the *Encylopaedia Judaica* terms 'terrorists'; but for both moral and tactical reasons, he opposed indiscriminate reprisals against the Arab population. Golomb supported all forms of cooperation with the British authorities that permitted secret stockpiling of weapons and military training, but never forgot the fundamental conflict existing between the alien regime and the clandestine *Haganah*. He always opposed giving of information to the

British concerning the strength and equipment of the *Haganah*. Golomb was among those who supported the enlistment of volunteers into the British Army during World War II and proposed the parachuting of Jews into occupied Europe. He was one of the founders and builders of the *Palmah* and prepared the *Haganah* for the future struggle of the Jewish people in Palestine. He inspired and educated many commanders of the *Haganah* and future officers of the Israeli Defense Forces.

Golomb was active in the *yishuv's* public life. He was a leader of *Ahdut ha-Avodah* (later of *Mapai*), and of the Histadrut, a member of the National Committee as well as a delegate to Zionist congresses. His articles appeared in the Hebrew labour press, and a number of them were collected into two volumes, *Hevyon Oz* (1950-54), which also included memoirs and reminiscences by his friends. His home in Tel-Aviv was turned into a *Haganah* museum.

Golomb's Brother-in-Law

Moshe Sharett (Shertok) (1894-1965) was born in Kherson, Ukraine. His father was one of the members of the legendary Bilu *aliya;* he immigrated to Palestine in 1882, but after the failure of the effort returned to Odessa in 1886 where he established himself as a prominent Zionist publicist and where he married and stayed until 1906. He returned with the wave of the second Zionist *aliya.* For a time he farmed a large estate from the leading al-Husseini family at Ayn Siniyya near Jerusalem, where he cultivated about a hundred acres and had the concession for the flour mill. Two years later he abandoned the farm and the family settled in Jaffa where he opened a building material business and then joined the group which founded *Ahuzat Bayyit*, the first Jewish quarter of what was to become the metropolis of Tel-Aviv. In Tel-Aviv he was a prominent public figure (died 1913).

His children were Rivkah, who married Dov Hos (see below); Moshe, who was to become Israel's Foreign and then Prime Minister; Yehudah, a noted composer; Adah, who married Eliyahu Golomb, founding leader of the *Haganah*, and then the Israeli Army (see above); and Geulah who died early.

His son, Moshe Sharett, graduated in the first graduation class of the Herzliyyah Gimnasiah (together with Dov Hos, Eliyahu Golomb, who married his two sisters Rivkah and Adah respectively), a feature he shares with many of the top political and civil servants in Israel. Following his graduation he went to study law in Constantinople (1913). With the outbreak of World War I he returned to Palestine, where for a time he taught Turkish at Hebrew schools. With the publishing of the War edict that all foreign nationals were to be expelled by the Ottoman administration, he entered his first hectic public activity in organizing mass Ottomanization of the Jewish population in Palestine. There were difficulties on a number of levels. There were those who refused to expose their families to the danger of Ottoman conscription, which Ottomanization involved; these were expelled to Egypt, and measures had to be taken by the Jewish institutions of the *yishuv* to ensure that they were not unduly harmed, harassed, blackmailed or robbed. Administration for the immediate Ottomanization of new immigrants had to be established. Jewish controlled offices had to be organized to avoid Ottoman bureaucracy blackmailing excessive graft from applicants, etc. Similarly, a network of connections with the Ottoman military and recruiting offices had to be maintained to arrange the dismissal of the new Ottoman citizens from active service, which was always possible by added *bakshish*. Sharett himself decided to join the Ottoman army and spent World War I as an Ottoman officer. In 1919/20 he was nominated Secretary of the Jewish Board of Deputies in Jerusalem, in 1920-25 Executive member of *Ahdut ha-Avodah* and in 1930, with the merger of *Ahdut ha-Avodah* and *Ha-Poel ha-Tzair*, Executive member of *Mapai*. He spent 1920-25 at the London School of Economics and during his stay in London he was nominated to liaise between the British Labour Party and the Histadrut, hoping to facilitate support for the Zionist policies and overall projects.

In 1922 he married Tziporah, daughter of Yeduah Leib Meirov and in 1931 he was nominated Secretary of the Political Department of the Jewish Agency (under Dr. Haim Arlosoroff as Director). After Arlosoroff's murder on the Tel-Aviv beach (possibly by a revisionist group) he replaced him as Director. He led the struggle against the British white papers restricting Jewish immigration and Zionist purchase of lands in Palestine, determined the Zionist policies vis-a-vis the various British commissions on Palestine and ranked second in the Zionist command after Ben Gurion, Chairman of the Jewish Agency. He represented the Jewish cause before the United Nations in 1947 and won political recognition for Zionism in the 1947 United Nations Partition Plan, which constitutes the legal basis for the establishment of the state. He became Israel's Foreign Minister, and in 1954, after Ben Gurion's resignation, he became Prime Minister.

Ben Gurion was reinstated Prime Minister in 1955 after the Lavon affair, which involved an abortive attempt by a Zionist underground movement to upset US-UAR relationships by placing bombs in the US library in Cairo *inter alia*. The attempt failed and erupted into an enormous international scandal. Persistent rumours attributed the scheme to a clandestine plot by Dayan and Ben Gurion behind Sharett's and Lavon's (then Defense Minister) backs.

As to the Lavon affair, one of the best available accounts is given by Uri Avnery. It offers an insight into the more shadowy aspects of Israeli policy, and a detailed quote would be, I think, in order:

> In the beginning of July, 1954, a man in a Cairo hotel turned on his radio and listened to a soft voice coming from Israel. What he heard was a code word ordering him to set in motion the plan he had brought with him to Egypt.

It concerned a small group of young Jewish Egyptians, recruited some time before by an Israeli intelligence officer who called himself John Darling. It was an efficient spy ring, well trained, one of the many which operate in all Middle Eastern countries and form an integral part of the omnipresent military preparedness.

What the group was now ordered to do was something quite unlike ordinary espionage. The idea was to plant bombs in American and British offices throughout Egypt, thereby creating tension between Egypt and the two Western countries. This tension was supposed to help the Suez rebels in the British Parliament and to provide ammunition for those parts of American public opinion that opposed arming Egypt. It would also create a general state of confusion and disprove the thesis that the Egyptian regime was a stable and solid base for Western policy.

The first few attempts were successful. But the members of the group, inexperienced in this special activity, could not really carry such a plan through. They also had misgivings; they loved Israel and risked their lives for it, but they were not anti-Egyptian and did not like to endanger the lives of Egyptian people. When the young man was accidentally captured at the Cairo cinema — betrayed by his homemade, premature incendiary — the whole ring broke up. Under questioning, perhaps helped by torture, some facts quickly came to light.

The man who had brought the orders escaped in time; the other members were captured. One committed suicide in his cell, two were hanged and the others condemned to long stretches in prison. A beautiful girl, Marcelle Ninio, a well-known figure in the more elegant sports clubs of Cairo, attracted special attention for her role in the group. After the Six-Day War, Israel secured her release from Egyptian prison as a condition of the return of the 5,500 Egyptian prisoners of war captured during the war.

The first inkling that something bad had happened in Egypt appeared in the Hebrew press on July 25. A small news item read: "According to Radio Damascus, six Zionists were arrested in Egypt. They were accused by the Egyptian police of trying to sabotage the Anglo-Egyptian negotiations. The arrested men were indicted for setting fire to the American Information Offices in Cairo and Alexandria."

The man who was the most upset upon reading this — or so he said — was Defense Minister Lavon. He did not remember ever having given the order to do this. In fact, the question, "Who gave the order?" has haunted Israel ever since, toppling governments, splitting parties and turning Ben Gurion into Public Nuisance No. 1. The Egyptian aspect of the affair is generally alluded to in Israel as "The Security Mishap." Its sequel in Israel is called "The Lavon Affair". It aroused passions such as no other affair in Israeli public life, before or since, ever did.

The failure of the operation destroyed Lavon. He was compelled to resign, and the government turned in despair to Ben-Gurion, begging him to reassume the post of Minister of Defense. Lavon himself and many others are convinced, to this day, that the whole intrigue was concocted to provide Ben-Gurion with a face-saving way to return from Sdeh Boke, where he had been waiting, with growing impatience, for his people to call him back.' (3)

With the deposition of Sharett as Premier, his position in the Government was effectively undermined and a year later he resigned as Foreign Minister. In 1960 he was elected Chairman of the Executive of the Zionist Organization and the Jewish Agency. He died in 1965.

Four in-laws, Sharett, Meirov-Avigur, Golomb and Hos, determined the course of the Zionist movement in many ways (see below). Avigur, Golomb and Hos were key figures in constituting and building the Zionist military arm — the *Haganah* — and subsequent to Israeli independence, the Israeli army. Meirov-Avigur was the brother of Ziporah Sharett, Eliyahu Golomb married Sharrett's sister, Adah, and Dov Hos married his other sister Rivkah. As we have seen Golomb's daughter Daliya married Asher Yadlin, Director of the giant Histradut corporation, The Workers Company, whose cousin Aharon Yadlin married Adah ha-Cohen and is today Israel's Minister of Education.

THE GREAT FAMILY

The following diagrams spell out the corporate kin connections outlined above. For ease of exposition the material is presented in a series of diagrams. The names of some persons who link one diagram with another are enclosed in a rectangle with the numbers of the linked diagrams in small circles attached. Quotes (complete or abridged) of entries from the *Encyclopaedia Judaica, The Encyclopaedia of The Pioneers of the Yishuv and Its Founders*, and *Who's Who in Israel, 1973* are provided where relevant for key members of the ha-Cohen corporate kin who have played a prominent role in shaping Zionist and Israeli economic, political and military history — except for those whose political biography has been already outlined in detail above.

NOTES TO DIAGRAMS

I.   RABIN, Yitzhak; Rav Aluf (Lieutenant General); Member of Knesset (Maarach) 74-; Ambassador to US, 68-73; formerly Chief of Staff, Israel Defence Forces; born Jerusalem, 1922; married; 2 children; education: Agriculture School Kfar Tabor, 36-40; took part in World War II Allied invasion of Syria and operations behind enemy lines, 41; active service and command, 1948 War of Independence; participated Israeli Delegation at Rhodes armistice negotiations, 49; Head, Tactical Operations Department, H.Q., 50-52; graduated from Staff College, England; Head of training department, Israel Defence Forces, 54-56; Officer Commanding, Northern Command, 56-59; Head, Manpower Branch, 59- 60; deputy Chief of Staff and Head General Staff Branch, 60-64; Chief of Staff, Israel Defence Forces, 64-68; Honorary Ph.D.: Hebrew University, Jerusalem; Dropsie College, Philadelphia, Pa.; Brandeis University, Waltham, Mass.; Yeshiva University, NYC.; Chicago, Ill., College of Jewish Studies; University of Miami, 70; Jewish Theological Seminary of America, 73.

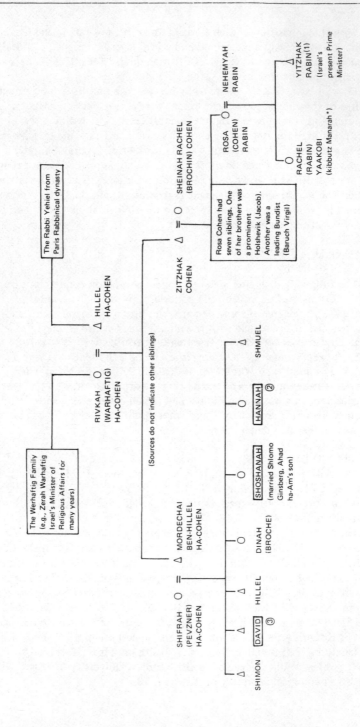

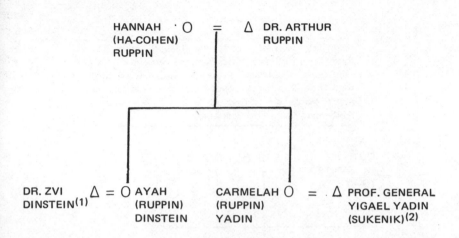

HANNAH ⃝ = △ DR. ARTHUR
(HA-COHEN)   RUPPIN
RUPPIN

DR. ZVI   △ = ⃝ AYAH   CARMELAH ⃝ = △ PROF. GENERAL
DINSTEIN[1]   (RUPPIN)   (RUPPIN)   YIGAEL YADIN
                   DINSTEIN   YADIN   (SUKENIK)[2]

II.   1. DINSTEIN, Zvi: Dr. Juris., Member of the Knesset (Parliament);
Deputy Minister of Finance, 67-; Deputy Minister of Defence 65-67; formerly Contr. Foreign Exchange, Director of Investment Authority, Ministry
of Finance; born Tel-Aviv, 1926; married Aya Ruppin; 3 children; education:
Hebrew and Geneva University; missions to Europe for immigration, purchase of arms supplies, 48-53; Assistant Director, Development Authority,
Head Foreign Aid Bureau, Ministry of Finance, 53-54; member of many
public bodies; Chairman Board of Directors, Industrial Development Bank of
Israel Ltd., 71-; Chairman, Israel Petroleum Institute and Israel Refineries;
also responsible for all petroleum affairs, Ministry of Finance.
       2. YADIN, Yigael: M.A.; Ph.D.; Archaeologist; Member, Inquiry Com-
mission into Yom Kippur War, 73; Professor of Archaeology, Hebrew Univer-
sity, Member, Israel Academy and corresponding member of French and of
British Academy, 65; Member: American Society, Old Testament Study,
Society of Old Testament, England; Hon. Dr.: Brandeis University and Hebrew Union College, USA; Witwatersrand University, South Africa; formerly
Chief of General Staff, Israel Defence Forces; born Jerusalem, 21.3.1917;
married Carmella Ruppin; 2 daughters; education: Hebrew University,
Jerusalem. Head, Planning Department Hagannah Resistance Movement and
Israel Defence Forces, 47-48; Chief of Staff, 49-52 (rank of Lieutenant Gen-
eral); Head, exploration and excavation mission, Hazor, 55-58, 68; 1 of leaders
of exploration in Dead Sea Caves, 60-61; Director Massada Expedition, 63-65;
publications exhaustive, internationally famed research works on the Dead Sea
Scrolls; papers and books on archaeology, collab. to scientific journals, laureate of
Israel Prize, 1956, and of Rothschild Humanities Prize, 1964.

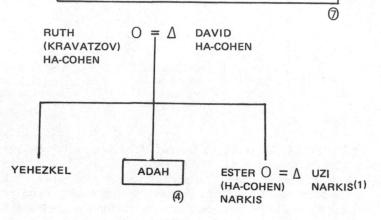

David ha-Cohen's second wife was Brachach Habas. His third wife is Ruth Arbel (Abuhav). His corporate affiliation to the Atlantic Fishers Co. Ltd. link him to the Meridor-Kremermann-Brener-Weizmann kin-corporate bloc of Maritime Fruit Carriers Co. Ltd. and the heart of right-wing (Revisionist) Zionism.

⑦

RUTH (KRAVATZOV) HA-COHEN O = Δ DAVID HA-COHEN

YEHEZKEL   ADAH ④   ESTER (HA-COHEN) NARKIS O = Δ UZI NARKIS(1)

III.   1. NARKISS, Uzi: Director General, Department of Immigration and Absorption, Jewish Agency; born Jerusalem, January 6, 1925; education: Hebrew University, 46-47; Ecole Superieure de Guerre, Paris, 53-55; married Esther ha-Cohen, October 6, 49; children: Itzhak, Ruth, Tamar; Member, Palmach, 41-46; Battalion Commander, Israel War of Independence, 47-49; Head, 'Operation' Division, General Headquarters, Sinai Campaign, 56; Military Attache, France, 59-62; Awarded Legion of Honor by French Government; Commander, National Defence College, 63-65; Commanding General, Central Command, 65-68; Commanding General of troops that liberated Jerusalem Six Day War; rank of Aluf (Brigadier General); contributions to military journals. 15 Hanassi Street, Jerusalem.

66

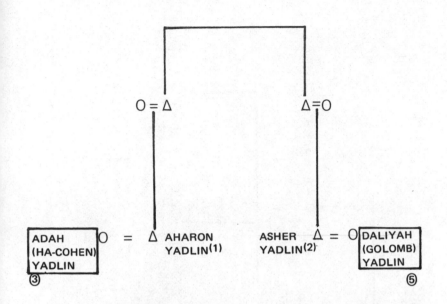

IV.   1. YADLIN, Aharon: Member of Knesset (Parliament); General Secretary of Israel Labor Party, 72-; Deputy Minister of Education and Culture, 64-72; born Ben-Shemen (Israel), April 17, 1926; married Ada ha-Cohen; 3 sons: Amos, Yoram, Amir; educated Hebrew University; co-founder, Kibbutz Hatzerim; for many years member of Presidium, Scouts Movement in Israel; formerly Director, Beit Berl (Mapai Educational Institute), 56-58; Member of Knesset, 56-59; member leading bodies of the Labor Party of the kibbutz movement 'Ihud'; Chairman, Israel Secondary Teaching Centre; Chairman, the Zionist Club in Israel; Chairman, Beit Berl Institute; author: papers, articles, on labour affairs, youth and educational problems; of 'The Aim and the Movement' (on Socialism) 1969; also 'Popular Sociology'. Kibbutz Hatzerim.

   2. YADLIN, Asher: M.A. (econ.); Secretary General of 'Hevrat ha-Ovdim' (highest supervising body of the Histradut-owned economics enterprises), 64-; Chairman, Kupat Holim Klalit, 72-; born Jerusalem, March 1, 1923; married Dahlia Golomb; children: Anat, Omri; graduate Hebrew Gymnasium 'Herzlia', Tel-Aviv; halutz, agriculture training at Kvutzat Hamadia; appointed Secretary of the 'United Youth Movement', Israel, attended New School of Social Research, New York (B.A.); City College, N.Y. (M.A.); appointed Secretary, Union of Government Employees (Histradut), 59-61; Administrative Manager of Kupat Holim, 64-66; publishes (on economic issues) in 'Riva'on Le-Kalkala' (Economic quarterly of the Histradrut); lectures at 'Bet Berl', etc.

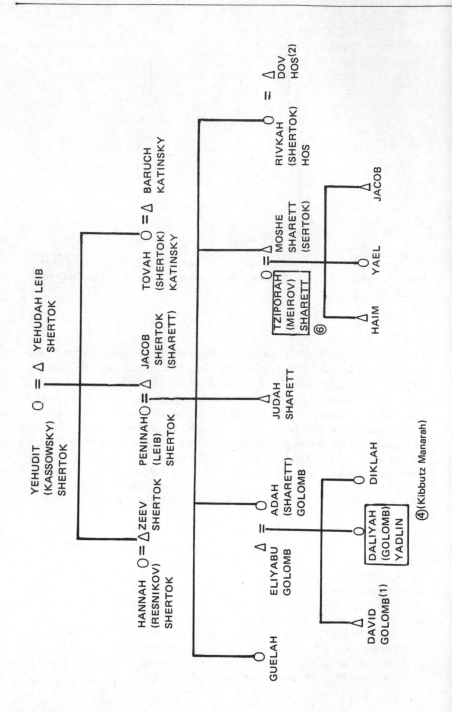

V.   1. GOLOMB, David: Economist; Head, Planning Centre, Hevrat
Ha-Ovdim (Histradrut); formerly Member of Knesset, -69; born Tel-Aviv;
married Miriam (Dr.); 2 sons, Eliahu, Israel; formerly Member kibbutz
Maayan Baruch; studied Economics, Hebrew University; formerly official
of the Research Department, Bank Israel; appointed Head, Institute for
Economic Research, Federation of Labour; President, Board of Directors,
MUFAT, Research and Industrial Development Ltd.; Member, Secretariat,
Labour Party.

2. HOS, Dov: (1894-1940), Labour leader in Eretz Israel. Born in
Orsha, Bielorussia of a Zionist family. He went to Eretz Israel with his
parents in 1906, and was among the first graduates of the Herizliyyah
Gimnasiah in Jaffa (1913). Upon the outbreak of World War I, together
with Eliyahu Golomb and others he founded the 'Jaffa Group', which
began military training in preparation for future events. Upon the advice
of the yishuv leaders, he volunteered for the Turkish army, where he
became an officer, but his activities in defending Jewish settlements led
to his being accused of a breach of military discipline. He was condemned
to death in absentia, but escaped. In 1918 he volunteered for the Jewish
Legion of the British army. In 1919 he joined the founders of the *Ahdut
ha-Avodah* Party, became a member of its executive committee, and was
active in the Histradut and the Hagannah. He was a founder of the Public
Works office of the Histadrut (later renamed Solel Boneh). Hos represented the yishuv vis-a-vis the mandatory authorities and was on several
occasions sent to Great Britain as a contact with the British Labour
Movement. He was a pilot and a pioneer of aviation in Palestine. A member
of the Tel-Aviv municipal council, he was a deputy mayor of the city
between 1935 and 1940. At the outbreak of World War II he worked for
the formation of Jewish units in the British army. Together with his wife
and daughter, he was fatally injured in a road accident. Kibbutz Dorot
is named for Hos and his family, and he is also commemorated in the
name of Tel-Aviv's airfield, Sedeh Dov.

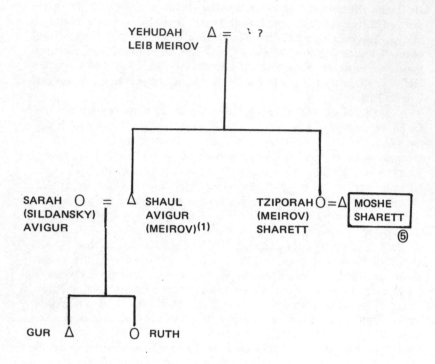

VI.   1. AVIGUR (MEIROV), Shaul: (1899-). Key figure in the Hagannah.
Avigur was born in Dvinsk, Russia. He went to Eretz Israel in 1912 and six
years later became a member of the *kevuzah* Kinneret. Later he took charge of
the Hagannah's central arms depot in Kinneret. He was an active member of
the *Ahdut ha-Avodah Party* and then of *Magai*. From 1922 Avigur was a member
of the national committee of the Hagannah. He devoted himself to purchasing
arms, to underground arms manufacture, and to the organization of the Hagannah's intelligence service (*Sherut Yedi'ot*). During World War II Avigur was
active in organizing 'illegal' *aliyah* from Middle Eastern countries. When the
war ended, he headed the vast underground operation for the transportation
of the survivors of European Jewry, working from Paris. In 1948, during the
Israel War of Independence, Avigur was in charge of the purchase of arms in
Europe; Until the mid-1950's he was a chief assistant to Minister of Defence
David Ben-Gurion, and thereafter served in special capacities on behalf of
the Ministry for Foreign Affairs and the Prime Minister's office. He was a
member of the editorial board of *Sefer Toledot ha-Hagannah* ('The History
of the Hagannah') and published a book of reminiscences, *Im Dor ha-
Hagannah* ('With the Hagannah Generation'), 1962.

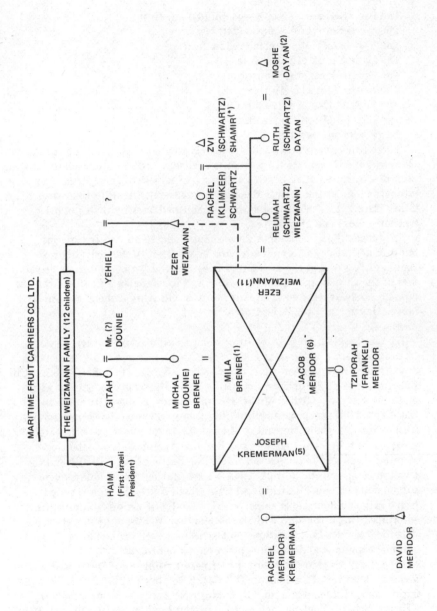

(*) Zvi (Schwartz) Shamir introduces us to the select league of the major
Israeli private law firms, namely:

The Dov (Bernard) Yoseph (Joseph (4)) law firm
The Jacob Shimshon Shaprio (10) law firm
The Yehoshua Rotenstreich (9) law firm
The Haim Zadok (12) law firm
The Gidon Hausner (3) law firm
The Arieh Pinkus law firm
The Michael Piron (8) law firm
The Eliyahu Miron (7) law firm
The Zvi Shamir law firm

These firms have the tendency not only to enjoy top Israeli Big Business,
Histadrut and Government operations as clients, but also to regularly provide
Ministers to consecutive Israeli Cabinets. The largest of these firms were
established under the British Mandate (e.g. Joseph, Shapiro, Rotenstreich).
Other firms in this select league were established later by their junior
partners before and after 1948.

Dov Joseph (4), Jacob Shimshon Shapiro and Haim Zadok (Present
Minister of Justice) all served *inter alia* as Ministers of Justice. Gidon
Hausner (3) served as the Israeli Attorney General. Arieh Pinkus as Treas-
urer of the Jewish Agency and Zvi Shamir, though never a Cabinet Minister
himself, could at least boast of two Minister and army General sons-in-law:
Moshe Dayan and Ezer Weizmann.

VII. 1. BREMER, Mila: Director of companies; Master Mariner; Deputy
Chairman, Managing Director and President of 'Maritime Fruit Carriers Co.';
Sea-Captain (rank of Sgan-Aluf, res.); born 25.6.1921, in U.S.S.R.; education:
London University, Southampton College and University, economic and
maritime subjects; married Michal Dounie; 2 sons, Abner, Dan; member
Hagannah, 1937; after nautical training school in United Kingdom; service
with British Navy and Mercantile Marine, 39-45; promoted to officers rank,
41(at age of 20); participated in naval military campaigns in Atlantic,
Mediterranean and Indian Ocean (including Battle of the Atlantic and the
invasion campaigns of Europe, 1944); 1948, during war of independence,
commanded an Israeli warship and with Israeli Navy, -54; commanded
Israeli cargo and passenger ships, 54-57; founder of various shipping, fishing
enterprises (in partnership with Jacob Meridor, Member of Knesset), e.g
Atlantic Fisheries Co., Maritime Oil Carriers Co., etc., contributor to international economic and maritime press on related topics.

2. DAYAN, Moshe: Member of Knesset, Minister of Defence (67-);
formerly Minister of Agriculture (59-64); B.Sc.; born 20.5.1915 in Degania,
Israel; married Rachel Korem, 73; 1 daughter; 2 sons; education Senior
Officers' School, England, School of Law and Economics (B.Sc.), Tel-Aviv;
three years at the Hebrew University; Farmer in Nahalal; joined Hagannah at
early age; among the first volunteers to General Wingate's Night Squads;

commander Palmach unit, defending road to Ras-el-Naqura during Allied invasion into Syria, lost left eye in action; detained in Acre by the British, 39-41; i/c Commando Unit, War of Liberation; appointed Brigade Commander, Jerusalem Arca, during Jerusalem siege, 1948; Head, Israel Delegation to armistice negotiations with Arab States at Rhodes, 1949; Chief Liaison Officer, mixed armistice commissions; Chief of General Staff, South Command, 1952; North Command, 52-53; Chief of Staff, 53-58, rank of Rav-Aluf (Major General) during Sinai Campaign (his account of that action, Diary of the Sinai Campaign, appeared in 1966).

3. HAUSNER, Gideon: Member of Knesset; Chairman, Parliamentary Faction Independent Liberals; Chairman 'Yad Vashem' Cl,; advocate; Lecturer in Commercial Law Hebrew University; legal consultant and advocate to national institutions and leading firms; Member of Knesset, 65-; member Presidium Cl. for Soviet Jewry; Chairman Israel-Sweden Friendship League; born Poland 26.9.15.; married Yehudit Lipshitz; children: Tamar, Amos; formerly military prosecutor, later President, Military Court; Attorney General of Israel, 60-63; Chief Prosecutor in Eichman trial; publications: 'Justice in Jerusalem' (in several languages); delegate to several World Zionist Congresses; member Trustees Hebrew University.

4. JOSEPH, Dov: B.A., Bachelor in Civil Law, Ph.D.; advocate and Barrister-at-Law; formerly Member Executive and Treasurer, Jewish Agency; Government Bank Leumi le-Israel, B.M., 'Mekorot', 'Zim'; born Montreal 1899; married Goldie Hoffman; 1 son, 2 daughters; education: London and McGill University, President 'Young Judea' Organization, Canada, 1919; adviser, Political Department, Jewish Agency to England, U.S.A., Canada and South Africa; member Jewish Agency Executive 1943-46; Military Governor, Jerusalem during siege 1948; member, first, second and third Knesset; Minister of Supply and Rationing (initiator of the austerity regime programme) 1949-50; formerly Minister of Communications, of Agriculture, of Health and Minister of Justice, 1952; Minister of Development, 1953-55; Treasurer, Jewish Agency 1956-61; Minister of Justice (61-65).

5. KREMERMAN, Joseph: Director and Chairman Etz Lavud Ltd. and affiliated companies; Treasurer of Herut Party; Member of Knesset, 64; born in Haifa; participated in Irgun Zevayi Leumi and active in War of Independence as Naval Captain in the famous 13th fleet; Graduate of Business Administration School, Seattle, Washington and Law School of Tel-Aviv University.

6. MERIDOR, Jacob: Founder and Chairman, Board of Directors 'Maritime Fruit Carriers Ltd.', Haifa; born Poland 1 September 1913; married Zipora Frenkel; 3 children; military training in Poland; to Israel, 1932; road builder joined Irgun Zevayi Leumi, -33; participated in Iraqi underground mission, -41; commander-in-chief Irgun Zevayi Leumi 41-43; second in command 44-48; exiled -45; escaped 5 times; author of 'Long

is the Road to Freedom'; past Member of the Knesset.

7. MIRON (Znamirowski), Eliahu: Advocate, admitted to Bar, 46; member Board of Directors Israel Electric Corporation; Mizrachi United Bank; board of trustees Bar-Ilan University; honorary counsel; Ort Israel; Magen David Adom; trustee Keren Shoshana Sapir; Maurice Polack Federation; born Warsaw 18.9.1921; married Shoshana Halpern; children: Ester, Itzhak, Mordehai; to Israel 1932; member Executive Council for 'Eretz Israel Hayafa', Chairman of Legislative Committee; formerly member High Court of Zionist Organization; formerly member of Central Committee and Chairman of Legislative Committee, Israel Bar Association; member board of directors Government Company for Financing of Industries, -54; formerly Director General Ministry of Interior; papers on local rule.

8. PIRON, Michael: Information unavailable.

9. ROTENSTREICH, Joshua: Doctor of Law; advocate; President Israel Bar Association; legal adviser Journalist's Association of Israel and of its Press Council; born Kolomyja (Poland), December 27, 1910; married Carmela Frostig; 3 daughters; education Sambor College, Lwow College, Jan Casimir University, Lwow; to Israel 1933; Middle East correspondent of various journals in Poland until 1933; contributes to legal periodicals here and abroad.

10. SHAPIRO, Ya'acob Shimshon: LL.B.; Minister of Justice 65-73; born 1902, Russia; education Medical School, Kharkov University; Law School, Jerusalem; to Israel 1924; co-founder kibbutz Givat Hashlosha; first Attorney General, member Labour Party; resigned mid term from 2nd Knesset; private lawyer until appointed to the Cabinet.

11. WEIZMANN, Ezer: Major General (res.); formerly Chairman Executive Committee, Herut Party; born in Haifa 1924; education 'Reali'¹ School, Haifa; joined 1942 at 18, British Army, RAF, fighting in the Western Desert; member first group of Jewish volunteers from Palestine, to Aviation School in Rhodesia, 43; pilot RAF, in Egypt and in India; released 1946; studied Aeronautics in Britain 46-47; took part in building the first nuclei of Jewish air force; appointed 1948 Commanding Officer of Negav air groups; sent to Czechoslovakia to fly Messerschmidts to Palestine 1948; participated 1st air attack of Israeli planes on the Egyptian column advancing in the Ashdod area; Commanding Officer of Fighting Squad 49; head, Air Force's Operational Department; July 1950; Commanding Officer of the Israeli Air Force 58-66; Deputy Chief of Staff Israel Defence Forces 66-69; married; 1 son, 1 daughter; resigned army December 69 to join the National Unity Government as Minister of Transport and Communications 69-70.

12. ZADOK (Wilkenfeld), Haim Joseph: advocate, Member of Knesset; formerly Minister of Commerce and Industry 65-66; born Poland 2.10.13; to Israel 1935; married Esther Berger; 2 daughters; education Second and High School, Philosophy and Judaica, Warsaw University; graduated Jerusalem Law School; joined Labour Zionist movement in 1930; with

Hagannah and Jewish Settlement Police -48; with Israel Defense Forces in War of Independence; Deputy Attorney General 49-52; Lecturer in Commercial Law, Tel-Aviv Law School 53-61; Chairman Knesset Foreign Affairs and Defence Committee; member of Knesset Constitutional Legal and Judicial Committee; member, Cl. of Inter-Parliamentary Union; Chairman Executive Committee, Hebrew University, Jerusalem.

ISRAELI 'SOCIALISM' : UTOPIA INCORPORATED

Misconceptions about the nature of labour Zionism and the role of its cooperative and collectivist frameworks are deeply entrenched in the West, perpetrated by official Israeli propagation of what can only be termed outright and brazen lies. We have traced various aspects of labour Zionism throughout the previous chapters of this book. It is now appropriate to complete our political and cultural analysis through a closer examination of its economic base. We shall examine in detail the business and ownership profiles of key Histadrut corporations and will then proceed to a detailed examination of kibbutz industries.

The economic enterprises of the Histadrut owned Workers' Company are divided into eight main categories:

1. parent institutions directly affiliated to the Workers' Company,
2. cooperative agricultural farms (affiliated to the Workers' Company through NIR, a cooperative company for the settlement of Hebrew Workers Ltd.),
3. production cooperatives (affiliated to Workers' Company through NIR),
4. central insurance funds and pension funds,
5. provident funds of wage labourers,
6. mutual aid and savings societies for workers at their workplace,
7. consumers' societies, and
8. housing societies.

These categories break down as follows:

1. **Parent Institutions Directly Affiliated To The Workers' Company:**

	No. of affiliated units
Workers' Bank Ltd. (Bank ha-Poalim B.M.)	10
AMPAL — American Israel Corporation	9
Ha-Mashbir ha-Merkazi, A Cooperative Society of The Hebrew Workers in Israel Ltd.	35
Building & Public Works Company Ltd. (founded by Sollel Boneh)	13
Overseas & Harbour Works Company Ltd. (founded by Sollel Boneh)	11

	No. of affiliated units
Shikun Ovdim (Workers' Cooperative Housing Society Co. Ltd.)	19
Tnuvah, A Cooperative Centre for Marketing Farm Produce in Israel Ltd.	21
Yakhin Hakal Ltd. (citrus and agricultural products)	7
Mekorot Water Co. Ltd. (now owned by the government)	7
Koor Industrial Holding Co. Ltd.	36
Ha-Mashbir — Industries Ltd.	10
Teus — Development Areas Ltd.	19
Zim, Israel Navigation Co. Ltd.	17
Nahshon Ltd. (fishing)	6
Ha-Sneh, An Israeli Insurance Co. Ltd.	3
Histour. (tourism)	1
Hevrah le-Melona'ut (Hotels Company) Ltd.	1
The Cooperative Fund Ltd.	23
Keren Ihud ha-Kevutzot ve-ha-Kibbutzim Ltd. (the holding and investment company of the *Mapai* affiliated kibbutzim)	8
Keren ha-Kibbutz ha-Meuhad Ltd. (the holding and investment company of the *Ahdut ha-Avodah* affiliated kibbutzim)	11
Keren ha-Kibbutz ha-Atzi Ltd. (the holding and investment company of *Mapam* affiliated kibbutzim)	14
Keren ha-Moshavim Ltd. (the holding and investment company of the Moshav movement irrespective of party affiliation)	4
Corporations Directly Affiliated to the Workers' Company	71
Nir, A Cooperative Society for Settlement of Hebrew Workers Ltd.	143
Total (for Category (1))	499
2. Cooperative Agricultural Farms	548
3. Production Cooperatives	203
4. Central Insurance Funds and Pension Funds	7
5. Provident Funds of Wage Labourers	183
6. Mutual Aid and Saving Societies for Workers At Their Workplace	60
7. Consumer Societies	69
8. Housing Societies	202
Grand Total (for all Categories)	1771

(Sources: J. Olitzky (ed) *The Histadrut Between Convention and Convention: Report Chapters 1959-1965* (Heb.) The General Federation of Hebrew Workers in Eretz Israel, The Executive Committee, pp.198-9)

A detailed description of at least some of the Histadrut corporations will offer us a concrete insight into the dimensions and the international affiliations of the Histadrut economic sector. The corporations described below are key corporations in the domain specified. Following their history, like following the history of the dominant lineages within the Israeli-Jewish ruling elite that have come out of the labour Zionist movement, will offer us an insight into Israeli economic history which cannot otherwise be gained. The illustrations will be based on official publications and promotion material of the corporations in question. Through these official descriptions the reader will discover that the economic structure of what is often acclaimed as the core of the so-called socialist effort in the only socialist democracy in the Middle East presents itself as straight forward multi-national, profit motivated corporate capitalist venture, which manifests little difference from the pattern followed by its equivalent in other countries.

The corporations chosen to illustrate the case are central to Israel's economy. They jointly own and control important industries, and the reader who would follow the evidence with some care would soon discover the outline of interlocking directorships. These, however, are not explicitly spelt out.

AMPAL — American Israel Corporation: Incorporated in New York February 6, 1942 as AMPAL — American Palestine Trading Corporation. Present name adopted January 29, 1954.

Formed to develop trade relations between United States and Israel, to assist in development of economic resources of Israel and to give financial aid to commercial, banking, credit, industrial and agricultural enterprises, cooperative or otherwise, concerned with colonization work in Israel. Company owns no property.

On August 16, 1949, company purchased from Palestine Economic Corporation the remaining 50% stock interest in Palestine Purchasing Service, Inc.

Subsidiaries: Israel Development Corp.; Israel Securities Corp.; Israel Purchasing Service; Ampal Israeli Development Corp.; Ampal Reality Corp.

Company owns 50% of voting stock of Canpal — Canadian Israel Trading Co., Ltd. (Can), principally engaged in shipment of consumer goods to Israel.

Also owns 50% voting stock of Israel American Industrial Development Bank Ltd. organized in 1956 to finance medium and long term credits to industries in Israel.

Affiliates: At January 31, 1973, company held direct or indirect interest in the following corporations: Zim-Israel Navigation Co. Ltd., Yakhin Hakal-Yakhin Mataim Ltd., Delek-Israel Fuel Corp. Ltd., Lapidoth-Israel Oil Prospectors Corp. Ltd., Sefen Ltd., Alliance Tyre & Rubber Co. Ltd., Dead Sea Works, Ltd., Koor Industries & Crafts Co. Ltd., Magal Israel Gas Enterprises Ltd., Electro-Chemical Industries (Frutarom) Ltd., Nesher Cement Works Ltd., Mekorot Water Co. Ltd., Tadiran, Israel Electronics, Middle East Tube Co., Makhteshim Chemical Works, Ltd., Israel Corp., Industrial Development Bank of Israel, Industrial Services Ltd., Shikun-Ovdim Ltd.

Officers: Abraham Dickenstein, Chairman; Ralph Wechsler, Hon. Chairman; Victor Packman, Chairman Executive Committee; Hymen Goldman, Vice-Chairman; I.H. Taylor, Vice-Chairman; Ralph Cohen, President; Jacob Katzman, Vice-President and Secretary; Louis Ludwig, Vice-President and Treasurer; Morris Lieberman, Vice-President; J.N. Mitchell, Vice-President; Hy Amitay, Assistant Treasurer; T.R. Ellis, Assistant Secretary; Max Zuckerman, Contr.

Directors: Aharon Becker, Ralph Cohen, A. Dickenstein, Jacob Feldman, Hymen Goldman, Jacob Katzman, Jack Kay, Jacob Levinson, Morris Lieberman, Louis Ludwig, J.N. Mitchell, Victor Packman, M.M. Schwartz, I.H. Taylor, Ralph Wechsler, Asher Yadlin, Abraham Zabarsky.

Income Account, yrs. ended January 31:

	1974	1973
Net interest earn.	$636,381	$686,552
Other income	204,493	223,669
Total	840,874	910,221
Net Income	299,142	389,628

Balance Sheet, as of January 31:	1974	1973
Total	$34,259,133	$35,542,545

(based on *Moody's Bank & Finance Manual*, 1974: 2384-5)

Most of AMPAL's affiliates are major Histadrut and Government owned concerns (see breakdown of Koor industries pp. 81-84 and Appendix A) AMPAL is the main finance agency directing US capital investments into the Histadrut Worker's Company concerns. A brief examination of one of AMPAL's main subsidiaries, the Israel Development Corporation will give us an idea of this US based company's control of the Histadrut economic sector.

Israel Development Corporation
History: Incorporated in New York, April 10, 1951, as Israel Industrial
Development Corp.; name changed to Israel Industrial & Mineral Develop-
ment Corp. June 27, 1952 and to above in 1956.

Business: Operates as a closed-end, non-diversified investment company,
confining investments to existing industrial, mineral, transportation and
other productive enterprises in Israel.

Income Account years ended November 30:

	1973	1972
Divs. & Int. rec.	$2,244,338	$1,892,211

Balance Sheet as of November 30:	1973	1972
Assets		
(1) Invests.	23,062,609	21,958,862
Cast, etc.	3,182,945	842,361
Accr. int. rec.	196,813	79,844
Acceptances	497,311	500,654
Fixed Assets net	20,597	14,353
Accts. receiv.	23,950	14,813
Deferred charges	267,599	321,601
Total	$27,251,824	23,732,488

Securities Owned as of November 30, 1973: (Unaffiliated Issuers) Agidev-
Agricultural Development Co.; Aguda Shitufit Chaklait Yakhin Be'Eravon
Mugbal. (Histadrut); Dead Sea Works. (Government); 'Delek' Israel Fuel.
(Government); Hamat Ltd. (Histadrut); Hamgaper Ltd. (Histadrut); Hevrah
Yisraelit Lepitaoch Kalkali; Industrial Development Bank of Israel;
Industrial Services Co.; Israel Ceramic Works 'Harsa'. (Histadrut); Israel
Corporation; Israel Portland Cement Works (Histadrut); Israel Sugar Works
(Histadrut); 'Koor' Industries & Crafts (Histadrut); 'Lapidoth' Israel Oil
Prospectors (Government); Makhteshim Chemical Works (Histadrut);
Merkavim Metal Works (Histadrut); Middle East Tube Co. (Histadrut);
Mifaleh Batim Tromiyim (Government); Naphtha Israel Petroleum (Govern-
ment); Nesher Cement (Histadrut); Paz Oil Co.; Real Estate Participation in
Israel; Solcoor Marketing & Purchasing (Histadrut); Sonol Israel Ltd.;
Suppliers & Agents; Tefahot Israel Mortgage Bank (Histadrut); Citadel Life
Insurance of N.Y.; Vulcan Foundries Ltd. (Histadrut); Yakhin-Hakal Ltd.
(Histadrut); Zim Israel Navigation.

Affiliates: Bank Hapoalim B.M. (Histadrut); Israeli Steel Mills Ltd. (Histadrut);
Magal Israel Gas Enterprises; Taal Manufacturers of Plywood (Histadrut);

Etz Vanir Ltd.; Industries & Investments of Sefen (Histadrut); Yakhin Mataim (Histadrut).
Total investments $23,062,609
(Based on *Moody's Bank & Finance Manual*, 1974: 1528-9)

The corporation has Ralph Wechsler as Chairman of its Executive Committee, Rudolf G. Sonneborn as Honory Chairman and Victor M. Carter as Chairman. Victor M. Carter is considered to be one of the main foreign investors in the Israeli economy, controlling large sections of its operation through capital investment of some $3.5 million in dozens of plants (cement, plastics, textiles and real estate).

The other two American based companies that have extensive interests in all sectors of the Israeli economy are PEC Israel Economic Corporation and Israel Investors Corporation. These latter two tend to invest more heavily in the Israeli private sector (e.g. the Discount Bank multinational empire). The Chairman of PEC Israel Economic Corporation is Joseph Meyerhoff and the Chairman of the Israel Investors Corporation is Louis H. Boyar. Neither are unknown quantities in US Big Business.

Having seen *how* US finance is channelled into the 'socialist' Histadrut economic sector, it would now be in order to examine the details of the largest (Histadrut owned) industrial corporation in the Middle East: Koor Industrial Holdings Co. Ltd. We shall outline the general structure of this giant corporation and follow the outline with a detailed description of one of its key subsidiaries: Tadiran — Israel Electronics Industries Ltd. Thereby the close connections between US capital and Histadrut industries, the militarization of the Israeli economy as well as the fast developing cooperation between the Israeli Histadrut owned industry and South Africa will be brought into sharper focus.

KOOR, INDUSTRIAL HOLDING CO. LTD.

Koor, it will be recalled, was established as an independent holding company with the re-organization of Sollel Boneh (see above) in 1958. It has established itself as the largest industrial concern in the country and in 1965 it had 36 affiliated subsidiaries and associated companies. Its diversification, the nature and size of its investments and the value of its assets place Koor as a sizeable corporation internationally. The table overleaf offers data concerning Koor subsidiaries for January-December, 1964.

A closer look at the Koor enterprises will reveal some interesting features. We shall confine ourselves to one of the Koor subsidiaries, namely Tadiran.

Tadiran, Israel Electronics Industries Limited
Tadiran, now a leading international industrial enterprise and Israel's largest electronics manufacturer, barely exceeded workshop size only a short dozen years ago when it was founded, in 1961,

Table offering data concerning Koor subsidiaries for January-December 1964

Name of Subsidiary	Ownership	No. of Workers	Annual Turnover (in 1000 IL)	Main Products
Israel Steel Mills	100%	583	43,100	round iron; profile iron
Nesher, Israel Portland Cement (Haifa & Ramleh)	45%	742	38,500	grey cement; special cement
Soltam	50%	679	19,000	metal products; sleeves for engines
Alliance (Haderah)	25%	737	32,700	tyres; rubber tubes; rubber belts
Middle East Tube	100%	485	23,600	steel pipes (seamed and seamless, black and galvanized up to 6"
Yuval-Gad Pipe Manufacturing	50%	296	4,600	concrete pipes; lamp-posts and other concrete products
Hamat Tool & Machinery	100%	548	12,600	sanitation, plumbing and taps; iron construction; wires; nails; pressure casting
Phoenicia Glass Works	100%	708	15,100	flat and hollow glass (every kind)
Telrad	50%	385	28,000	telephone switchboards; telephones; intercoms etc.
Vulcan Foundries	100%	479	10,720	metal casting (iron and non-iron); bath tubs; construction machinery; cast pipes etc.
Zrifin Pipes	100%	322	11,400	seamed steel pipes 4"-12"
Makhteshim	100%	221	8,650	insecticides; herbicides (for household and non-household use)
Ashkelon Plywood	100%	436	12,000	plywood (every kind); chip-board
Harsah	100%	322	6,620	sanitary ceramics of all kinds; tiles; art ceramics
Tadiran	50%	630	10,200	electronic products; radio communication; dry batteries; car radios; air conditioners
Hamegaper	50%	272	5,880	rubber footwear; rubber products for sports and recreation
Merkavim	100%	261	5,000	bus bodies; containers

82

Name of Subsidiary	Ownership	No. of Workers	Annual Turnover (in 1000 IL)	Main Products
Mif'alei Handaseh (Engineering Works)	100%	196	4,250	iron constructions; rail carriages; cranes
Yizrom	100%	87	2,350	electric and flourescent bulbs of every kind
Alliance (Caesarea)	25%	76	2,550	(a section of Alliance Haderah) rubber foam mattresses; upholstery etc.
Batteries	100%	49	1,800	batteries for motor vehicles
Engines (Ramleh)	100%	82	1,430	electric engines of every kind
Gamid	100%	71	1,800	rubber hoses of every kind; rubber belts and carpets; rubber mattresses etc.
Lapid	100%	90	1,700	household ceramics; sanitary ceramics; art ceramics
Hasin Esh (Fire Proof)	—	59	1,700	kiln bricks and fireproof bricks of every kind
Solgon	100%	31	1,410	paint (construction painting, ship painting etc.)
Zekhukhit Bitahon (Safety Glass)	150% (sic)	24	1,230	safety glass
Simat	50%	47	1,130	metal sheet processing machinery
H.M.H.	50%	42	1,100	stainless steel cutlery
Ramim	100%	50	470	iron construction
Fenikiyah	100%	73	700	glassware for laboratories and industry
Hishulei ha-Karmel (The Carmel Iron Works)	100%	115	1,350	iron products; tools etc.
Solkoor	100%	—	—	

Sources: J. Olitzky (ed) *The Histadrut Between Convention and Convention 1959-1965*, General Federation of Hebrew Workers in Eretz Israel, The Executive Committee, pp.221)
Up-to-date data (the 1970's) has not to my knowledge been published. According to Olitzky, (1965-1969) the number of Koor Subsidiaries in 1969 has increased only slightly: thirty six subsidiaries in 1969 as compared with thirty three in 1965.

83

through the merger of two small Israeli companies, Tadir and Ran. Tadir, producing quartz crystal products for communications, was owned by Koor Ltd., the industrial concern of the general federation of labor, whereas Ran, producing batteries for civilian and military use, was owned by the Ministry of Defense. Through this merger they became equal partners in Tadiran. Tadiran, under Mr. Caspi's continuous leadership, has since expanded into other products and new markets, and has achieved an ever increasing sales volume and continuous profitability. Its sales soared from IL2 million in 1961 to IL 265 million during 1972. In 1972 the company had a net income, before income tax, of IL16 million, paid up capital of IL34 million, and a balance sheet of IL287 million. The area and personnel, which had both grown tenfold during these dozen years, reached in 1972 one million sq. ft. and 3800 employees respectively, the employees consisting of 250 engineers and other professionals, 1000 technicians and other skilled workers, 2000 production workers, and the remainder — clerical and service employees.

Growth has continued especially in international operations and in foreign sales around the world. Tadiran's exports now approach 25% of its total sales.

With this international trend, Tadiran's ownership itself became increasingly international. In 1969 the Ministry of Defense sold 35% of Tadiran's shares to General Telephone and Electronics International Incorporated (GTEI), an international USA corporation, with whom Tadiran had previously concluded significant know-how agreements. In 1972 GTEI acquired the remaining shares held by the Ministry of Defense. Thus, Tadiran's shares are now held as follows:

Voting shares— 50% by Koor Industries Ltd., Tel Aviv, and 50% by GTE International Inc., New York. Preferred non-voting shares — IL7.7 million by GTEI; Employee shares — partly paid 280,000 shares of IL10 each.

Principal officers of the Company are: Board Chairman — since 1970, Meir Amit, general manager of Koor; Managing Director — since 1961, Elkana Caspi.

Tadiran produces four major product lines: tactical communication systems, telecommunication equipments, electric & electronic consumer products, and power sources & electronics components. (1)

As the reader will soon realize, Tadiran's ownership structure and business history is typical of the Histadrut Workers' Company owned corporations. In the following subsections similar profiles of other Histadrut (kibbutz based) firms will be examined. They all betray the same pattern, including, as we shall later see, strong business interests in South Africa.

KIBBUTZ INDUSTRY

Against this background we shall now examine the economic reality underlying the core institution of labour Zionism: the kibbutz Federations. As noted above (p.82-83) 92 per cent (548 out of the total of 597) of the cooperative agricultural farms (kibbutzim and moshavim) are affiliated to the Histadrut Workers' Company. The Kibbutz Federation industries constitute an industrial body of considerable size. In the years 1960-1972 the number of kibbutz-owned industrial plants increased from 108 to 197 and the number of employees in these industries increased from 4860 to 9944. In the period 1966-1971 production increased from IL248 million to IL475 million and investments in the period 1969-1972 increased from IL53.3 million to IL73.0 million. During the period 1960-1972 kibbutz population increased only by 32.7 per cent(from 39.421 members in 1960 to 54,093 members in 1970). Approximately 30 per cent of the kibbutz productive manpower is currently employed in industry and in some kibbutzim industrial production constitutes 80 per cent of the total kibbutz production.

The annual economic survey conducted by the Association of Kibbutz Industry (1973) provides various table relevant to the growth of kibbutz industries during the period 1968-1973 (see below). In the introduction to the survey Dan Karmon notes that:

> 'The number of kibbutz plants to date (Oct. 1, 1973) . . . incorporated in the Association of Kibbutz Industry is 247 . . . There is now at least one industrial plant in 186 out of the total of 223 kibbutzim in the country. In other words only 47 kibbutzim have remained without any industrial plants. Despite the war one can assume that in the current year some of these kibbutzim will be industrialized as well.'

He further notes that the fast growth of kibbutz industry has continued in 1973 (34% in current prices, 17% in fixed prices). The turnover in sales has correspondingly grown from IL825 million in 1972 to IL1,125 million in 1973. Kibbutz industry exports increased from $34 million in 1972 to $45 million in 1973, which is 7.1% of the total Israeli export for that year. Export target for 1974 is $66 million (increase by 50%).

The Association of Kibbutz Industries is a roof organization incorporating all kibbutz owned industrial concerns in the four major Kibbutz Federations: *Ihud ha-Kevutzot ve-ha-Kibbutzim* (The Federation of the Kevutzton and the Kibbutzim) affiliated to the Labour Party, formerly to Mapai (The Eretz Israel Workers' Party): 81 kibbutzim and 5 Nahal outposts; *Ha-Kibbutz ha-Me'uhad* (The United Kibbutz Federation), affiliated to the Labour Party, formerly to Ahdut ha-Avoda (The Labour Union): 59 kibbutzim and 2 Nahal outposts; *Ha-Kibbutz ha-Artz*; *Ha-Shomer Ha-Tza'ir*, (The National Kibbutz Federation/The Young Guard) affiliated to *Mapam*, the United Workers' Party, since 1969 in alignment with the ruling Labour Party: 75 kibbutzim; *Ha-Kibbutz ha-Dati* (The Religious Kibbutz Federation) affiliated to the National Religious Party — 11 kibbutzim and 2 Nahal outposts (All figures for 1969).

In the adjoining pages the reader will find some relevant tables quoted from the Annual Report of the Association of Kibbutz Industry (1973).

When we come to examine the finaneial structure of specific kibbutz industries we find that they do not vary from the pattern that has emerged above and is typified by the ownership structure of Tadiran, Israel Electronics

Distribution of No. of Plants by Branches of Industry (Data until 1.10.1973)

	1969	1971	1972	1973	Index 1973 1969
Metal & Printing	51	58	68	73	143
Electricity & electronics	15	22	27	25	167
Wood & furniture	14	14	16	19	136
Plastics & rubber	25	32	41	53	212
Textiles & leather	9	11	12	14	156
Quarries & building materials	8	8	12	11	138
Decorative artifacts	—	—	—	9	—
Food	19	20	21	22	116
Chemistry	5	5	6	4	80
Miscellaneous	18	22	22	16	89
Total	164	192	232	246	150

(Notes: Until 1972 decorative artifacts plants were incorporated into 'Miscellaneous')

Distribution of Plants by Kibbutz Federation

	1969	1971	1972	1973	Index 1973 1969
Ihud ha-Kevutzot ve-ha-Kibbutzim	49	56	74	82	167
Ha-Kibbutz ha-Me'uhad	42	50	54	61	145
Ha-Kibbutz ha-Artzi/Ha-Shomer ha-Tza'ir	62	78	80	85	202
Ha-Kibbutz ha-Dati	4	6	7	9	225
Total kibbutz plants	157	185	215	235	150
Total moshav plants	7	7	10	9	129
Grand total	164	192	232	246	150

(Note that in 1973 only nine industrial plants were owned by moshavim throughout the country.)

Distribution of kibbutzim by No. of Plants per Kibbutz (Data for 1973)

No of plants per kibbutz	No of kibbutzim
1	138
2	40
3	7
4	1
Total	186

Distribution of Plants by Year of Establishment (Data for 1973) (Slightly adapted)

Year of establishment	No of plants	average sales per plant	average sales per worker	average no of workers	kibbutz member workers	hired wage workers	% of self employ- ment
Until 1951	48	10,691	101,819	105	45	60	43
1951-1960	45	5,104	89,544	57	21	36	37
1961-1965	45	4,956	123,900	40	28	12	70
1966-1970	47	2,132	92,695	23	19	4	83
1971-1974	61	954	95,400	10	8	2	80

Distribution of Investments in the Years 1969-1974 (in IL millions) (slightly adapted)

Branch	1969	1970	1971	1972	1973	forecast 1974
Metal & printing	15.8	21.5	22.2	27.2	34.4	55.1
Electricity & electronics	1.8	2.4	2.9	4.6	5.2	9.6
Wood & furniture	7.6	8.6	10.0	24.8	19.2	30.6
Plastics & rubber	13.3	18.0	11.7	22.2	41.7	70.7
Textiles & leather	2.1	1.3	2.4	1.9	1.5	4.8
Quarries & building materials	9.5	10.4	6.0	21.5	22.5	24.9
Decorative artifacts	0.4	0.4	0.7	0.6	0.8	0.8
Food	5.7	6.0	17.1	22.7	23.2	30.1
Chemistry	0.4	0.3	0.7	1.2	1.1	3.1
Miscellaneous	0.4	2.5	2.5	4.1	3.0	10.1
Total	56.9	71.5	76.2	130.8	152.6	239.8

Industries Ltd. We are literally facing a Utopia Incorporated. In fact, the legal identity of the spearhead of labour Zionism — the kibbutz — as registered with the Israel Registrar of Companies is none other than 'A Group of Workers for Cooperative Settlement Ltd.'

A partial synopsis of kibbutz industry ownership pattern and an illustration of its corporate nature is provided by Elizer Levin, the economic analyst of *Ha-aretz*. Under the title: 'Mapai and the Labour Party Properties' he reports as follows:

> The Kor-Oz refrigerator factory produces thousands of refrigerators every year. Its turnover in 1973 was IL 9 million, and it has since increased considerably . . . Who is the owner of this successful plant? It is not easy to answer the question, because the ownership is held by companies, whose shares are owned by other companies and so on several times. But the person who will have the patience to examine the files of one company after the other will finally discover that Kor-Oz is owned by the 71 kibbutzim of the Ihud ha-Kevutzon ve-ha-Kibbutzim Federation (Mapai) through a company called the Ihud ha-Kevutzot ve-ha-Kibbutzim Foundation . . .
>
> The properties of the 70 kibbutzim include, in addition to the said refrigerator factory and its distribution agencies other businesses as well. The Foundation owns 18% of the shares of the plywood factory Taal . . . 34% of the shares of a company called "Yitzur u-Pituah" (Production and Development), which owns a plant for vegetable dehydration, Deco, at Kibbutz Brur Hayyil. . . and 25% in the canned food factory Pri ha-Galil at the Hatzor development township in the Galilee . . . (2)

Some illustrations of the ownership profile of typical kibbutz industries will further illuminate the case. We have chosen the three kibbutz owned plants of Sefen, Taal and Deco for this purpose. For further reference concerning the ownership structure of Histadrut controlled companies (kibbutz companies included) see Appendix B.

Sefen Ltd. (Wood and laminated wood industries). Ownership (in 1968): AMPAL — American Israel Corporation. Massadah, the Gordoniah Group (*kevutzah*) for Cooperative Settlement Ltd. Ashdot Yaakov, *Ihud ha-kevutzot ve-ha-Kibbutzim* (*Mapai* affiliated), a Group of Workers for Cooperative Settlement Ltd. Afikim, *Ha-Shomer ha-Tza'ir* (*Mapam* affiliated), A Group of Workers for Cooperative Settlement Ltd. Beit Zera', A Group of Workers for Cooperative Settlement in Kefar Nathan Lassky Ltd. Deganiyah B, A Group of Workers for Cooperative Settlement Ltd. Deganiyah A, A Group of Workers for Cooperative Settlement Ltd. Kinneret, A Group of Workers for Cooperative Settlement Ltd.

Ta'al, Manufacturers of Plywood, Kevutzat Mishmarot Ltd., Kevutzat Mishamarot, Pardes Hannah. Ownership (in 1963). Mishmarot, A Group of Workers for Cooperative Settlement Ltd. Keren Ihud ha-Kevutzot ve-ha-Kibbutzim Ltd. (the holding and investment company of the *Mapai* affiliated kibbutz federation). Israel Saharov and Partners Ltd. Elihahu Saharov Properties Ltd. H.G.M. Properties Ltd. Zvi Properties Ltd. Israel Company

Ltd. Feuchtwanger Registration Company Ltd. Bearer Shares (public).

Deco — A Swiss-Israeli Company for Dehydration Ltd. (translated from the official name in Hebrew). Ownership (in 1968): Brur Hayil, A Group of Workers for Cooperative Settlement Ltd. Uviko — An Israeli-Brazilian Company for Investment and Development Ltd. (trans. from Hebrew). Masga AG (Zurich). Yitzur u-Pituah (Production and Development) Ltd. Wolfgang Messer (Geneva). Ernest Selinson.

Parenthetically I must add that it is both amusing and revealing that except for Santa Josephthal (Deco) from kibbutz Kefar Gil'adi, who formally notes in the Registry's records her profession as Company Administrator, all other kibbutz members serving as Directors describe themselves as 'farmers'.

THE NATURE OF KIBBUTZ SOCIALISM

The kibbutz, and the cooperative movement in Palestine in general, are indeed — to borrow Buber's phrase — 'a signal non-failure'. Only not at all in the sense that Buber had in mind when he pointed to the kibbutz and the cooperative federations in Palestine as examples of socialism. The kibbutz is not, and has never been, an 'all out effort to create a full cooperative which justifies our speaking of success in the socialist sense' (3) Contrary to Buber's misleading presentation the Jewish village commune in its various forms as found in Palestine did not escape and indeed could not escape the fate invariably in store for all colonial utopian communal efforts.

Buber notes that:

> The repeated attempts that have been made during the last 150 years, both in Europe and America, to found village settlements of this kind, whether communistic or cooperative in the narrower sense, have mostly met with failure.'

He adds that

> 'I would apply the world "failure" not merely to those settlements or attempts at settlements, which after a more or less short-lived existence either disintegrated completely or took on a capitalist complexion, thus going over to the enemy camp; . . . (4)

And yet, divorcing himself completely from the concrete context in which the kibbutz is situated, he insisted on characterising it as 'a signal non-failure'. Buber was not the only one to share the blindness concerning the nature and the implications of the kibbutz and cooperative Jewish colonization movement in Palestine. He stands in the company of Spiro, Bettleheim etc. However, Buber's failure in properly accounting for the kibbutz reality is particularly grave, since he, for one, must have known the reality of the venture. After all, he was a co-founder of *Brit Shalom* (see glossary). In perpetrating the sort of mystification quoted above Buber is guilty of deliberate falsification.

The kibbutz shared many features of all utopian efforts. These are, as Buber correctly notes, either shortlived and disintegrate completely, or cross over to the capitalist enemy camp. The only thing the kibbutz was determined to avoid was the collapse into a shortlived attempt. As the core founding elite institution of the envisioned state of Israel, its signal non-failure was precisely in its success in establishing the Jewish state.

'The essential point is to decide on the fundamentals: a restructuring of society as a League of Leagues, and a reduction of the State to its proper function, which is to maintain unity; or a devouring of an amorphous society by the omnipotent State; Socialist Pluralism or so-called Socialist Unitarianism. The right proportion, tested anew every day according to changing conditions, between group-freedom and collective order; or absolute order imposed indefinitely for the sake of an era of freedom alleged to follow "of its own accord". So long as Russia has not undergone an essential inner change — and today we have no means of knowing when and how that will come to pass — we must designate one of the two poles of Socialism between which our choice lies, by the formidable name of "Moscow". The other, I would make bold to call "Jerusalem".'(5)

Let us examine concretely the 'socialist' nature of Buber's 'Jerusalem'. First, the question of hired labour employed by the kibbutz. According to Levitan (6) 52 % of the labour force employed in kibbutz industries is hired labour. Although most of the kibbutz hired labour force is concentrated in industry, kibbutz agriculture employs hired labour as well: 6.5 % of the labour force employed in agriculture at the Ha-Kibbutz ha-Artzi Federation; 20 % in the Ikhud Federation. The corresponding figure for hired labour in industry are 21 % and 76% respectively (see tables below).

Official kibbutz statistics, however, do not reveal the full picture relevant to this matter. Most kibbutzim enjoy a regular supply of foreign volunteers, who in return for a full day's labour are provided with their food, lodging and a token amount of pocket money. The nature of the volunteers' contribution to kibbutz life can be learned from the following report in *Davar*, the official daily of the Histadrut.

'. . . In the internal bulletin of kibbutz Yagur we read . . . the following:

"We do not employ Arab workers from the territories [post -1967 occupied territories — U.D.], but we are aided by volunteers and Ulpan [new immigrants' language school — U.D.] students. Gradually we are getting used to the fact that there are certain jobs that a kibbutz member does not do, "black jobs" in slang. Today, there are certain jobs that are done exclusively by volunteers. This is particularly prominent in the services . . ." ' (*Davar* 10.3.76)

Kibbutz hired labour statistics are further improved through sale of kibbutz plants with high concentration of hired labour to the Histadrut Workers' Company. *Haaretz* carried the following report:

'Negotiations to sell the controlling share in the Nun canned food plant owned by kibbutz Neveh-Yam to the food division of Koor

Industries are now in advanced stages. The negotiations concern the sale of 74% of the plant's shares . . . For some time now there have been negotiations to bring into the administration of Nun other elements in addition to kibbutz Neveh-Yam, which is struggling with manpower problems. The plant employs some 300 hired labourers, as against some 30 kibbutz members, and the Ihud ha-Kevutzot ve-ha-Kibbutzim Federation is exercising pressure on kibbutz Neveh-Yam for some time already to find a solution to the problem . . . It was reported that kibbutz Neveh-Yam intends to use the sums of money received in return for the sale of 74 per cent of Nun shares in order to develop resort facilities on the kibbutz.' (7)

The tables opposite, quoted from the Annual Report of the Association of Kibbutz Industries, 1973 give the details of hired wage labour in kibbutz industries and its distribution by Kibbutz Federation.

After 1967 reliance on cheap Arab labour from the post-1967 occupied territories has been fast increasing throughout the Histadrut economic sector. The following report on the Histadrut owned *Hishuelei ha-Karmel* is illuminating and instructive.

'Hishulei ha-Karmel, at Tirat ha-Karmel near Haifa is owned by the Koor Industrial concern jointly with a Finnish Company. It is one of the plants which expanded after the Six Day War because of orders from the Ministry of Defense. Its smooth running and its increased production are possible, to a large extent, because of the relatively large increase of workers absorbed from the West Bank who have succeeded in integrating in the plant. Its sales turnover has increased fivefold in the past three years: from 1.7 million to 9.3 million last year . . . Hishulei ha-Karmel is today the largest forging plant in the country and probably in the Middle East . . .

The heat, the deafening noise and the exceptional physical exertion required in such work make it difficult for the management to find workers. In 1971 the plant employed only 80 workers, and when it was decided to expand the plant — which the management was requested to do at the earliest feasible date — consideration was given to the possibility of importing workers from Cyprus. Jewish workers, and even local Arab workers do not tend to take difficult jobs, especially not under the terms which Hishulei ha-Karmel can offer, since the plant is committed to pay wages strictly according to official pay guidelines. After re-examination (however) the Israeli security agencies authorized the plant to employ workers from the West Bank. Today out of the total of some 200 workers at Hishulei ha-Karmel, 90 are Arabs from Jenin and neighbouring West Bank villages, about 20 are Druze and the rest are Jews. The plant employs about 70 more people in administration — engineers and technicians — all of them Jews . . .

At the beginning the Jewish workers objected to the employment of Arabs at the plant, and there were some slight scuffles. The local (trade union) Labour Council significantly assisted in changing the Jewish workers' attitude and they came to realize that the Arab workers do not replace them, and in reality even relieve them to some extent, in that they usually do the unskilled, hard and dirty jobs. This is largely because they still lack a sense for industry, except for a few who worked in Germany . . . But in fact this is

Distribution of Member-Workers (Self-Employment) by kibbutz Federation 1969-1974

Kibbutz Federation	Year 1969	% of self-employment	1970	% of self-employment	1971	% of self-employment	1972	% of self-employment	1973	% of self-employment	forecast for 1974	% of self-employment 1974
Ihud ha-Kevutzot ve-ha-Kibbutzim	973	24	1007	24	1050	26	1341	27	1467	28	1647	29
Ha-Kibbutz ha-Me'uhad	1056	66	1198	68	1292	67	1510	69	1689	71	1819	72
Ha-Kibbutz ha-Artzi/Ha-Shomer ha-Tza'ir	1704	79	1780	78	1918	80	2175	80	2374	81	2583	82
Ha-Kibbutz ha-Dati & Moshavim	196 ?	56 ?	102 ?	28 ?	158 ?	37 ?	94 115	49 36	104 144	49 31	113 140	52 31
Total	3929	48	4087	48	4418	48	5235	50	5778	52	6302	52

only one of the reasons that the West Bank Arabs are employed
almost exclusively in "black jobs". They are very disciplined, says
the management. They are obedient, there is no truancy from work.
One can assume that an important reason for this is that they have no
trade union defense and backing and they can be dismissed from their
job from today or tomorrow... The overhead on their wage with
social benefits just slightly exceeds half of the overhead on Jewish
workers wages ... Nevertheless, their wage is by far higher than the
wage they used to get in the past. This is the labour pool that the
plant can expect to have in the future (excluding the possibility of
political changes), and the plant's continued development depends
on these workers. But by all indications, if this situation becomes
permanent, it will not be possible to maintain for long the different
(wage) levels; one for Jewish workers and one for the workers from
the (occupied) territories.' (8)

As to labour conditions in kibbutz industries, one can safely say that the
terms of employment of hired labour on kibbutz industries are in no way
superior to those prevalent in the private sector. In fact they are quite often
worse. An illustration of the case can be found in Atallah Mansour's
report on labour conditions in Pri ha-Galil

'The director of the plant admits that the workers do not have a
decent dining hall ... half of the workers in the plant are members of
minorities (euphemism for Arabs — U.D.). Most of them are recruited
to the place through labour contractors, but one does not get the
impression that the manager of this Histadrut publicly owned plant,
or the Histadrut officials ... mind in any way that these workers are
exploited by "middlemen" who suck their blood and take a share of
their meagre income. On the contrary, I got the impression that the
manager is satisfied with the arrangements with the labour contractor
since the latter is under obligation to supply a regular number of
hands, and when a woman worker is sick or pretends to be sick he is
under obligation to provide a substitute. These women labourers
receive after the subtraction of legal and illegal deductions from their
income a net daily wage of some IL20.' (9)

Further, the Eshkol District Council, which incorporates the kibbutzim
and moshavim of Chad, Beeri, Gevulot, Diklah, Yesha, Kisufim, Kerem
Shalom, Mivtahim, Magen and Nahal Sinai, published in 1974 a circular
listing recommended standard wages for hired labour employed by its
member settlements. The recommended hourly wage is IL 12.50, but the
recommended hourly wage for an Arab is IL 5.00 (10). It is also important
to know that the Eshkol District Council incorporates settlements established in the Negev within the borders of Israel proper (the 'Green Line')
and settlements established after June 1967 in the Gaza Strip and the
Rafiah Approaches. Both categories are incorporated in the Eshkol
District Council and are listed in the said circular without distinction.

Other problems facing kibbutz socialism relate to the presence of a non-
Jewish volunteer labour force on the kibbutz premises. As we have already
noted above, the kibbutz volunteer labour force is employed as cheap
labour for the execution of dirty 'black' jobs. However, some kibbutzim

have discovered that their presence is a mixed blessing. *Yediot Aharonot* reports as follows:

> 'By tacit agreement concluded some years ago at the kibbutz Netzer Sireni General Meeting it was decided that the kibbutz will not accept non-Jewish volunteers or Ulpan students. The kibbutz which was then in favour of promoting "common understanding" was badly affected by a number of instances where kibbutz members married Danish (non-Jewish) girls and left the kibbutz. The "Danish trauma" moved the majority at the General Meeting to decide in effect on introducing prior selection of foreigners coming to the kibbutz, the guiding criterion being whether or not they are Jewish.' (11)

The reader will recall out cultural and political analysis of the kibbutz and will therefore not be surprised to discover at the core of kibbutz ideology and practice a deeply entrenched racist sentiment. The kibbutz together with the Jewish National Fund are the two key institutions where racism is formalized as legal Apartheid in Israel. Jewish National Fund holdings in land and properties cannot, as the reader will recall, be legally sold, leased or subleased to non-Jews and kibbutz membership is similarly legally barred to any person who does not happen to be of Jewish origin. These two institutions constitute the pillars of the Zionist effort in Palestine. They have determined and continue to determine, throughout the specific patterns of the Zionist colonization, its specific political, ideological and cultural configurations, and, in important ways, the legal structures of the state of Israel.

Unlike South Africa Israel has avoided out and out indiscriminate legal Apartheid. It confined legal Apartheid to key essential areas: the kibbutz, the Jewish National Fund, the Israel Nationality Law and the Law of Return. It was this procedure which enabled the Zionist movement to mislead, betray and cheat large sections of liberal and the radical western public opinion for so many years into supporting the Zionist effort in Palestine as a basically humanistic and progressive effort. It will be our business in the following section to illustrate and outline the ideological, political and economic ties sustained and cultivated between Israel and South Africa as two settler colonial polities facing similar existential predicaments.

ISRAEL AND SOUTH AFRICA: THE HISTADRUT AND KIBBUTZ CONNECTION

We have considered the importance of US capital investments in the Histadrut owned economic sector. It is in order to mention, however, that since 1967 a very marked and fast expanding complementary process is taking place, namely, the development of extensive Israeli-South African political, military and business relations. As the *Jewish Affairs*, the official organ of the South African Jewish Board of Deputies, notes in its November

1970 issue:

> 'The argument that Israel and South Africa have a basic community of interest in the Middle East and further south has more than a grain of truth in it. There is nothing secret or sinister about it. The strong ties between the two countries, closer than ever since the 1967 war, are inseparable from their geographical and strategic position, from their anti-communist outlook, and from all the realities of their national existence . . . In short, the destinies of the two countries, so different in many ways, but so alike in the fundamental conditions of their survival, are interwoven in a much more meaningful sense than any enemy propagandist could conceive, or, for that matter, would be happy to see.
>
> . . . Israeli and South African interests converge not just on the eastern fringe of the African continent, but still more positively in the heart of the continent itself. Both share an interest in the material and social development of those among the 200 million Africans who wish to seek their help and co-operation . . .
>
> It is on African soil that the paths of Israel and South Africa are certain to cross in the 70's, and, to an increasing extent, in the more distant future. It is not, and never has been, a question of rivalry, but rather of the one complementing the other where they happen to meet.'

Similarly, the Israeli Hebrew press is quite explicit on the subject of the development of Israel-South Africa relations, and the various reports published recently offer an illuminating insight into their scope and depth. Israeli relations with South Africa, extend to developing a Mirage type combat-bomber, concessions to produce the Uzi sub-machine gun, supplies of Gabriel sea-to-sea missiles, and, judging by the reported increase in the flow of Israeli nuclear scientists to Pretoria in the past eighteen months, close cooperation in the development of South Africa's nuclear programme. *Davar* and *Yediot Aharonot* (26.11.1976) report on the departure of a high ranking official Israeli delegation to South Africa headed by the General Director of the Ministry of Finance Mr. Amiram Sivan to discuss economic and trade interests common to both countries. *Maariv* (21.12.1976) reports that the South African and Israeli governments have concluded an agreement whereby South Africa will make provisions to enable South African Jews to invest up to R20 million in Israel. Given South Africa's very stringent foreign currency and foreign investments regulations this is indeed a very special agreement. According to *Maariv* this is in fact the second agreement of this type. The first agreement made provisions for investments by South African Jews in Israel up to R11 million.

And as the following report in *Maariv* clearly demonstrates, Histadrut owned corporations have important contributions to make to this unholy alliance:

> 'The Tadiran company has built a plant in Rosalene, near Pretoria. The activities of the Tadiran company in South-Africa are in partnership with the South-African group Kalen and both of the partners will operate together under the name Consolidated Power. The director of this new company is J. Brosh and the engineering manager

is David Frankel. (Both Israelis — U.D.)

Mr. Frankel has declared that the new company will manufacture systems for emergency lighting but refused to answer questions about communication equipment. According to him some of the most sophisticated types of equipment will be imported from Israel, and the combined company will sell them. ' (13)

Out of the three large kibbutz federations affiliated to the various labour Zionist parties, the Mapam affiliated Ha-Kibbutz ha-Artzi/Ha-Shomer Ha-Tsa'ir Federation is always hailed in pro-Zionist propaganda as the best and relatively least corrupted communitarian and socialist network in Israel. The truthfulness of this claim can be judged against the following report

'Many plants in Israel, are trying recently, quietly but intensively, to increase their commercial relations with South-Africa. One of the most active enterprises in this field is Asia-Ma'aharot belonging to the kibbutz Ma'abarot of Hashomer-Hatzair. The plant has set itself an objective: to increase every year by 20% the export of its mixture for cattle feeding to South-Africa. According to the scientific director of the plant David Shim'oni, the export of its produce to South-Africa was worth one million dollars.' (13)

In this context it is also interesting to note that the Association of Kibbutz Industries organizes its exports to South Africa through Afitra, the Histadrut owned Koor subsidiary in South Africa. The Annual Report of the Association of Kibbutz Industries for 1975 carried a short report by Mr. Amir Segev on Afitra's activities in South Africa:

'One can note with satisfaction that there is a sympathetic attitude towards trade with Israel (and not only among Jews). We have entered into partnerships with local firms which will enable us to extend a wider and more professional coverage of the very extensive market of this state (in textiles, chemicals, and parts of agricultural equipment). We hope to reap the fruits of our activity at the end of 1975 and in 1976. Our office represents today some 50 Israeli producers, of which 24 are kibbutzim.'

In the Association's 1976 Annual Report Amir Segev can already report that the Afitra offices in South Africa now represent 27 kibbutz firms and the projected estimated export of kibbutz industries to South Africa for 1976 totals some $900,000. Special attention is given to 'technical and electronic products of special nature'. The informed reader will find the euphemism quite telling.

THE MILITARIZATION OF THE ISRAELI ECONOMY

No outline of the Histadrut economic sector can be considered complete unless examined, *inter alia*, against the dominant processes of militarization of the Israeli economy. Again we are assisted by the excellent work of Tamar Guzansky, who points out that the process of enrichment of the Israeli bourgeoisie and the impoverishment of the Israeli working classes has rapidly accelerated since 1967, parallel to the militarization of the Israeli economy and the rapid increase of its dependence on foreign capital investments. Her calculations, based on official data, are indicated in the following table:

	1967	1968	1969	1970	1971 estimate
Military expenditure (in milliard IL)	2.8	3.2	4.5	6.0	7.5
% of military expenditure in GNP	23	23	28	31	33
% of military expenditure in the government budget	29	30	36	49	48

(Adapted from Guzansky, 1971)

She points out that approximately 10% of the civilian labour force is directly employed by military industries and that in 1970 the military sector (excluding the giant state-owned Military Industries (Taas) which does not appear in official statistics) purchased and financed 7% of the total Israeli industrial production and 25% of the building construction and public works. The level of militarization of the Israeli economy is close, in fact, to that of the US where the military industrial complex contributes 10% of the GNP (in Israel 8%) and employs 14% of the total labour force (in Israel 10%).

The sharp increase in military expenditure is correlated with a similarly sharp increase in foreign capital transfusion, primarily from the US. After 1967 one witnesses a very rapid penetration of western multi-national interests into key sectors of the Israeli economy which is qualitatively distinct from the traditional dependence of the Israeli economy on the regular transfusion of foreign capital. This was rendered possible (and necessary) with the rapid militarization of the economy immediately after the 1967 war. Heavy multinational investments concentrated mainly in the military industrial sector of electronics and light and heavy metal industries.

Some illustrations are in order: Tadiran, as we have already spelt out in the profile of this corporation above, is owned by the US General Telephone and Electronics International (GTEI) (50%; the other 50% is owned by the Histadrut Workers' Company (Koor)). GTEI is listed 21st in the US list of corporations. Motorola (9th on the US list of corporations) operates independently in Israel. Control Data operates in Israel through two subsidiaries Albit and Contal. Miles Laboratories (359th on the US list) operates in Israel through their Miles Yeda and Miles Chemical subsidiaries. Miles Yeda entered into an agreement with the Israel Atomic Energy Commission, for the purpose of production and marketing of radioactive materials. Monsanto (the 3rd largest chemical complex in the US controlled by the First National City Bank) operates in Israel through

Monsol. (Gusansky, 1971). All the corporations mentioned are major Pentagon contractors and suppliers and their penetration of, and often outright control over major Israeli military industries again underlines Israel's dependence on the US on the one hand, and the size of US support, economic military and political, to Israel and post-1967 Israeli foreign and internal policies.

WHO RULES THE HISTADRUT?

To round off our survey we must attend to the question 'who rules the Histadrut?'. It must be pointed out again that until 1973 the ruling elite of the state of Israel consisted of members of the first generation founding Zionist colonial pioneers and that the short history of the polity studied allows at best for the emergence of the first generation of dominant corporate lineages. In the concrete identification of these lineages I was assisted by Steven Benjamin Schecter who has kindly made his field notes available to me. In his study (14) Schecter undertook to examine the Israeli corporate elite, which he selected in the following manner:

'a list of the top companies in industry, commerce and banking, construction, transport, insurance and services and utilities was compiled according to the number of workers employed or total assets, depending on the type of economic activity involved. Agriculture was omitted because of its specific pattern of ownership and difficulty of classification, and my desire to concentrate on the industrial corporate elite. The list of the 111 top companies in industry consisted of all those employing 150 workers or more. To this were added 12 government owned companies engaged in industrial activity with assets valued at IL 10,000,000 or more. The top banks were selected . . . The top 5 investment companies . . . The top 16 contractors . . . employing 300 workers or more in 1965 . . . The top builders were included in the list if they either built above IL 1,000,000 worth or employed more than sixty five workers; in all they also totalled 16 . . . The top 4 companies in transport . . . The top 3 insurance companies . . . owning assets worth more than IL 50 million . . . (and) the top (7 companies) in service and utilities, covering food, hotels, department stores, water and electricity. The total number of companies representing the corporate elite in Israel came to 178.'

To Schecter's list of 178 top Israeli companies I have added seven: Koor, Ampal — American Israel Corporation, Te'us — Development Areas, The Trustee Company of the Workers' Company, The ha-Kibbutz ha-Meuhad Fund (controlled by *Ahdut ha-Avodah*), The ha-Shomer ha-Tzair Fund (controlled by *Mapam*) and the Ihud ha-Kevutzot ve-ha-Kibbutzim Fund (controlled by *Mapai*). Schecter's omission of the first four is quite inexplicable. Our standard figure for the total number of companies representing the corporate elite in Israel is, therefore, 205. Although in some cases the year for which the companies were selected varies from 1965 to 1968, the various sources consulted by Schecter assented that the list compiled on the basis of 1965 figures accurately reflects the situation in 1968 as well. Most of Schecter's data refer to entries registered at the Israel Registrar of Companies between 1967-1969. Similarly most of the available secondary source material (e.g. Guzansky, Levinson, Olitzky) date to 1970 at the latest. In reality the situation remained stable from the late 1960s through the early 1970s. Caution, however, must be exercised in extrapolating from this study to the post-1973 Israeli economic and political reality, which probably marks the historical decline of Zionism.

Of the 205 top companies, 54 (data available for 51) are owned fully or in part by the Histadrut sector. In order to determine the dominant corporate lineages that have emerged out of this Histadrut controlled economic sector, information rendered available by the Israel Registrar of Companies has to be retabulated. The Registrar offers an index of Israeli companies, and lists under each entry the members of its Board of Directors. For our purposes a reverse index had to be computed listing under every member of the Boards of Directors of the 51 top Histadrut companies the name of the company of whose Board of Directors the person in question is a member. Having effected this procedure sixteen persons have emerged as members of Boards of Directors of four or more of the above top 51 Histadrut companies. The choice of multiple membership in four Boards of Directors or more is reflected in the following J-shaped frequency distribution graph. (see over leaf) It shows that the upper 'a-typical 5%' (reflected in the graph as a tail that demonstrates a distinct reluctance to 'die out') are concentrated in multiple membership of four Boards of Directors or more. The choice of the upper 5% as the a-typical tail of a frequency distribution is a 'subjective' statistical convention used in hypothesis testing and the construction of confidence intervals. I am indebted to Dr. David Jerwood, Dept. of Mathematics at the University of Bradford for assisting me in the technical statistical interpretation of the data.

AMIT, MEIR: — Levidei Ashkelon, Machteshim, Chemical Works; Merkavim; Alliance; Israel Ceramic Enterprises 'Harsah'; Israel Steel Works; Koor.

BADER, MENACHEM: — New Printing Company; Ha-Shomer ha-Tzair Fund; Yitzhar; Na'aman; Yakhin.

BLUMENTHAL, NAPHTALI:— Levidei Ashkelon; Machteshim, Chemical Works; Merkavim; Hishulei Hacarmel; Israel Ceramic Enterprises 'Harsah'; Israel Steel Works; Alliance; Koor.

COHEN, HILLEL:— Stone and Lime Company; Hatzatz Israel-American; Trustee Company of the Workers' Bank; Investment Fund of Hevrat Ovdim; Workers' Bank.

EILAM, YITZHAK:— Israel Ceramic Enterprises 'Harsah'; Israel Steel Works; Hamegaper; Levidei Ashkelon; Machteshim, Chemical Works; Merkavim; Soltam; Alliance; Hishulei Hacarmel; Koor; Investment Fund of Hevrat Ovdim; Workers' Bank.

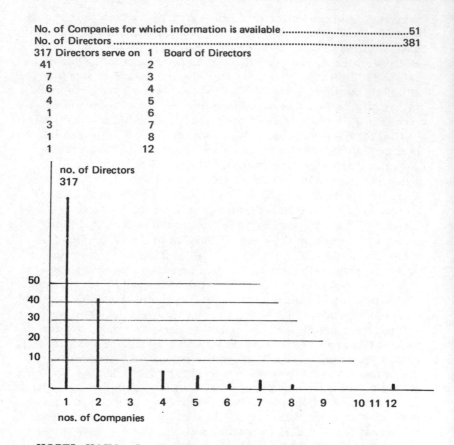

No. of Companies for which information is available 51
No. of Directors 381

317	Directors serve on	1	Board of Directors
41		2	
7		3	
6		4	
4		5	
1		6	
3		7	
1		8	
1		12	

KOPEL, HAIM:— Levidei Ashkelon; Soltam; Alliance; Israel Ceramic Enterprises 'Harsah'; Israel Steel Works; Hishulei Hacarmel; Koor.

LEVINSON, JACOB:— Trustee Company of Workers' Company; Ampal — American Israel Corporation; Investment Fund of Hevrat Ovdim; Te'us Development Areas; Workers' Bank.

MARINOV, RAPHAEL:— Slilim; Hamashbir Latzarkhan; Hamashbir Hamerkazi; Hamegaper.

OPHIR, GID'ON:— Trustee Company of Workers' Company; Ha'argaz; Jerusalem Shoes; Amkor.

ROSEN, SHLOMO:— Ha-Kibbutz Ha-artzi Building Company; New Printing Company; Ha-Shomer ha-Tzair Fund; Gal'am.

SCHTREIPLER(SHAVIT), YITZHAK EDI:— Machteshim, Chemical Works; Israel Steel Works; Soltam; Alliance; Hishulei Hacarmel; Koor.

SHAHAR, ZE'EV:— Slilim; Hamegaper; Israel Sugar Enterprises, Shemen.

SHAPIRA, ZE'EV:— Yakhin; Yakhin-Hakal; Ha-Kibbutz Hameuhad Building Company; Shikun Ovdim.

SHIFFMAN, ZVI:— Levidei Ashkelon; Machteshim, Chemical Works; Israel Ceramic Enterprises 'Harsah'; Alliance; Israel Steel Works; Merkavim; Koor.

YULISH, MOSHE:— Israel Ceramic Enterprises 'hersah'; Israel Steel Works; Koor; Workers' Bank.

ZABARSKY, ABRAHAM:— Ampal — American Israel Corporation; Trustee Company of Workers' Bank; Investment Funds of Hevrat Ovdim; Zim; Workers' Bank.

We have begun our study with David ha-Cohen as point of departure for our research. Through tracing his kin and pseudo-kin relations and through our related analysis of the commanding heights of the Histadrut controlled corporate economy and their interlocking directorships we are now in a position where our study could be pursued further covering much larger scope and wider grounds. Using similar procedures and following the political biographies, kin affiliations and corporate pseudo-kin relations of the sixteen people who have been traced through our study thus far, we would expect that further refinement of the interlocking dominant labour Zionist lineages be revealed and new lineages ('tribes') identified. However this project could be systematically further pursued only through instituting an Israeli equivalent to Lewish Namier's *History of Parliament* project. This is quite clearly beyond the capacities, the time limitations and the financial resources of a single researcher.

ISRAEL AND THE U.S.

Raphael Bashan interviews Rabbi Baruch Korf, Nixon's Jewish Advisor:

Bashan: 'Would you now, in retrospect, say that Richard Nixon was a true friend of Israel?'
Korf   (Storming): 'Yes, yes, yes, without a shadow of a doubt. More than Truman Eisenhower Johnson and Kennedy.'
Bashan: 'Why?'
Korf   (Smiling): 'I too asked that once, and do you know what he told me? (He said): "Why not? Israel costs the US less than the Sixth Fleet." ' (1)

Analyzing capital inflow into Israel, Oscar Gass, an American economist and one time economic advisor to the Israeli government wrote as follows:

'What is unique in this development process is the factor of capital inflow. During the 17 years 1949-65 Israel received $6 billion more of imports of goods and services than she exported. For the 21 years 1948-68, the import surplus would be in excess of $7½ billion. This means an excess of some $2,650 per person during the 21 years for every person who lived in Israel (within the pre-June 1967 borders) at the end of 1968. And of this supply from abroad only about 30 per cent came to Israel under conditions which call for a return outflow of dividends, interest or capital. This is a circumstance without parallel elsewhere and it severely limits the significance of Israel's economic development as an example to other countries.' (2)

The fact that a large proportion of this unilateral capital transfer consists of Jewish donations raised by the Zionist fundraising outfits, predominantly in the US (See Table on opposite page) raises the question of why the US Treasury should permit such a massive transfers of funds under the obviously fictitious guise of 'charitable donations'. (3). The answer to the question reveals itself quite plainly when we examine the role of Israel in the Middle East as a whole. This has been plainly formulated as early as 1951 by the editor in chief of Israel's leading Hebrew daily, *Ha-Aretz*, in a leading article that is now classic.

'Israel has been given a role not unlike that of a watchdog. One need not fear that it will exercise an aggressive policy towards the Arab states if this will contradict the interests of the USA and Britain. But should the West prefer for one reason or another to close its eyes one can rely on Israel to punish severely those of the neighbouring states

	Capital Import to Israel 1969-1970 and Forecast for 1972 ($millions)				Capital Import to Israel, 1971-1972 Estimate for 1973 and Forecast for 1974 ($millions)			
	1969	1970	1971	1972 Forecast	1971	1972	1973	1974 Forecast
1. Unilateral capital transfer	474	678	745	760	774	1,061	2,217	1,760
a. United Jewish Appeal and other institutions	175	296	265	280	234	310	680	420
b. Personal compensations from West Germany	138	202	220	210	231	292	275	275
c. US Government grant	—	—	—	50	—	60	912	790
d. Private transactions	161	180	260	220	309	399	350	275
2. Gross foreign investments	82	81	130	120	98	189	200	100
3. Long and medium term loans	443	900	1,030	915	988	949	1,354	1,098
a. The independence and development loan	184	231	280	280	285	300	500	400
b. Food surplus	32	49	55	55	95	48	46	8
c. Import & Export Bank loans	17	18	45	25	30	30	35	40
d. AID loans - housing					—	35	15	50
e. US Government loans	56	320	305	300	258	252	300	300
f. Loans from international agencies	29	5	30	20	37	37	55	50
g. World Bank	6	5	20	20	13	16	18	25
h. Loan from Germany	35	38	40	45				
i. Other loans	90	239	275	190	306	231	385	225

(Source: 'Israel National Budget', *The Bank of Israel Survey*, nos 40, 41 & 42, Jerusalem, 1972, 1973 & 1974 respectively)

whose lack of manners towards the West has exceeded the proper limits'. (4)

Israel in other words, is financed economically by US imperialism in order to execute a specific political role in the area. The Israeli-Jewish society is thus locked into a double bind. Given its colonial history and the fact that both the rich man's villa and the poor man's shack are built on the ruins of the dispossessed native Palestinian-Arab homestead, the Israeli-Jewish society as a whole, above and beyond its class contradictions, is pitted against the native resistance and the Arab world at large. In order to survive the conflict and continue to maintain de facto supremacy over the Arab world it must benefit from consistent and generous economic and military support of that imperial power in whose interests it is to be able to 'punish severely those of the neighbouring states whose lack of manners towards the West exceeds the proper limits.'

Recent developments in the area since 1973 demonstrate the case quite dramatically. The 1973 war did not in any way end in an undisputed Israeli victory. Quite clearly Israel would have suffered a smashing defeat without the massive airlift of US arms and ammunition flown directly from US warehouses to the frontline airfields in the Sinai Peninsula. The United States, through its direct involvement in the 1973 war, saved Israel from a military defeat, and the United States has since brought the area under its undisputed dominance, driving the USSR very rapidly from its positions of paramount influence in Egypt and Syria. In complex and uneven ways the continued existence of the state of Israel as an exclusively Jewish state in direct confrontation against the dispossessed native Palestinian-Arab population and the neighbouring Arab states serves US interests as is clearly manifested by the post-1973 developments. This need not remain the case forever. Much of continued US support to Israel is a matter of costs (see quote above),costs which are rapidly increasing. A comparative examination of Israel's National Budget for the years 1969 through 1974 reveals interesting information on the matter. As the table on page 105 indicates, the first direct US Government grant to Israel, $60 million given in 1972, makes up 2.7 per cent of the total capital import to Israel for that year (unilateral capital transfer, capital loans and foreign investments). In 1973 Israel received $912 million by way of direct US Government grant, which makes up 24 per cent of the total capital import to Israel, and the estimate for 1974 is $790 million (26 per cent of the total capital import for that year).

Simultaneously, since 1974/5 there seems to be troubles in the Jewish fundraising scene in the United States. The following press reports are indicative and illustrate the gravity of the situation.

'The Jewish Agency is seeking the state of Israel's surety for commercial loans it plans to take from foreign banks in order to cover the deficit of $64 million in the estimated income from the Emergency Appeal. The Emergency Appeal has been running since 1967. Through this Appeal the Jewish Agency recruits funds abroad to finance education and social projects in Israel. Recently it emerged that the income from the Emergency Appeal for the current year will be some $64 million short of the estimate.' (5)

Israel Bonds are sold for a period of 10-15 years and carry an interest of 4%. Every Bond owner is permitted to demand immediate redemption in Israeli Pounds for the purpose of investment in Israel or tourism in Israel. Most of the Bonds are indeed redeemed in Israeli Pounds. Income from the Bonds since their first issue in 1951-2 up to 1966-7 was $933 million. During that period, $404 million were redeemed, which leaves a net capital gain of $529 million for the said period in Bonds held by the public, mainly in the US.

'If we examine the accounts of sales and redemption of the Bonds for 1976, which was a peak year in the sales of the Bonds, we find that the income to the Israeli Treasury from the sales of Bonds last year will not exceed $276 million approximately, whereas the expenditure on redemption of Bonds, payment of interest and allocations for payment of interest in the future exceeds $253 million. In other words the total net contribution of the Bonds to cover Israel's foreign currency deficit in 1976 was in the order of some $25 million — against the total deficit of $3.2 milliard.' (6)

Israel's dependence on the United States is now almost total, especially after 1973, when the mobilization of Jewish foreign capital support cannot even remotely constitute a material alternative to direct US underwriting of Israeli military expenditure and foreign currency deficit. Nevertheless, there is an important and fundamental difference that distinguishes the US — Israel alliance from any other alliance between the United States and other states in the area. The current alliances between the United States and Iran, Saudi Arabia or Egypt for instance, depend on the continued existence in power of appropriate political regimes in these states, and would be seriously jeopardized should the nature of these regimes significantly change through internal developments. On the other hand, given the colonial underpinnings of the Israeli-Jewish society, the state of Israel cannot hope to continue to exist as an exclusively Jewish state in total confrontation with the Palestinians and the neighbouring Arab States without continuous massive imperial protection — British from 1917 until 1948 and American since the 1950s onwards. This, of course, is realized full well by all parties concerned. It guarantees complete allegiance of the whole body of Israeli-Jewish society to western, primarily US, imperial interests irrespective of any change of regime within the state of Israel itself. Put in other words, the states of Iran or Saudi Arabia can suffer a radical change of regime that will jeopardize their continued alliance with the United States without risking in any serious manner the dismantling of the Irani or the Saudi states per se. In the case of Israel, as for the cases of South Vietnam, South Korea, Rhodesia, Algeria or South Africa (and allowing for all relevant differences in context), a change of political regime that could imply a break-away from the continued alliance with the

United States necessarily implies the dismantling of the settler-colonial state and its transformation into a different political entity. Rhodesia will not escape its fate and will soon be transformed back into Zimbabwe. Similarly Israel will not escape its fate, and it will be, though not in the near future, transformed back into Palestine. Israel's continued existence as an exclusively Jewish state is critically dependent on continued imperial under-writing and active imperial support. Israel under any government will therefore always be a completely dependable local ally to the United States. This, however, does not necessarily imply it must be, or in fact is, a docile, passive and completely reactive ally.

The structure of the relations maintained between the settler-colonial body and its imperial metropolitan patron is complex and determined by a set of important contradictions. Yet, as Arghiri Emmanuel argues convincingly (7) the terms of the relationship cannot be understood unless one realizes that they allow the colonial settlers considerable leeway for action as an independent political factor.

From the imperial point of view extension of support to the settler colonial policy is a straightforward matter. In the case of Palestine, the motivation for British imperial support of the Zionist colonial efforts there was quite plainly articulated by the former military governor of Jerusalem and later of Palestine, Sir Ronald Storrs, already in the 1920s:

> 'The enterprise was one that blessed him that gave as well as him that took, by forming for England "a little loyal Jewish Ulster" in a sea of potentially hostile Arabism.' (8)

From the settler colonist point of view the colonial situation sustains a fundamental underlying contradiction. On the one hand the colonial settler policy could not have emerged in the first place except within the universe determined by imperial political interests and through continued imperial protection and support. On the other hand, as the history of every settler-colony invariably manifests, imperial and settler colonial interests are bound to conflict, at which time the settler colonial policy has no other option except taking up arms in a unilateral declaration of independence. As Emmanuel points out various colonial settler communities have already faced this problem:

> 'Their numbers and their means of action certainly differed widely according to whether they were in a settlers' or a mainly administrative colony, but their position and their attitude were essentially the same, while their aggressiveness and efficacy depended on the relation of forces at a particular time. There were few of them in the Congo, and they were beaten, but only after obliging the imperialists to use all the means at their disposal. They were scarcely more numerous in Rhodesia, but they succeeded with disconcerting ease. While although they were far more numerous in Algeria, both in absolute and in relative terms, they nevertheless succumbed, though not until they had endangered the parent country itself and obliged a French Prime Minister to scurry to the radio in the middle of the night so as to stir up the population against a hypothetical descent

of parachutists over the capital . . .

As for Israel, it is all too often forgotten that if this country represents a spearhead of imperialism in the particular international context of today, with the antagonism between the two great blocs, this is only a result of special circumstances. Its true nature is to be a mass of small "white" settlers spreading out more and more to colonize an under-developed territory. It is this that makes their conflict with the peoples of the region so ruthless, even where the latter live under pro-Western regimes which are themselves the satellites of imperialism. In spite of its circumstantial and unnatural alliance with American imperialism (which is not all that reliable, as the recent quarrel about frontiers with William Rogers shows), Israel is a secessionist colonial state. Its foundation was the object of a long and bloody struggle with England, who played the role of the imperialist parent country.' (9)

Both parties to the US-Israel alliance are aware of the terms of the relationship. We shall not go into the question of why the United States did not force immediate Israeli withdrawal from all territories occupied through the Israeli victory in the 1967 war, as it did after the Israeli conquest of the Sinai Peninsula in the 1956 war, although the answer is not difficult to determine. It emerges clearly from a comparative political analysis of the balance of power in the 1950s as against the 1960s, among the various local political forces in the Middle East on the one hand and the Great Powers on the other. The details of such a comparative analysis, however, are beyond the scope of this study.

Since continued US political, economic and military support of Israel has to date never been conditional upon the modification or cessation of Israeli fast colonization programmes in the post-1967 occupied territories, US policy on this matter can only be interpreted as tacit de facto support of Israel's colonial policies. In the period 1967-1976 over eighty new Israeli settlements were established in the post-1967 occupied territories, excluding the Greater Jerusalem Metropolitan area, which now extends from Bethlehem to Ramallah (See official map of the new settlements 1967-1976, Appendix C). This de facto tacit support, official US declarations on the matter notwithstanding, need not be maintained forever. It could be the case that it is maintained by force of the unveiled threat by Israel that any serious US pressure on Israel to force Israeli withdrawal from these settled territories in the framework of an attempted settlement of the Israeli-Palestinian conflict will immediately result in an unilateral declaration of independence by Israel in the form of an Israeli initiated war whose results and consequences would be very difficult to gauge. True, such prospects could be suicidal — but they need not be, especially should the Israeli operation be manifestly effective and achieve undisputed military success and possible political advantages to the American Empire, at least ex post factum. Yoel Marcus, the leading Ha-aretz commentator presents the case in succint and lucid terms:

'There is no doubt that there will now be a period of significant tension, and pressures will be brought to bear on us which have nothing to do with the question as to whether we are right or wrong; rather they have to do with the process of the decline of the West. We shall have to mobilize American Jewry — still a powerful force — and make clear to the Americans the basic difference between us and Cambodia . . . We shall have to explain again and again that a strong Israel is not only in the American interest, but also still the only way to convince the Arabs to find some form of coexistence with her. Secondly, on the level of relations with the Arabs, we shall have to deprive them not only of those achievements that result from the use of force, but we must also prevent the successful implementation of military actions whose aim is to terrorize the world. This is not only a matter of proper military deployment on our part, but also one of principled readiness to be slightly mad. We must make it clear — and first of all to ourselves — that we do not necessarily intend to play according to Arab rules. We shall determine which Arab move is from our point of view a *Casus Belli*, in what form of a war of attrition we shall refuse to take part, and at what point we shall play the game differently from the way others expect us to. If the Free World is frightened and the West is in a process of decline, it may be that we have a number of means available to terrorize it more than the Arabs could. A word to the wise is enough.' (10)

In the light of such brinkmanship, of which both parties to the alliance are fully aware, one can expect to witness continued US support for the current status quo in the area so long as its costs, financial and political, are exorbitant. The only political factor that can ultimately render these costs exorbitant from the US point of view is the Palestinian resistance.

Should the Palestinian resistance achieve better successes than hitherto, the prospects of US abandonment of Israel (very much along the lines of French abandonment of Algeria) can be considered quite realistic.

The day-to-day workings of the Israel-US alliance, do not usually manifest themselves dramatically. Some aspects came to light recently in the United States, and were then reported extensively in Israel. The following is Evans and Novak's original report:

'WASHINGTON — Secret, under-the-table CIA payments amounting to "tens of millions" — far more than any sums paid to Jordan's King Hussein — have been regularly funneled to Israel's intelligence service for control and disbursement by the Prime Minister's office.

What is important about these payments, which started around 1960, is not their secrecy or even their existence. It is their purpose: to give the anti-communist West, through the highly effective good offices of Israel, competitive equality in political penetration of newly independent states in black Africa.

. . . Anti-Israel sentiment began rising in black Africa soon after Israel seized the Egyptian Sinai, the Syrian Golan Height and the Palestinian West Bank in 1967. It boiled over after the Yom Kippur War of October, 1973. Long before then, however, Israeli activities in black Africa had fulfilled expectations as a counterweight to Soviet-Chinese penetration. Black Africans were taught special Israeli talents, such as frontier fighting and farming skills, developed in Israeli kibbutzim.

One of the best dividends from this CIA investment came in Zaire (the former Belgian Congo). President Mobutu of Zaire, leader of moderate forces in the Congo's civil war against communist backed radicals might never have emerged the victor without Israel's help.

The questions answer themselves: A public request for such funds would have exposed Israel as a proxy missionary for the US, frightened black Africa into refusing cooperation for fear of political backlash and sharpened one of Moscow's propaganda pictures of an imperialistic Uncle Sam with Israel as his tool.' (11)

THE FUTURE

I have examined in detail the position of the Oriental-Jewish society in Israel, and pointed out that given Israel's colonial history, not only is the ruling elite's allegiance to imperialism secured, but much more significantly the allegiance of the society as a whole is guaranteed insofar as it predicates its existence on maintaining a privileged position against the colonized. The fact that these privileges are unevenly distributed does not, in a colonial context, make for a particularly revolutionary working class. Class conflicts within Israel are further constrained by the fact that the society as a whole is subsidized from outside through huge regular unilateral inflows of capital. The Israeli working class shares directly and indirectly the benefits of this capital transfusion. People are clearly aware that their employment, the level of their wages and consumption, their housing and the general level of the standard of living they enjoy in no way correspond to the Gross National Product of the country and would be clearly untenable without this kind of unilateral foreign capital inflow. Their allegiance to the system is therefore deep seated.

All this can be expected to change if the system betrays signs of an impending defeat. First indications that this may come to pass sooner than many envisaged became apparent in the 1973 war. But one must not fail to note that the popular response to the war and the indication that the system could conceivably be defeated on the battlefield or through a major economic crisis resulted in an enormous upsurge of support to the right in the 1973 post-war elections.

As Teodor Shanin correctly observes:

> 'What next? How about the Israeli "masses", those old and young, who grew up mostly within the norms and values of moderate (labour) Zionism? There are always some to whom anything beyond their immediate existence and environment is highbrow. These follow and will follow any governmental authority, responding to the ever-repeated call for national unity against the ever hostile world. Faced with the collapse of an ideology they have lived by (moderate labour Zionism), some, especially the older ones, will simply hide from the horrors of recognition, negating a life span. Others, especially those who went through the social education of the Israeli school and army will "drop their dreams", become "pragmatic" in the sense of do-your-job-efficiently, look-after-your-family-and-to-hell-with-them, any "them". Thoughts about emigration to a softer spot of the world

112

will often follow. At the same time the explicit and outspoken fundamentalism (of right-wing Zionism) will proceed, making new converts in a creeping advance towards parliamentary power.' (1)

It is similarly recognized within the Israeli socialist left that as long as Israeli's privileged status in the region continues to be defined in the terms outlines above

'there is little prospect of internal social conflict acquiring a revolutionary character. On the other hand, a revolutionary breakthrough in the Arab world would change this situation . . . (It) could change the balance of power . . . (and) make Israel's traditional politico-military role obsolete, and would thus reduce its usefulness to imperialism. At first Israel would probably be used in an attempt to crush such revolutionary breakthrough in the Arab world; yet, once this attempt had failed, Israel's politico-military role vis-a-vis the Arab world would be finished. Once this role and its associated privileges had been ended, the Zionist regime, depending as it does on these privileges, would be open to mass challenge from within Israel itself.' (2)

Yet, as the 1973 war indicated, there may be a flaw in the reasoning. The Zionist polity can conceivably be defeated through developments other than a revolutionary breakthrough in the Arab world. It could, for instance, be defeated through realignment of American imperial interests in the area with existing Arab regimes at the cost of the abandonment of its traditional Israeli 'watchdog'.

When it comes to speculative overall perspectives of the medium and longer-term future of the state of Israel and US-Israel relations two broad theories seem to be dominant in the field. The first suggests that since it is becoming increasingly expensive and politically counter-productive for the US metropolis to continue its support to its Israeli colonial satellite at the level which seems necessary if its *de facto* military supremacy in the area is to be maintained ($2.5 billion per annum in 1974-5), and, no less important, since there is now, since 1973, a real option of replacing the long-standing axis of Irani-Israeli *de facto* alliance under US sponsorship with an Irani-Saudi Arabian-Egyptian *de facto* alliance under US control, we shall increasingly witness a gradual abandonment of Israel by the US. In terms of this theory, if such gradual abandonment proves for a variety of reasons to be impossible in practice, the US may actually welcome, if not precipitate, another Israeli-Arab military confrontation, which will be engineered to result in an unambiguous Israeli defeat and the conclusion of an Israeli surrender peace treaty. Such a peace treaty will probably not involve the dissolution of the state of Israel as a legally, internationally recognized sovereign political entity, but will basically result in the implementation of the UN Resolution 242 strictly interpreted to involve Israeli withdrawal from all post-1967 territories, perhaps the bi- or inter-national-ization of Jerusalem, the establishment of a Palestinian state alongside Israel on the West Bank and the Gaza Strip and possibly the implementation of the right of the 1948 refugees to return to Israel proper. There are very few people who doubt that in the event of another Middle East war Israeli contingency plans of utilizing the war in order to engineer mass removal of the Palestinian-Arab population from the West Bank and the Gaza Strip will be implemented. In terms of this scenario, however, the destruction will be rampant, but not of long-term consequence, since under the terms of an Israeli surrender settlement, whatever may be achieved by resort to such policies during the actual time of war and fighting will shortly thereafter be undone.

The alternative theory outlining the long-term prospects of US-Israel relations argues that given the fact that as a result of the post-1973 renegotiations of the terms of oil production and marketing by the OPEC cartel, effectively acting in concert, there now emerges in the Middle East a new *industrial bourgeoisie*, which utilizes the finance capital it has now available not primarily to facilitate service and luxury consumption, but to establish in the Middle East a new industrial and military base, which will in the near future effectively compete with the existing industrial centres of Euro-America and Japan.

In the history of capitalist production, major re-divisions of markets and global spheres of economic influence prompted by the emergence of a new industrial bourgeoisie have always been decided by recourse to a World War. In terms of such a scenario, not only is it nonsense to consider the abandonment of Israel by the US subsequent to the 1973 war, but precisely the contrary is true: in such a scenario Israel has a critical role to play, since it is the only state in the area, which, due to its position as a colonial society in confrontation with a native Palestinian-Arab population and the neighbouring Arab states, can be trusted to maintain unwavering popular allegiance to its metropolitan shield and protector, irrespective of whatever changes in its political regime may take place. Most extrapolations of this scenario involve a US takeover of key oil-fields in the Gulf, with Israel playing a central role both militarily and geo-politically. It may very well be that US marines transported by air could find *en route* refuelling facilities only in Israeli airfields; and, of course, in terms of such a scenario, the Israeli army will play a significant role in the overall allocation of attack responsibilities (the takeover of the Kuwaiti oilfields is usually postulated).

Opinion varies largely as to the outcome of such an attempt and as to whether indeed it can be efficiently and smoothly carried through. If, however, it is the case that such or similar motivations will in fact underlie the next Middle East war, we shall be witnessing a very rapid Vietnamization of the area. These are also the only circumstances which will enable the state of Israel to successfully implement plans to render the West Bank and the Gaza Strip *Arabrein* and in the process transform Israel to what can be only described as a Zionist political monster, very much akin to the Thieu regime in South Vietnam. The revisionist Zionist dream (or better: nightmare), widely shared since 1967 within labour Zionism, of a Jewish state extending from the Nile to the Euphrates would indeed become a reality, which would necessitate the coming into explicit political power of the worst fascist elements both in Israel and the Zionist movement; elements which would not only, like labour Zionism, effectively implement Zionist colonial and occupation policies, but which would implement them without being hindered in any way be even a semblance of moral scruples.

It is in our opinion also true that so long as none of the various relevant factors determining the terms of the Israeli/Palestinian conflict do not significantly alter, the Israeli ruling authorities, under labour Zionist leadership or fundamentalist right-wing revisionist Zionist leadership, can remain quite confident that however intolerable the circumstances of living and the hardship imposed upon the greater majority of the Israeli (predominantly Oriental) Jewish population, its ultimate loyalty to the continued existence of the state of Israel as a Zionist (Jewish) state is not at risk. This is not to say that protest and recurrent rebellion has been mild or inconsistent. Quite the contrary is true. The cyclical uprising of various Oriental-Jewish communities and sectors has been (correctly) perceived by the predominantly Ashkenazi Israeli ruling authorities as extremely dangerous. Since the early 1970s the situation worsened considerably, and the Government decided to employ Border Police Units, 'The Green Berets' to oversee the increasingly boiling and volatile belts of Oriental-Jewish slums. The Israeli Border Police consists of crack units who have had, since 1967, the opportunity to refine their skills in the maintenance of law and order through the repression and attempted destruction of the Palestinian-Arab resistance in the post-1967 occupied territories of the Gaza Strip and the West Bank. A few random citations of relevant headlines from recent Israeli Hebrew press will adequately illustrate the point:

WHAT'S GOING ON HERE? IS THIS NABLUS? — ASKED AN OLD MAN IN ROSH HA-AYYIN IN RESPONSE TO THE MASS RIOTING OF THE TOWNSHIP'S PUPILS
'At the end of a day of demonstrations and strikes: sabotage of installations, arson, uprooting trees, road blockades, and rioting for its own sake.' (3)

BURNING TYRES — THIS TIME IN TEL AVIV
'The columns of smoke that rose from the tyres set on fire by the residents of the Sheikh Munis quarter have achieved their purpose. The Tel Aviv Municipality accepted the demands of the residents. (Sheikh Munis is an evacuated Arab village, inhabited predominantly by Oriental Jews now forming a part of the Tel-Aviv slum belt.) (4)

TEAR GAS USED TO EVACUATE INVADING SQUATTERS IN LYDDA.
'Fights between the policemen and the evacuees. 60 people detained 200 policemen and policewomen from the Central Police Area evacuated yesterday by force the scores of families who last week invaded empty apartments in the center of the city of Lydda. The policemen, wearing helmets and armed with batons, were compelled to use tear gas.' (5)

And yet, I submit, the confidence of the Israeli ruling authorities in the *ultimate* loyalty of the greater majority of the Israeli-Jewish population, and especially its internally colonized and impoverished Oriental-Jewish masses is well warranted. This is so because, as noted earlier, given Israel's colonial history, both the rich and the poor, the Ashkenazi and the Oriental Jew, unevenly share the gains of the colonial enterprise. Both are fully aware that the rich man's villa in Zahalah and the poor man's badly over-crowded slum apartment in Kiryat Shmoneh (Khalisa); are situated there in the first place only and directly because the native Palestinian-Arab was dispossessed of his lands and property and his right of return denied. The example below illustrates this point.

When the Tel-Aviv Municipality decided to crack down on unauthorized building, the new legal rigours did not fall on hotels which got building permits for 14 stories, but in fact built 16, 17 and over, or on millionaires who add an additional story to their luxurious penthouses, but on the widespread, often makeshift unauthorized building in the metropolitan slum belts. For instance, it affected a workshop built (by the Harari brothers) in the Ezra (slum) quarter, no different from the hundreds of workshops and thousands of flats built in this quarter and in similar quarters. It was built without permit, and like many of the buildings in the same street and neighbouring streets, it too is built on public land. Many families get their livelihood from this workshop, which produces television aerials. Eight of the Harari twelve brothers and seven sisters, who were born in Brazil to their Syrian parents, are linked in one way or another to the workshop. In addition, twelve hired workers depend for their livelihood on the workshop.

> ' "Why do they wish to destroy our life?" — ask the Harari brothers with sincerity. They truly believe, as do many in the slum quarters of Tel-Aviv, that squatting on public land entitles them to occupancy rights on the land. "Did the state of Israel buy all the lands now owned by the Israel Land Authority?", I was asked again and again during my visit in the Ezra quarter; "Did the state not take these lands by force in the war against the Arabs? We too, or our elder brothers, participated in the war for the conquest of the land which we are now occupying." '

The attempt by the Tel-Aviv Municipality to demolish the unauthorized building did not go unchallenged:

> 'Much was written this week on the violent resistance of the brothers to the execution of the demolition order: fortifying themselves in the workshop behind welded door and seizing photographers and news-paper correspondents as hostages ("we were treated superbly", said the hostages who were allowed out of the workshop when the police crack forces began their attack). Much was written about the riots that broke out around the workshop; on the ditch which prevented the bulldozer from approaching the site; on the tyres that were set on fire to block the way before the Tel-Aviv Municipality vehicles; on the molotov cocktails thrown at the police force, and on the hand grenade that was used and wounded three civilians and two policemen.' (6)

The Oriental-Jew is crippled through systematic structural policies of economic exploitation, political repression, ethnic discrimination and cultural mutilation. Yet he is likely to be much more rabidly anti-Arab than his rich Ashkenazi compatriot. It is not difficult to see why. Official political statements by the PLO leadership notwithstanding, there is little in the *de facto* Palestinian strategy of armed struggle that adequately answers his fundamental existential fear. He is (properly) afraid that the victory of the Palestinian resistance would simply result in forcing him out of his poor and overcrowded shelter and alienating job back into the tent camp and the lifetime idle unemployment of the refugee. After all, the Oriental-Jewish citizen of the state of Israel is more likely than not to have a vivid living memory of what it means to live in a refugee camp, euphemistically termed in Israel 'transit camp' (*Maabarah*). Many thousands of Oriental-Jewish families lived 'in transit' as refugees for close to a decade after their transfer to Israel in the early 1950s.

The implications of a possible Palestinian resistance victory for the affluent and rich Ashkenazi Jew are significantly different. A Palestinian victory will destroy all that he stands for: the continued existence of the exclusively Jewish state of Israel as a solution to the Jewish problem (though the vision and idealism are now very much corrupted and largely fabricated); and such a victory would undoubtedly rob him of his privileged political and economic position as a participant in the administration of the state. It is not, however, likely to place him in material jeopardy. Given his class position, his professional skills and his contacts, he is likely to be able to escape material misery both in the event that he chooses to remain in Palestine after the defeat of the state of Israel or alternatively, re-establish himself and his family abroad. Short of complete devastation and genocidal Arab occupation of Palestine, he has options that are not available to his Oriental-Jewish compatriot. These options are not abstract or irrelevant. The figures of the levels of immigration to and emmigration from Israel, especially after 1973, bear ample witness to that. *Yediot Aharonot* reports that 'according to the forecast of the Ministry of Finance 16,000 people will emmigrate (from Israel) and the net population growth through immigration will amount to only 8,000'. Professor Joseph Dan sums up the situation as follows:

> 'In March 1976, thirty one years after the Holocaust and twenty eight years after the establishment of the state of Israel, 1511 new immigrants arrived to the country. Had the British Mandate still administered the country, and had it continued to maintain its 1946 immigration quota, this would mean that in March 1976 only eleven Jews who wished to immigrate to Israel would not have received immigration certificates (from the British Mandate authorities in 1946). It is the existence of the state of Israel and the Law of return which entitle these eleven immigrants the right to enter the country. These eleven immigrants are the only beneficiaries (in March 1976) of all the sacrifices made by the people of Israel in order to maintain its state — a state where the Law of Return is paramount.' (7)

Areih Zimuki reports that:

> DRASTIC STEPS AGAINST (SOVIET JEWISH IMMIGRANT)
> DROP-OUTS IN VIENNA ARE DISCUSSED

> 'The suggestion that an unequivocal binding commitment be taken from Jews who wish to leave the Soviet Union, stating that their aim is to immigrate to Israel will be considered in the framework of the current discussion on the new policy towards the "drop-outs" that should be adopted by the Government and the Jewish Agency. The opinion that is forming at the Jewish Agency is that drastic steps must be taken against the "drop-outs" which now make up some 60 per cent of those who receive immigration certificates from the Soviet Union to immigrate to Israel and who subsequently arrive in Vienna. The "drop-outs" abuse the immigration certificates given to them by the Soviet authorities, and thereby damage the possibilities of those Jews who want to immigrate to Israel in the future as well as endanger the future of (Jewish) immigration (to Israel).
> A more stringent treatment of those (Soviet) immigrants who leave Israel and arrive in Rome is also being considered. In Rome they are seeking assistance from Jewish welfare societies. The problem is how to influence Hais, the Jewish welfare association, and other institutions to cooperate in the implementation of the policy that will be determined in Jerusalem.' (8)

As Professor Amnon Rubinstein notes:

> 'Most of the emmigrants from Israel (yordim) represent a stratum of the Israeli society that has above the average professional skills. The fact that they have been successful in obtaining work abroad in the West testifies to this. (Thus) the reservoir of talented labour force which we so badly need is badly crippled.' (9)

For the overwhelming majority of the Oriental-Jewish citizens of Israel, for whom the maintenance of adequate subsistence is a major, and often insoluble problem, the option of travel and emigration simply does not exist. They are destined to remain in Palestine, and they can reasonably be expected not to ultimately betray their loyalty to a political system that condemns them to second-class citizenship, of the only realistic alternative made available to them is refugee statelessness.

It is interesting to note to what extent Oriental-Jewish racism against the Arab is derivative and largely situated in the specific colonial circumstances into which they were administered. As we have already mentioned, in 1975 both the Moroccan and the Iraqi Governments took official legal measures to secure the possibility for Oriental-Jewish citizens of the state of Israel of Moroccan and Iraqi origin respectively to return to their country of origin as equal citizens under law and under the UN Universal Declaration of Human Rights. (See Appendix C). The response of the Israeli authorities bordered on hysteria:

> 'The Secretary of the Association of Moroccan Immigrants, Mr. Moshe Asolin, made a statement in the name of his organization, in which he said "Anyone attempting to organize and encourage

ethnically motivated emigration, puts himself in collaboration with the designs of the PLO and elements hostile to the state. We did not emigrate when we lived in tents, corrugated tin and tarpaulin huts. We shall definitely not do so today. We have established in the country glorious projects both in development towns and in settlement (agricultural) settlements, and we shall continue to do so." ' (10)

Yet, a week later, *Yediot Aharonot* reported that

EMIGRANTS FROM ISRAEL RECEIVED MOROCCAN PASSPORTS

"There is no organized emigration out of Israel, and all the publicity concerning an organization orchestrating emigration from Israel to Morocco is a balloon that has exploded" — said yesterday Mr. Asher Hasini, the President of the North African Immigrants' Association at a press conference at Beit Agron in Jerusalem. Nevertheless it was stated on that occasion that some one hundred families who emigrated from Israel in recent years turned to the Moroccan Embassy in France and received Moroccan passports. Some returned to Morocco and others continued on their way to other destinations, primarily Canada. The Moroccan passport offers easier access to Canada. In return for their Moroccan passports these emigrants deposited their Israeli passports at the Moroccan Embassy in Paris.' (11)

Illiteracy has never necessarily indicated lack of political sophistication, and conversely, a literate public is not necessarily well informed politically. Take for instance the following statement made by the spokesman for a group of families who have made public their resolve to return to Morocco:

' "Why do you, the Ashkenazim make such a fuss when we (declare our resolve) to return to Morocco? When (Israeli) Jews return to Germany, a country where six million Jews were murdered, everyone swallows his tongue and does not make a squeak. Why, then, do you make a fuss when we return to Morocco? There was no Holocaust there. On the contrary, there Jews were treated with respect.". (The spokesman's uncle) Albert adds: "We have never suffered in Morocco. If there was in Morocco any oppression, it was perpetrated by the French regime. The Arab policemen always treated us with great respect". "And what" — I (the interviewer) dare to ask — "if King Hasan is ousted and a madman like Colonel Qaddafi gets to power?". "And what" — they respond — "if the Arabs settle scores with Israel? You take a chance and remain here. To your good health. We take a chance and return to Morocco. History will tell who was wiser. Anyway, you should know that we have always gotten on well with the Arabs. Wonderful people. It is only the Ashkenazim that we have never gotten on with" '. (13)

The Oriental-Jewish citizens of Israel listen regularly to Arab radio stations and are ardent viewers of Arab TV programmes, and thus are probably better informed about the Arab world than many of their Ashkenazi anti-Zionist socialist compatriots. The Oriental-Jewish citizens of Israel are particularly keen observers of hypocrisy and deceit and like all people subject to crippling economic exploitation and political domination, they are not easily fooled. They have the long experience of three decades of second-class citizenship in a state which committed itself in its political credo — the Israeli Declarations of Independence — 'to promote the development of the country for the benefit of all its inhabitants uphold the full social and political equality of all its citizens, without distinction of religion, race or sex guarantee the freedom of religion, conscience, education and culture, etc.' It will take more than the mere propagation of an abstract political slogan to undermine their loyalty to a Zionist political regime in Palestine. Further, the *de facto* priorities of the Palestinian armed struggle could hardly encourage Oriental-Jews in Israel to believe that the PLO has their welfare in mind. After all it is the impoverished Oriental-Jewish settlements and development towns along the Israeli borders that are the primary victims of Palestinian guerrilla and terror operations, not the hated affluent neighbouring kibbutz, whose flourishing industries rely heavily on Oriental-Jewish hired labour from the surrounding *moshav* and development town hinterland. Similarly, when the victims of the Palestinian resistance tend to be the impoverished Oriental-Jewish inhabitants of Kiryat Shmoneh rather than the top military brass and civil servants residing in Zahalah, or the poor guests of the Savoy Hotel, which offers cheap overnight accommodation to Oriental-Jewish and Arab guest labourers in Tel-Aviv rather than the guests of the neighbouring Hilton Hotel, one could hardly be surprised that those identified by the Palestinian resistance as its potential allies within Israel are highly suspicious of the offer.

To my mind, at least, there are specific conclusions to be drawn from the above analysis. To the extent that the Palestinian resistance identifies itself as a revolutionary organization, it cannot shrug off the responsibilities that go with that. If it seriously considers that the undermining of the loyalty of the Oriental-Jewish citizens of Israel to the ultimate defense of the polity where they are doomed to second-class citizenship is of critical importance to the success of its struggle, it will plainly have to demonstrate, not only through its political statements, but simultaneously through its Constitutional pronouncements and its *de facto* political and military strategy, that it does in reality offer a better alternative than refugee statelessness to the people in question. We have already an indication of the possible response of at least certain sectors of the Oriental-Jewish citizens of the state of Israel to such possible developments, namely, the public and widespread affirmative to the legal measures taken by the Moroccan and Iraqi Governments concerning the rights of Israeli Moroccan and Iraqi Jews to return to their respective countries of origin as equal citizens under law and under the UN Universal Declaration of Human Rights. It must, however, be emphasized that if the Palestinian resistance is to put a convincing case, it must answer concrete and specific questions, e.g.: What does the implementation of the rights of the Palestinian-Arab 1948 refugees to return to their family place of origin exactly mean; will the present Jewish occupants of the houses in question be evacuated; if not, how would the return and repatriation of the Palestinian-Arab refugees be in fact effected; if the family home in question has been razed, and the site is now situated under the asphalt of a metropolitan parking lot — how would that effect the terms of the Palestinian-Arab refugee return and repatriation; in what terms would Palestinian citizenship be defined; what would be the criteria of land distribution and property ownership; what would be the nature of the political economy and political regime; in what terms would cultural self-determination for the Palestinian-Jew and the Palestinian-Arab be politically and constitutionally guaranteed in the new secular democratic and socialist regime; what would be the nature of the relationship between state and religion in a secular democratic and socialist Palestine, etc. In a recent discussion among Palestinian-Arabs and Israeli-Jews the following basic elements towards a definition of Palestinian citizenship for a projected Socialist Republic of Palestine were suggested: Any person who (1) lives in Palestine at the date of the establishment of the new regime, and/or (2) holds an Israeli passport, and/or (3) is a descendant to any person who was either born or lived in Palestine in the period beginning with the first Zionist Congress (1897) until the date of the establishment of the new regime, is a Palestinian national. Note that this skeleton definition covers all relevant constituencies without postulating a Palestinian-Arab Law of Return. It is only by meeting the challenge in such specific terms that a Palestinian resistance can hope to achieve a critical object which is essential for the success of the struggle towards a secular socialist and democratic Palestine Republic. The object *is not* to create a situation whereby large sectors of the Oriental-Jewish Israeli citizens will actively mobilize in cooperation with the Palestinians in a joint resistance to Zionism. Such cooperation, given appropriate circumstances, may take place, but then it would involve only a small minority of Oriental-Jews. The realistic object must be understood to be the constitution of a political situation where the Oriental-Jewish citizens of Israel will withdraw their loyalty and cooperation from *active defense* of the state of Israel either through direct mass passive resistance, or, what is more likely in the foreseeable future, through widespread draft avoidance, incompetent soldiering and refusal to die on the battlefield for a cause that is not their own ('cowardice').

Given the colonial nature of the state of Israel and the specific position of the Oriental-Jews as second-class citizens in the Zionist polity, which in many ways condemns them as a public (allowing, of course, for significant exceptions) to what I have earlier termed 'structural passivity' — one cannot reasonably expect more. But one must also be wary of foolishly underestimating the worthwhileness of the prospects. If a Palestinian resistance can create a political context wherein the loyalty of the majority of Israel's Oriental-Jewish citizens can be effectively undermined and find its expression through the various forms of passive resistance to the state and passive support for the Palestinian resistance and for the resistance organized by the small groups and organizations that are likely to emerge within the Ashkenazi as well as the Oriental communities in Israel in co-operation with the Palestinian-Arab in active resistance (armed resistance included) — it would have thereby constituted the preconditions for its victory.

The emergence of significant anti-Zionist socialist forces from within the Israeli-Jewish society in collaboration with sections of the Palestinian-Arab resistance very much depends upon the concrete circumstances of the decline of Zionism and the state of Israel. One hopes that the process will be that of gradual stagnation, corruption and demoralization; one fears the nightmare of a murderous, bloody defeat and counter-occupation. Those who are today leading the struggle against the violation of Palestinian human, civil and political rights under Israeli rule, may, within their lifetime, be placed in a position of leading the struggle to defend Israeli-Jewish rights under Arab rule. Against such a contingency, responsibility — political and intellectual — dictates modesty. It is not at all certain that the anti-Zionist socialist left in Israel will be able to build up sufficient power to curb the worst suicidal developments now in full swing within mainstream Zionism. Responsibility similarly dictates a consistent and un-flinching commitment by the Israeli anti-Zionist socialist left. Successful developments in the growth of socialist opposition to what can only be termed 'suicidal Zionism' in Israel are inconceivable without the development of similar processes within Jewish communities throughout the world, and within western public opinion at large. Quite clearly an important motivation underlying this study is the hope that it will, upon publication, significantly contribute towards this end.

I would like to conclude by quoting in full an anonymous leaflet published in Israel under the title: *The Israeli Socialist Organization for the Liberation of Palestine — Publication No. 2*. It reads as follows:

> 'The establishment of the Israeli Socialist Organization for the Liberation of Palestine is based on the awareness that a necessary condition for an overall social change in Israel is the defeat of the Zionist political regime which dominates the country: the defeat of the state of Israel as an exclusively Jewish state. One of the important tasks of an Israeli revolutionary organization is to struggle against the Zionist administration and disrupt its regular operation. This struggle must be based on a clear and very precise analysis of the Israeli social and economic structure and its class stratification. The Israeli Socialist Organization for the Liberation of Palestine was established with the aim of putting forward an alternative to the reality of life in Israel which is primarily determined by the Israeli-Arab conflict and the struggle against the Palestinians. It is our duty, therefore, to outline clearly the nature of our relations to the Palestinian-Arab struggle against Zionism.
>
> The political line adopted by the Palestine Liberation Organization (PLO) since 1970 defines the object of the PLO struggle as the establishment of a secular and democratic political regime in

122

Palestine which will guarantee equality of rights to Jews, Muslims and Christians. For us, as socialists, this is not a sufficiently adequate slogan. We do not believe that democratic rights can be in fact established in a regime that is not explicitly socialist by name and deed. Furthermore, we believe that the disregard of the national nature of the conflict has far-reaching negative political implications. From our recognition of the existence of an Israeli-Jewish people in Palestine and its aspiration for national self-determination, it does not follow that we support the implementation of this aspiration in the framework of a separate Israeli-Jewish state, namely: separate Israeli-Jewish army, taxation and judiciary systems. Racism and national discrimination originate when a community of national, religious or ethnic particularity gains monopoly over a state administration. We make a clear distinction between the aspiration of a community to maintain cultural autonomy and national self-determination on the one hand, and the implementation of this aspiration through monopolistic control over a state administration which is defined as Jewish (or Arab). Hence the slogan of our struggle: "For a socialist, multinational secular and democratic Republic in Palestine". It seems to us that the necessary conditions for the establishment of a social order of this kind are (1) a Constitution that will determine that no national, religious or ethnic group will be given rights which are denied from other groups, and, (2) social ownership of the means of production and equal distribution of material resources among all members of society as individuals and among the different national and cultural communities of which the society in question consists. It follows that whereas the different cultural institutions will be in principle open to all, and in reality largely controlled by the members of the specific culture or nationality in question (schools, missions, press, etc.), the institutions of the Republic will be based on a hierarchy of constitutive assemblies elected on the basis of "one person — one vote". The Republican state administration will be completely secular, and there shall not be any representation in the institutions of the Republic that will be based on national, religious or ethnic criteria.

A socialist solution to the conflict must take into account the fact of the creation of an Israeli-Jewish national entity in Palestine as well as the existence of the Palestinian-Arab national entity. Every struggle for social change must be based on a theory of social change in order to be able to outline a consistent strategy that will indicate how it would be possible to move from a given situation (the Israeli-Palestinian and the Israeli-Arab conflict) towards a desired social order. We share with others the definition of the state as a social institution based on exploitation and oppression. The socialist vision to which we subscribe is the establishment of a social order that will not rely upon the national state as a centralist institution holding monopoly over the army, taxation and judiciary systems; a social order that will be based on communual ownership of the means of production, councils of workers, peasants, students, free professions, etc. organized in a hierarchy of constitutive assemblies. We are nevertheless convinced that in the specific historical context of the conflict between Zionism, the Palestinian-Arab people and the Arab world, a desirable and reasonable stage of transition towards a fully socialist solution is the establishment of a socialist, multi-national, secular and democratic Republic in Palestine *and not* the establishment of two separate nation-states: an Israeli-Jewish state and a Palestinian-Arab state side by side.

We have no doubt that the measure of success that can be achieved by the Organization in Palestine depends very much on the development and achievements of the socialist struggle in the area as a whole. The Organization will therefore aim to develop its link with socialist revolutionary organizations in the area and throughout the world. It is not inconceivable that Zionism will be defeated not through what we as socialists would like to see, namely: through the popular common struggle of Israeli-Jews and Palestinian-Arabs. It is possible that Zionism will be defeated, for instance, through Arab occupation. The defeat of Zionism through such developments will bring suffering and calamity on large sections of the Israeli-Jewish people. It is possible that Zionism will ultimately succeed in bringing calamity on precisely the public it purports to redeem. The chance to avoid such a calamity is through the establishment of an Israeli socialist organization that will stand in the front-line of the struggle against Zionism; an organization that will constitute in fact a history of common Israeli/Palestinian struggle which will establish the base for a common future of equality and brotherhood between the oppressor and his victim.

This is in our opinion one of the tasks of the Israeli Socialist Organization for the Liberation of Palestine. We hope to succeed where others have failed or have not been sufficiently successful.'

GLOSSARY

Ahad ha-Am — Ascher Hirsch Ginsberg (1856-1927)

Hebrew essayist, thinker, and leader of the pre-political Zionist Hibbat Zion (qv) movement. He served as a point of reference for many liberal critics of Zionism, primarily due to his systematic critique of political Zionism and his emphasis on the cultural-educational requirements of the Zionist endeavour and the Jewish secular revival. Born in Skvira, the district of Kiev, Russia, he received traditional Hassidic education throughout his youth in parallel to his secular studies programme and Haskalah (qv) preoccupation. As a result of his powerful rationalist tendencies, he first gave up traditional observance, and subsequently abandoned all religious faith. About 1889 he was persuaded to undertake the leadership of the Benei Moshe — The Sons of Moses — secret society, which was founded in Russia the same year, to ensure personal dedication of its members to the spiritual renaissance of the Jewish people and the return of the Jews to their historic homeland, but with prior spiritual preparation and a commitment to a broader scope of nationalism, elevated to an ethical ideal based on the love of Israel and embracing moral values.

Despite its small membership (about 160) the order exerted considerable influence on the Hibbat Zion movement, whose leaders were also members of Benei Moshe. Both the order and the Hibbat Zion movement strongly opposed Herzl's political Zionism, and Ahad ha-Am consciously placed himself at the forefront of opposition to Herzl throughout his life. In 1891 and 1893 he visited Israel and made sharp critiques of the Zionist colonization of the country:

> 'We are used to believing abroad that Eretz Israel is now almost totally desolate, a desert that is not sowed, and anyone who wishes to purchase lands there may come and purchase as much as his heart desires. But in truth this is not the case. Throughout the country it is difficult to find fields that are not sowed; only sand fields and stone mountains that are not fit (to grow anything) but fruit trees; and this, only after hard labour and great expense of clearing and reclamation — only these are not cultivated.' (1)

Ahdut ha-Avodah — The Labour Union — Established in 1919 by merger of Poalei Zion (qv) with a minority of Ha-Poel ha-Tzair (qv).

Merged with Ha-Poel ha-Tzair in 1930 to form the Eretz Israel Workers'

Party — Mapai (qv).

In 1944 'Faction B' split off from Mapai renamed itself Ahdut ha-Avodah/Poalei Zion and merged with Ha-Shomer ha-Tzair (qv) to form the United Workers' Party — Mapam (qv).

In 1954 Ahdut ha-Avodah withdrew from Mapam and established itself as an independent member in the government coalition from 1959-1965. In 1965 it entered into an Alignment with Mapai, and in 1968 the Mapai-Ahdut ha-Avodah Alignment united with Rafi (which split from Mapai in 1965 with the withdrawal of David Ben Gurion from Mapai leadership) to form the ruling Israel Labour Party. (see political parties chart: p. 168).

Aliyah — Ascent — Term designating immigration to Israel. Emigration from Israel is termed Yeridah (Descent). The organization of Jewish immigration to Israel is administered by the Jewish Agency (qv), which is the executive arm of the World Zionist Federation. Youth Aliyah is a specialized administration focusing on immigration into Israel of minors, including Jewish orphans.

Avneri, Uri/Ha-Olam ha-Zeh — This World — Uri Avneri was born in 1923 in Beckum, Germany, as Helmut Ostermann; 1933 — settled in Palestine; 1938-1941 — member of the IZL-Irgun (qv); 1941-1946 — regular contributor to the fascist Hebrew periodical *Ha-Hevrah* (Society) and the right-wing Revisionist organ *Ba-Ma'avak* (In The Struggle); 1948-1949 — company commander of the motorized commando Samsom's Foxes; 1951 — co-founder and editor with Shalom Cohen of the photographic news weekly *Ha-Olam ha-Zeh* (see below); 1958 — founding member of the anti-French Israel Committee for Free Algeria; mid-1960s — founding member of the League Against Religious Coercion and the Committee Against the Military Government (see Defence (Emergency) Regulations (1945)); 1965-1973 — Member of Parliament for Ha-Olam ha-Zeh/New Force Movement.

Uri Avneri and Shalom Cohen, an Israeli-Jew of Iraqi origin and Egyptian education, bought *Ha-Olam ha-Zeh* in 1951 and immediately transformed it into the best muckraking independent Israeli paper, exposing corruption and attacking both foreign and home policies of the Israeli government. Throughout the 1950s and mid-1960s the paper led the struggle against violation of human and political rights of the Arabs under Israeli-Jewish rule, against religious coercion, bureaucratic corruption, etc. In its better days it advocated the recognition of the rights of the Palestinian-Arab 1948 refugees for return and/or repatriation, took an unequivocal anti-Zionist position, and argued systematically for the identification of the Israeli-Hebrew people as a distinct body-polity, nationality and culture from the Jewish people at large. Did not hesitate to attack the expropriation of Arab lands, the Defence (Emergency) Regulations (1945) (qv), and the military government imposed since between 1948-1966 on the Arab

126

population under Israeli-Jewish rule.

In 1965 the Israeli government passed a new libel law which, though formulated in universal terms, was primarily directed to close down the paper. Under the circumstances, the only avenue open to the editors was to get into the Knesset (Parliament) and protect themselves and the paper by Parliamentary immunity. The original platform of the new movement Ha-Olam he-Zeh/New Force had three points: Peace (Shalom), Equality (Shivyon), Freedom (Shihrur). The platform was changed into a ten point platform, the first of which demanded uncritical loyalty to the state of Israel, its army and security, in an attempt to cleanse the movement's image from a public scandal involving one of the campaign officer's violating military security codes. Uri Avneri was elected into the Israeli Parliament in 1965 and since 1965 Ha-Olam ha-Zeh politics have become increasingly more conservative and Zionist. During the 1967 War Ha-Olam ha-Zeh issued a daily news sheet titled *Daf* (Page), which came out with an issue carrying a huge headline: 'On to Damascus' advocating the Israeli occupation of the Syrian capital. When the annexation of East Jerusalem came to a vote in the Israeli Parliament shortly after the 1967 War, Uri Avneri joined the national coalition government and voted for the annexation of the city — a decision which he has later publicly regretted. He has since 1967 consistently advocated the establishment of a Palestinian Arab state (in reality a Bantustan) next to the Jewish state of Israel with Jerusalem as a common capital.

The 1969 elections carried both Uri Avneri and Shalom Cohen into Parliament, with Amnon Zichroni (qv) third on the list and acting as the movement's Parliamentary counsel.

Shortly after the movement split with an avalanche of public scandals and recriminations. Shalom Cohen established the Israeli Democrats List, which has recently merged with the more militant faction of the Israeli Black Panther Organization (qv). In the 1973 elections both Uri Avneri and Shalom Cohen lost their seats.

Balfour Declaration — see Zionist Congresses.

Berit Shalom — Covenant of Peace — Organized group that supported the bi-national idea during the 1920s and early 1930s. Group's membership never reached the 200 mark and it had a strong influence only within the German Zionist Federation which was relatively small in numbers and influence. In 1933 Berit Shalom faded out of existence, the main reasons being lack of funds and gradual desertion of its members. The rise of National Socialism in Germany and growing pre-occupation with the situation of the Jews in Europe were also responsible.

Bilu (Beit ya'akov Lekhu ve-Nelkha) — The House of Jacob, come ye and let us go (Isa. 25) — Russian-based immigration attempt (1882-4), usually called the first Aliyah (qv). The first of the group to arrive in Palestine was Jacob Shertok (see Sharett), who preceded the first group of 14 Bilu settlers by a few weeks. The attempt disintegrated within two years. The Bilu association in Russia died out in 1883, and out of the estimated 53 Bilu members who left Russia for Palestine during the early 1880s, about half either returned to Russia or left for the United States. A Bilu nucleus, however, did finally succeed in establishing the agricultural settlement of Gederah (1884).

Bir'im and Iqit — Two Maronite villages whose populations cooperated with the Israeli Army in 1948 when they were asked to leave their homes for fifteen days and go to the nearby village of Gush Halav until things subsided. Those fifteen days have lasted twenty five years. The villages turned to the Israeli Supreme Court of Justice. In 1952, the Court gave a verdict in their favour and pronounced their right to return to their villages, subject to permission from the Ministry of Defence. The response of the Ministry was the systematic destruction of the villagers houses. The churches, however, were spared. The lands of the two villages are now cultivated and controlled by the neighbouring Jewish kibbutzim (qv) and moshavim (qv). The lands of Bir'im, for instance, are being cultivated by the Mapam (qv) kibbutz Bar-Am and moshav Dovev. There are at least 21 similar cases of Arab internal refugee populations in Israel.

Buber, Martin (1878-1965) — Israeli philosopher, theologian, author, educator, leader, Zionist thinker and major spokesman for Hebrew humanism. Born in Vienna, 1878; Founder of the Zionist weekly *Die Welt* and co-editor of *Judischer Verlag*, 1901; Co-founder of the Jewish National Committee, Germany, 1914; Founder and editor of *Der Jude*, 1916-24.

Established himself as the leading philosopher, theoretician and spokesman for Zionist utopian socialist (with A.D. Gordon (qv) and Gustav Landauer) in opposition to the predominant commitment of the labour Zionist movement to state socialism as expressed at the Convention of Ha-Poel ha-Tzair/Ze'irei Zion (qv), Prague, 1920. Professor of Comparative Religion, Frankfurt University, 1924-33; Editor of *Die Kreatur*, 1926-30; Director of Judisches Lehrhaus, Frankfurt, 1933-38; Settled in Palestine, 1938; Professor at the Hebrew University in Jerusalem, 1938-1951; Co-founder with Judah L. Magnes (qv) and others of Ihud (qv), advocating a bi-national state in Palestine, 1942.

Professor Emiritus of Social Philosophy at the Hebrew University in Jerusalem, 1951; PhD, Hebrew University in Jerusalem, 1952; D. Hum. L. 1958; First President of the Israel Academy of Sciences and Humanities, 1960-62.

Buber's advocacy of bi-nationalism as well as that of Ihud at large, must be taken in context. Ihud was a Zionist organization, at the periphery of the Zionist movement, and, at a certain stage, its members were leading administrators of the Zionist campaign in Palestine Eretz Israel, such as Arthur Rupin (the father of Zionist settlement in Palestine). However, Arthur Rupin noted as early as 1928 that 'It became clear how difficult it is to realize Zionism and still reconcile it with the demands of general ethics' and in 1936 he had to admit that it was not only difficult but simply impossible: 'On every site where we purchase land and where we settle people, the present cultivators will inevitably be dispossessed.' (2)

Cheder — Room — The traditional Jewish boys' school of Ashkenazi Jewry, both in the West (until the end of the eighteenth century) and in the East (until the Russian Revolution and the Holocaust). An equivalent institution of a somewhat different nature existed in Jewish Sephardi communities in Asia, North Africa, and the Balkan countries. The Cheder was privately run as opposed to the Talmud Torah (Talmud Toyre), which was the school for the children of the very poor, financed and supervised by the congregation. Cheder education consisted mainly of the study of certain parts of the Pentateuch (the Hebrew original interpreted through an old traditional Yiddish translation) and of certain sections of the Babylonia Talmud. The teacher (Rebe) was also supposed to acquaint his scholars with all the benedictions and prayers and, in general, to introduce them to Yiddishkeit (Jewish way of life). The child spent most of his waking hours in the Cheder from early childhood (age 4-5) to puberty.

Communist Party — see Rakah.

Defence (Emergency) Regulations (1945) — The body of legislation known as the Defence (Emergency) Regulations (1945) was introduced into Palestine by the British Mandate Administration in an effort to curb both Arab and Zionist political and armed resistance. They were preceded by the Emergency Laws of 1936 and the Defence Laws of 1939 enacted primarily to suppress the Arab Revolt in Palestine (1936-9) during which significant parts of the country were effectively controlled by the Palestinian-Arab rebel administration.

The response of the Jewish Yishuv (qv) to the Defence (Emergency) Regulations was harsh and unequivocal. To quote Mr. Jacob Shimshon Shapirah, a leading Zionist lawyer at the time and later Israel's Attorney General and Minister of Justice:

> 'The system established in Palestine since the issue of the Defence Laws is unparalleled in any civilized country; there were no such laws even in Nazi Germany. There is indeed only one form of government which resembles the system in force here now — the case of an occupied country. They try to pacify us by saying that these laws are only directed against malefactors, not against honest citizens. But the Nazi Governor of Occupied Oslo also announced that no harm would come to citizens who minded their own business. It is our duty to tell the whole world that the Defence

GLOSSARY

> Laws passed by the British Mandatory Government of Palestine destroy the very foundations of justice in this land. It is pure euphemism to call the Military Courts "courts". In fact they are nothing more than, (to use Nazi nomenclature), "Military Judicial Committees Advising the Generals" '. (3)

With the Israeli Declaration of Independence (May 14, 1948) and with the assumption of legislative power by the Israeli Parliment (Knesset) immediately thereafter, the Defence (Emergency) Regulations (1945) were not repealed. All Israeli Parliaments have continually resisted every attempt to remove the Regulations from the Israeli Statute Books. The Regulations (with the exception of the sections dealing with immigration and land acquisition) have passed into the body of Israeli law, only now they are applied almost exclusively against the Arab population under Israeli rule. These Regulations give the Israeli Military Governors (Commanders) complete control over life and property. Until 1966 their authority was supported by a specialized military administration (the Military Government). In 1966 this administration was disbanded and the execution of the Military Governors orders was handed over to the regular civilian police. Some of the more notorious regulations are:

Detention	111 — (1) A Military Commander may order direct that any person shall be detained for any period not exceeding one year in such place of detention as may be specified by the Military Commander in the order.
Deportation	112 — (1) The High Commissioner shall have power to make an order under his hand (hereinafter in these Regulations referred to as 'a Deportation Order') requiring any person to leave and remain out of Palestine.
Taking possession of land	114 — (1) A District Commissioner may if it appears to him to be necessary or expedient so to do in the interests of the public safety, the defence of Palestine, the maintenance of public order or the maintenance of supplies and services essential to the life of the community — take possession of any land, or retain possession of any land of which possession was previously
Gaz: 26.8.39 p. 659	taken under regulation 48 of the Defence Regulations, 1939, and may, at the same time or from time to time thereafter, give such directions as appear to him to be necessary or expedient in connection with, or for the purposes of, the taking, retention or recovery of the land.
Forfeiture and demolition of property, etc.	119 — (1) A Military Commander may by order direct the forfeiture in the Government of Palestine of any house, structure, or land from

130

which he has reason to suspect that any firearm
has been illegally discharged, or any bomb,
grenade or explosive or incendiary article
illegally thrown or of any house, structure or
land situated in any area, town, village, quarter
or street the inhabitants or some of the inhabitants of which he is satisfied have committed,
or attempted to commit, or abetted the
commission of, or been accessories after the
fact to the commission of, any offence against
these Regulations involving violence or intimi-
dation or any Military Court offence; and when
any house, structure or land is forfeited as
aforesaid, the Military Commander may destroy
the house or the structure or anything
growing on the land.

Closed areas

125 — A Military Commander may by order
declare any area or place to be a closed area
for the purposes of these Regulations. Any
person, who, during any period in which any
such order is in force in relation to any area or
place, enters or leaves that area or place
without a permit in writing issued by or on
behalf of the Military Commander shall be
guilty of an offence against these Regulations.
(4)

Druze — The Druze tradition identifies the origin of the sect in the reve-
lation visited upon the Fatimid Caliph al-Hakim bi-Amr Allah (996-1020),
who nominated Hamza Ibn Ali and al-Darazi as chief propagandists of his
teaching. The sect is named after the latter.

The Druze religious tradition developed from Ismailism and its official
name is Din al-Tawhid — ('The religion of divine unity: monotheism').
The Druze religion is known only to a select few, and the community is
clearly divided between the few initiates ('The Knowing') and the mass of
'The Ignorant' who have no access to Druze religious scripts and are bound
only by a minimal traditional code of behaviour and ethics. Both men and
women may belong to the select initiates. In 1960 the total number of
Druze was estimated at 300,000: 155,000 in Syria, 110,000 in Lebanon,
and 33,000 in Israel, mainly upper Galilee. Under the Ottoman Empire
founded by the Turkish tribal chief Uthman I (1288-1326) and officially
ended with the flight of Caliph Muhammad VI in 1922 from Constantinople, the Druze sustained a semi-autonomous and powerful emirate,
based in Mount Lebanon.

Attempts to co-opt the community into serving as local mercenaries
for the colonial administration were made during the reign of the British
Mandatory colonial administration of Palestine. These overtures, however,
as compared to the success of the Israeli colonial administration in that
domain, seem in retrospect almost negligible. The Israeli professional

soldier unit, the Israeli Border Police (The Green Berets) recruits heavily from the Druze and the Bedouin communities under Israeli rule (its higher ranks of course are almost exclusively Jewish). Also a Minorities Unit operates within the Israeli army, recruiting primarily from these two constituencies as well as admitting Christian Arab volunteers. Of the Muslim Arabs, only Bedouins may serve in the Israeli military or Border Police.

The Israeli Border Police and the Minorities Unit of the Israeli Army like all native mercenary units of a colonial power, are charged with the dirtiest jobs. Before 1967 they constituted the hard core of the Israeli border patrols, whose main job was to close the borders as effectively as they possibly could and bar infiltration and return of Palestinian-Arab refugees. Throughout the 1950s a constant thin flow of refugees succeeded in infiltrating back and joining their extended families in pre-1967 Israel. In most cases they were soon discovered (the Israeli secret police network within the Arab community was quite effective) and charged with illegal infiltration, bringing long jail sentences. Also, pre-1967 Israeli border Nahal (qv) outposts and kibbutzim (qv) had to rely on the patrolling of the Israeli Border Police, Army Minorities Unit and (exclusively Israeli-Jewish) reconnaisance units to supplement their internal patrol system against what proved to be at times large scale thefts. The rich and affluent Israeli kibbutz settlement had to sustain a tight system of patrolling to prevent its wealth being redistributed via the institution of theft among the people whose dispossession had rendered such accumulation possible.

After 1967 the Israeli Border Police, the Army Minorities Unit, and reconnaisance units played a crucial role in the destruction carried out in the newly acquired territories. Their most notorious operations were carried out in Gaza, where the post-1967 Israeli occupation met the strongest political and military opposition. It is worthy of note that the Israeli Border Police units which performed their murderous job in Gaza (1970-1) were transferred to Tel Aviv to maintain law and order in the metropolitan slum belts heavily populated with Israeli-Jews of Asian and African origin.

Lending itself to the mercenary service of the colonial power has never protected a native community from suffering the brunt of colonial policies, and the Druze are no exception. The lands of their villages were no better spared than the lands of predominantly Muslim or Christian Arab villages, and they of course could not escape the discrimination built in to the state of Israel. The Jewish city of Karmiel for example was established in the early 1960s on lands expropriated from the three Arab villages Deir al-Asad, Bi'na, Nahaf.

On February 8, 1971, *Yediot Aharonot* carried the following:

'Closed to Non-Jews' the answer given to a retired Druze officer who wanted to start a quarry:
This area is closed to non-Jews — thus replied in writing the director of Israel Land Authority to Mr. Ismail Qablan, a Druze from

Usafiyya, who wanted to start a marble quarry next to the development town of Karmiel.

Mr. Qablan, recently retired from the Israeli Border Police with the rank of officer after 20 years of service, has decided to start a business and after deliberations and consultations decided to start a marble quarry in the Galilee. He turned at first to the Israel Land Authority office in Nazareth, and the Director there gave him a written authorization to start the quarry and asked him to locate and prepare the land.

From the office of the Israel Land Authority Mr. Qablan turned to the Regional Planning Office, and the engineer prepared for him (the required) contour plan. For final authorization he had to turn to the Ministry of the Interior in Acre, and after filling our all the required forms at the Regional Office, he was told that within four-five months he would get a reply. Toward the end of this period the reply finally arrived, and it said that the Israel Land Authority does not authorize the plan. The reason: the quarry area is closed to non-Jewish citizens.

Mr. Qablan was deeply hurt by this reply, and turned immediately to the security authorities, the Chief of Staff, the director of the Israel Land Authority, and all other relevant officials asking "why did the Nazareth office of the Israel Land Authority give me the 'green light' (to go ahead) and the main office in Jerusalem refuses to recognize that."

In response Mr. Qablan received a simply reply from the Director of the Israel Land Authority: "The matter is under consideration." '

Under these circumstances one could hardly be surprised that discontent is mounting. Some grievances are:

Since 1948 the process of expropriation of the Druze lands has progressed incessantly.

The Ministry of Interior gives to the Jewish sector a municipal grant of 40-70 Israeli pounds per capita, whereas the grant for the Druze village is only 4-5 Israeli pounds per capita.

The Druze are paid 3.8 Israeli pounds for a kilogramme of tobacco against 5 Israeli pounds per kilogramme paid to their Jewish neighbours. Also there is the official Druze challenge to subjecting the community to compulsory conscription. As a matter of fact the situation came close to open mutiny when the religious leader (Imam) of the community, Sheikh Farhud Qasim Farhud, made a public statement (January 1972) calling upon members of his community to resist the draft. Obviously draft avoidance is now commonplace, with mounting resistance to the community being used as a source of native mercenaries. The Druze, from the Israeli point of view, can no longer be considered trustworthy. Some of the leading leftist Arab radicals under Israeli-Jewish rule are of Druze origin.

Fatah — (1956-1973) — Al Fatah grew out of a group of Palestinians mainly, but not exclusively from the Gaza Strip, and was founded in or about 1956. Its founders or early activists included Yasir Arafat (Abu

Ammar), Saliah Khalaf (Abu Iyyad), Faruq Qaddumi (Abu Lutuf),
Muhammad Yussuf Najjar (Abu Yusuf), Khalil al-Wazir (Abu Jihad), the
brothers Khalid and Hani al-Hasan. All remain leaders of the movement
and consequently, following the Fatah dominance in the Palestinian
Liberation Organization since 1969, leaders of the PLO, apart from Abu
Yusuf, who was killed in the Israeli raid on Beirut in April 1973. Despite
political divisions, they remain at least publicly united.

Their origins were among Palestinian students in Cairo, where Arafat
was President of the Palestinian Student Federation. Some had been
marginally active in the 1947-48 war — Arafat was a gun-runner in
Jerusalem — and their experience at that time, coupled with their experience of attempts by the Egyptian authorities to dominate the Palestinians
in Cairo, led them to believe in the need to create an independent Palestinian political entity, free of the Arab states. By 1956, Fatah was not yet
a separate entity, more a circle of friends, and Arafat fought as a lieutenant in the Egyptian army in the Suez campaign. Their emergence as a
separate political group was in 1958, with the publishing of a magazine,
Filistinuna, (Our Palestine) which expressed disillusion with the Arab
Governments.

Spreading through the Arab world as graduates, particularly in the Gulf,
they formed underground cells of other Palestinians, and also spread into
West Germany among the many Palestinian students living there. The
nucleus of Fatah was never Nasserist. Some of its leaders, including Arafat,
had been at one time members of the Muslim Brotherhood, while their
Gazan and Egyptian experiences made them suspect Egypt. Equally they
had few illusions about other Arab states, who found their assertion of the
independent status of Palestinians either unacceptable, or, in the case of
Jordan, a direct threat.

Their contacts with Arab movements began with the outbreak of the
Algerian revolution. By 1958, close links were established with the FLN,
who gave them their first training camps in 1962. The experience of the
Algerian revolution, coupled with their own belief in the need for armed
struggle moved Fatah towards preparation for actual military operations.
The decision to open military activity came through the crisis in 1963-64
over Israel's plan to divert the head-waters of the River Jordan. When the
Arab states were evidently unwilling to take action in 1964, the decision
was taken to move from a stage of armed reconnaissance to actual combat.
The first actual military operation took place on January 1st, 1965. The
first casualties were inflicted on Fatah, which had named its military wing
al-Asifa, (The Storm) to preserve at least some pretence of separate
identity, in the second week of January 1965, but not by Israel. A Fatah
patrol, returning from Israel, was attacked by Jordanian troops, and two
men were killed. Concomitant with their insistence on the right of the
Palestinians to determine their own struggle, Fatah's leaders also adopted
a policy of non-interference in the affairs of Arab states. This was partly

a practical decision, hoping thereby to avoid Arab governmental hostility, but also partly ideological. Jordan, after the annexation of the West Bank by King Abdallah (1951), had always claimed to represent the Palestinians. Fatah's very existence posed a challenge to that claim, a fact recognized by both sides, and this fact has always underlain the relations between the Hashemite Government and the Palestinian movements, Fatah included. After the launching of guerilla activity at the beginning of 1965, the Jordanian Prime Minister, Wasfi Tal, later assassinated by Black September in Cairo in November 1971, embarked on a hunt of Fatah members.

Within the Middle East as a whole, despite Fatah's insistence on the policy of non-interference, it had enemies. At the beginning of 1964, the Palestine Liberation Organization was formed under Egyptian tutelage, to control the Palestinians more effectively. The PLO was hostile to Fatah, as was the Arab Nationalist Movement of Dr. George Habash, then in a Nasserist phase. Following Fatah's embarkation on guerilla activity, the Arab League, on Egyptian prompting, and with the backing of the PLO, asked all Arab states not to publicize the al-Asifa military communiques. In 1966 Arafat was imprisoned for a short time in Syria, even though the Ba'athist regime which took over in March 1963 had by the summer of that year permitted Fatah to open some training camps.

Arab hostility, coupled with the popular strength of Nasserism before 1967 kept Fatah both relatively small and isolated from both the Arab masses and the Palestinian masses before 1967.

The 1967 War was a turning point. During the war itself Palestinians did fight. Fatah, which then had about 400 guerillas, fought in the Golan, especially in Queneitra. In Gaza the PLO controlled Palestine Liberation Army also fought stubbornly.

In June and July 1967 Fatah discussed with a number of other small guerilla groups, which were later to form the Popular Front for the Liberation of Palestine, PFLP, the formation of a united front. Failing to agree, they went their separate ways, and Fatah resumed attacks against Israeli forces in August 1967 — then the only Arab force to be fighting the June victory. While their underground network was swiftly dismantled, as a result of the Israeli capture of Jordanian intelligence files in Jenin in June, their resumption of fighting had two immediate results: it gave the Palestinians as a whole some hope that a course of action still lay open, and it meant that the Arab states — even, reluctantly, Jordan, could not turn so openly against them, since they were the only standard bearers for the entire Arab people in the military sphere. March 1968 saw the full emergence of the Fatah on to the Arab stage, with the battle of Karameh, in Jordan. An Israeli expeditionary force crossed the Jordan to destroy Palestinian guerilla bases. According to Palestinian sources the total number of Israeli soldiers deployed in the operations across the river was 15,000. Fatah guerillas in the town of Karameh, with some support from Jordanian regular units, forced Israel to withdraw with considerable casualties. The political and military credit went to Fatah: for the first time an Arab force had stood, fought and defeated the Israelis — that, at least, was how it was presented and Fatah overnight gained recognition from the Arab states.

From March 1968 until September 1970 Fatah and the remainder of the guerilla organizations were at their political and military peak. Infiltration into Israel grew to its highest level. Large numbers of Palestinians and other Arabs flocked to join, many to be turned away. They were given a kind of semi-state status by other Arab Governments including, again reluctantly, Jordan. Among the Palestinians in Jordan and to a lesser extent in Lebanon, Fatah took on the role of a government — building schools, establishing the Palestinian Red Crescent as a rudimentary medical service, levying taxes — generally freely paid — and negotiating on an apparently equal basis with Arab Governments. Fatah's ideology at this time became more international in its outlook. It forged links with other guerilla movements, in Vietnam and South America for example, and also with some left-wing groups in Europe. In June 1968, Fatah took control of the PLO, at a meeting of the Palestine National Council which ousted Shuqayri, the racist who had been appointed its original leader, and this control was strengthened in February 1969 at a meeting of the Council in Cairo. A short trial of strength with the Jordanian Government in November 1968 ended with a recognition by both sides of the need for at least a temporary truce.

Two developments within this period are important for understanding the political development of the Fatah. The first was the conscious attempt by a number of Arab Governments, afraid of losing all control over the Palestinians, to create their own docile guerilla groups.

In 1968, the Syrian Ba'ath founded al-Sa'iqa (The Thunderbolt) as an ostensibly independent Palestinian organization. In practice, however, it was a wing of the Ba'ath party, and as such, subject to Syrian Government control. While it did carry out operations against Israeli forces, its foundation gave the Syrians an excuse for not recognizing Fatah as the major representative voice in the executive Committee of the Palestine Liberation Organization. Early in the same year, a member of the PLO executive before the June war, Bahjat Abu Gharbiyya, founded the Popular Struggle Front, and received support from Egypt. Early in 1969, the Iraqi Ba'ath followed suit, with the creation of the Arab Liberation Front. This body never showed any independence from the Government in Baghdad, whose attitude was shown shortly after the ALF's foundation when they forbade Fatah to commemorate the Karameh battle in Iraq. Two other pro-Egyptian organizations emerged at this time, the Action Organization for the Liberation of Palestine, and the Arab Palestine Organization. All of these groups arose from, or depended for their existence on, an unwillingness among the Arab states to let the Palestinians develop and control their own political institutions, something that was to lead to major political strife within the Palestine Liberation Organization and the resistance movement as a whole. Arab interference in the Palestine cause changed form after 1967 — it did not cease.

Another development within the same period is also vital — the emergence of a new attitude towards the Jews living in Israel. The racist statements of Ahmad Shugayri were recognized to be not only counterproductive, but also politically undesirable and unacceptable. Following the Israeli victory in the June war, a new political mood began to spread within Fatah which recognized the need to abandon the old Shugayri line of a Palestine cleared of Jews. Early in 1968, Fatah began to develop its ideology of a 'democratic secular non-sectarian state in Palestine', composed of Muslims, Christians and Jews — recognizing the right of the Jews to stay, but regarding them as a community bound by religion, rather than a separate people, with their own right to nationhood: the distinction is evident in the use of the three religions to distinguish the future component parts, rather than Israeli-Jews and Palestinian-Arabs.

The democratic state idea was first publicly proposed at a conference in Cairo in January 1969, and was adopted by the Palestine National Council later in the year. It was criticized from two sides: the ALF and Sa'iqa, indicated that they believed that the structure of any future state in Palestine should not be for the Palestinians alone to decide, while the Popular Democratic Front, a Marxist-Leninist group that emerged in February 1969 has from time to time referred to the Jews in Israel as a nation. The discrepancy between the Fatah political line based on a secular democratic state for Jews, Christians and Muslims on the one hand, and the legal constitutional stipulations of the Palestine Liberation Organization on the other has remained. The Palestinian National Covenant (1968) which is still in force, recognizes as Palestinians only those Jews who lived or came to Palestine before the Zionist invasion. Until this discrepancy is removed and legal constitutional recognition is extended to all Israeli-Jews living in the country, there is little hope that the PLO political line advocating a secular democratic state will gain credibility. In late 1969 and early 1970 the Fatah dominance within the Palestinian movement was fully consolidated through the various bodies of the PLO, including its regular army, the Palestine Liberation Army (PLA), and its military activities against Israel reached their height.

In the summer of 1970, however, Fatah, and the whole movement was faced with a major threat from within the Arab world — the acceptance by a number of Arab states, including Egypt and Jordan, of the American-backed Rogers Plan for a peace settlement. The guerillas warned that such a settlement could only come after they had been crushed in Jordan, and between June 1970 and September the Hashemite government prepared for a showdown with the guerillas. At the beginning of September, the guerillas effectively held a position of dual power in the country, with their own police, schools, army, militia, and health service and showed signs of undermining the government by organizing among the East Jordanians.

When the Jordanian government launched their major attack in September, the Palestinians had some 18,600 men, of whom 5,000 were guerillas, 3,600 from the PLA, 8,500 militia, and 1,500 'Lion Cubs' — junior militia and guerillas. Against them the Government had a total strength of 100,000. During the ten day civil war, while the guerillas were able partly to hold their own, they were forced onto the defensive, and slowly lost ground over the subsequent ten months. The Arab states had shown that they were prepared to stand aside and allow King Hussein to kill the guerillas. Israel, with guerilla strength sapped in Jordan, had far less incursions across the borders. Since then the guerillas have been under major attack, from Jordan in July 1971, when their last remaining areas of control were wiped out, and in Lebanon. Early in 1973 at a meeting of the Arab Defence Council the Palestinian representative, from Fatah, indicated that the PLO was not prepared to accept any concept of joint Arab defence strategy which involved King Hussein, whose overthrow was essential to any development of a common front against Israel. The non-interference policy adopted in the pre-June war period had disappeared. The Jordanian attacks had discredited those leaders who had for years upheld the non-interference policy. The position of Arafat himself came under criticism, not only from other smaller and more left-wing groups, but also from within Fatah, where Abu Iyad in particular emerged as an advocate of a more left wing policy. The strong hold that the leadership has been able to establish during the period of that rapid expansion of the movement from March 1968 until September 1970, came under attack, with serious criticism being made by militants in the ranks. Coupled with the reverse suffered on the Arab political front, this disillusion led to some defections, and a growth in strength of the left-wing within Fatah, particularly on the question of non-interference.

Today Fatah has changed significantly from 1970 although the leadership is the same. It is smaller — the 'fair-weather friends' have dropped away in the face of the military and political reverses. It is weaker inside the territory occupied by Israel, although sporadic action continues. In the framework of Arab politics, the Palestinian movement has become more closely linked with revolutionary Arab groups, such as the Popular Front for the Liberation of Oman and the Arabian Gulf, despite the large subventions that continued to be paid by the Gulf sheikhdoms and Saudi Arabia. While one sector of the leadership still publicly maintains the non-interference policy, another sector is engaged in political activity inside the Arab world, not only against Jordan, but in Egypt, for example, where Palestinians were active in the early 1973 demonstrations against President Sadat.

Contradictions remain: Arafat moved swiftly to mend the PLO's fences with the Saudi Arabian Government after the Khartoum Black September incident in the Saudi Arabian Embassy early in 1973.

The publicity-conscious movement of 1968-1970 has virtually gone underground in most Middle Eastern countries. The changes in the political thinking of the leadership have been to some extent a reflection of the changes at base level, where refugees and guerillas alike have become more radical. Arafat suffered a severe political challenge as a result of his temporary reconciliation with Hussein after the 1970 civil war, while large sectors of Fatah opposed any subsequent 'peace talks' between Jordan and the PLO. Concomitant with the changing attitudes towards the Arab scene have come changes in attitudes towards the world, with the desperation engendered by the refugee camps and the frustration of the 1970 defeat leading to the emergence of groups like Black September — probably initially a rank-and-file body, even if now under some form of central control.

The organization although changed significantly since 1970 still faces major problems: the majority of its support, apart from Palestinian intellectuals, comes from the refugees but its leadership comes from the petty-bourgeoisie, and even the bourgeoisie. Thus far the leadership has fought hard and successfully to maintain its position. While Fatah's members are mainly refugees, finance still comes largely from Arab Governments. Yet the non-interference policy has failed, and the leadership is obliged to treat diplomatically with Arab Governments which have displayed their hostility to the Palestinians. Although the military and political strategy of the movement has become more revolutionary vis-a-vis both Israel and the Arab states, much of the current activity verges on the classically terrorist — divorced from mass involvement and participation. This applies both to the Arab states and to Israel, and having lost the initiative the movement has been forced into a position of reacting to the moves of others.

The recognition of failure of previous strategy and tactics has now been made, but a new policy has not yet been put into practice. The old ties of the leadership group to the Arab states in the post-June War period up till 1970 is partially responsible, and a major change in the leadership may be necessary before a new policy can be put into practice. As the political attitudes at the base of the movement continue to change, however, similar changes may be expected from the leadership.

Provided that such a change takes place the Palestinian movement may move over to a policy of placing the need for revolutionary change in the Arab world, or at least some Arab states, before the problems of facing Israel. If the longstanding analysis of the Marxist groups within the Palestinian resistance were adopted as policy by Fatah, it would show how far the movement had advanced from its origins of national unity within the Palestinian context, and isolation from the shifting political currents and changes within the Arab states.

Haganah — Defence — The Pre-state military infra-structure established in 1920 in the Ahdut ha-Avodah (qv) Convention at Kinneret under the leadership of Eliyahu Golomb and Dov Hos. Its establishment constituted a break from the Ha-Shomer (qv) tradition and most Ha-Shomer members withdrew from the organization in dispute over its administration and military policies. After the 1929 Arab revolt the Haganah established itself as an all-Zionist organization where labour and non-labour Zionist movements were equally represented. In 1931, however, a section of the Haganah command headed by Abraham Tehomi seceded over what they considered to be the Haganah's policy of restraint towards the Arabs and established the Irgun Zeva'i Leumi (see Irgun). Between 1931-32 the Haganah organization consolidated rapidly and virtually controlled all adults and youths in the Jewish agricultural settlements as well as several thousands in the major cities. It established arms depots, underground production (Ta'asiyyah Tzeva'it), and a countrywide hierarchy of command, subject to the political control of the Histadrut (qv), the Yishuv (qv) National Executive and the Jewish Agency (qv), all at that point under the firm control of Mapai (qv) and under David Ben-Gurion's leadership.

During the Arab revolt of 1936-39, close collaboration was established between the Haganah and the British Mandatory administration. The British established the Jewish Settlement Police (JSP) mostly from the Haganah recruits to guard railways, airfields, and various British installations against Arab attacks. With the intensification of the latter, Jews were incorporated into the regular British army units, and when the Arab revolt reached its peak in 1938 the British sponsored the establishment of the Jewish Special Night Squads (SNS), under the command of Captain Orde Wingate, which received specialized training in counter-insurgency guerilla warfare methods. By that time the JSP had become a militia of twelve battalions including a mobile armoured unit equipped with machine guns.

In 1937 the Irgun split, dissenters returning to the Haganah. In 1939 the Haganah General Staff was appointed, with Ya'akov Dori as Chief of Staff. During World War II the Haganah put its major effort into the Jewish Brigade (qv) under British command, which fought on several Allied fronts in the Middle East, Greece, and Italy. This gave the Haganah close acquaintance with methods of organization and command of large units, as well as training in aspects of warfare which could not be practiced secretly (e.g. artillery). During this period the Haganah first regular units were instituted (Palmach) (qv).

With the termination of World War II the Haganah and the Jewish Yishuv felt sufficiently strong to launch countrywide military operations in order to demonstrate de facto political control in Palestine. The three Zionist military outfits: the Haganah, the Irgun and Lehi (qv) established the joint Hebrew Revolt Movement (Tenu'at ha-Meri ha-Ivri), which through 1945-1946 launched massive countrywide terror operations against the Arab urban and rural population and the British Mandatory administration of Palestine. Zionist control in Palestine was recognized in 1947, with the adoption of the 1947 United Nations Security Council partition plan. With the official establishment of the state of Israel on May 15, 1948, the Haganah became the state's military arm under the title Tzeva Haganah le-Israel (ZHL) ('Israeli Defence Forces').

Herut — Freedom — The right-wing Herut party, the largest opposition party in the Israeli Parliament, was established in July 1948 by the disbanded Irgun (qv), under the leadership of Menahem Begin. Except for a brief interlude Begin has headed the party, which in 1949 formally joined with the Zionist Revisionist Party (the Irgun was this group's military arm in the pre-state period) to establish the Herut ha-Tzohar alliance which forms a part of the World Zionist Organization. Betar (abbreviation of Berit Trumpeldor ('The Trumpeldor Covenant') is its youth movement both in Israel and in the Diaspora. In 1965 the Herut-Liberal Bloc (Gahal) was established, winning 26 seats in the Israeli Parliament both in the 1965 and 1969 elections. The party is notorious for its systematic advocacy of establishing a Jewish state in what it terms the historical borders of Israel (both banks of the Jordan). Herut in 1967 within the framework of Gahal was admitted as a member of the National Unity Government, from which it withdrew in August 1970 when the Israeli government voted to accept the Gunar Jarring United Nations mandate to enter into negotiations with the parties involved towards the implementation of the UN Resolution 242 of November 22, 1967 (qv). Menahem Begin, though fully aware that in reality the Jarring mission and the UN resolution could only serve as an effective camouflage to mask the consolidation of the post-1967 status quo, refused to sign a document which would, even nominally, relinquish the claim for Israeli-Jewish domination over all of post-1967 occupied territories.

Herzl, Theodor — Benjamin Ze'ev (1860-1904). Father of political Zionism and the founder of the World Zionist Organization.
    Born in Budapest 1860, Doctorate in Law from Vienna University, but soon ceased to practice law to devote himself to a literary and publicist career. In 1891 he was sent to Paris as a correspondant for the Viennese *Neue Freie Presse*, the influential liberal paper of the time, for which he worked from 1891-1895, to cover the Dreyfus trial (1895). This experience proved to be a critical turning point in his life, from which he developed his concept of the Jewish problem and what he considered to be its global, ultimate solution. *Der Judenstaat* ('The Jewish State') was published in 1895, and it set out the programmatic political underpinnings of the Zionist movement, to which he devoted his life thereafter. In 1895 he established the Zionist weekly *Die Welt* and in 1897 succeeded in organizing and convening the first Zionist Congress (see Zionist Congresses) in Basle. In 1899 the Jewish Colonial Trust was founded and registered in

London. Its subsidiary, the Anglo-Palestine Company, was established in Jaffa in 1903. In the course of consolidation of the Zionist movement and the state of Israel, the Anglo-Palestine Company developed into the Bank Leumi le-Israel, the biggest in Israel. In 1903 Herzl's willingness to seriously consider the implementation of his solution of the Jewish problem under British auspices in Uganda rather than Palestine nearly split the Zionist movement (1903-sixth Congress). He lived to see the split avoided and died in 1904. His remains have been brought from Vienna and re-interred on Mount Herzl in Jerusalem in 1949.

It should be noted that up until the sixth Zionist Congress possibilities of implementing this proposed solution in Argentine, Sinai, El-Arish, and Uganda were seriously considered. Der Judenstaat (1895) was originally written as an address to the Rothschilds in an effort (which failed at the time) to gain their financial backing.

Histadrut — The Federation — Established in 1920 as the General Federation of Hebrew Workers in Eretz Israel as an effort by the two rival major labour Zionist parties, Ahdut ha-Avodah (qv) and Ha-Poel ha-Tzair (qv), to coordinate Jewish labour matters.

Until 1948 the Histadrut was the administrative backbone of the Jewish Yishuv (qv) in Palestine, controlling its colonization effort, economic production and marketing, labour employment and defence (Haganah (qv)). An interview in the London *Observer* of January 24, 1971, quotes Golda Meir:

'Then (1928) I was put on the Histadrut Executive Committee, at a time when this big labour union was not just a trade union organization. It was a great colonizing agency.'

The name of the organization was changed in 1966 to The General Federation of Workers in Eretz Israel when the decision was made to legally accept Arab workers as members. The Histadrut is an economic empire controlling much of the country's holding corporations, banks, industrial concerns and agro-industries; an industrial giant which, among others, has a department for labour unions. According to the *Encyclopaedia Judaica*, the Histadrut-controlled industries employed 23.5% of the Israeli labour force and produced 20.8% of the net national product (in 1968-69).

As the second largest employer (second only to the State), it controls the nation-wide wage policy together with the private sector organised in the (national) Association of Industrialists. The *Encyclopaedia Judaica* euphemistically states that the Histadrut is bound to (bear in mind) the position of the country's economy and national economic policy. The Histadrut has virtual monopoly over health insurance services (there is no national health insurance in Israel) and operates mutual aid funds and pension funds for its members (75 per cent of the total Israeli labour force). For systematic analysis of the Histadrut see for instance Hanegbi, H.,

Hachover, M. and Orr, A. 'The Class Nature of Israel', *New Left Review*, No. 65, January-February 1971).

Ihud — Union — Founded in 1942 by Judah L. Magnes (qv), Martin Buber (qv), Henrietta Szold (qv), Rabbi Binyamin, Menahem Raphael Cohen, Ernst A. Simon (qv), Moshe Smilansky, and others, in an effort to revive the activity previously pursued by the League for Jewish-Arab Understanding and Berit Shalom (qv). One of the results of the Biltmore Programme (see Zionist Congresses), the first official Zionist declaration calling for the creation of a Jewish state, was that all the bi-nationalists (a very small number), left, right, and centre, got together in a last attempt to reverse what had become the official Zionist policy. That last attempt was Ihud.

Until the adoption of the Biltmore Programme in 1942, commitment to a bi-national state in Palestine and the principle of parity between the Jewish and Arab populations regardless of numerical population ratios was not necessarily an anti-Zionist position, nor did this seemingly run counter to the official aim of the Zionist movement: 'To establish a national home for the Jewish people in Palestine secure under public law'. (Basle Programme; see Zionist Congresses). The bi-national position was identified as treason and officially excluded from the Zionist context by the Biltmore Programme demanding that Palestine be a *Jewish* commonwealth. Ihud had its own periodical, 'Problems of the Day' (*Be'ayot ha-Yom*). The name was later changed to 'Problems' (*Be'ayot*) and appeared until 1948. Ihud resumed periodical publication in 1950 under the title *Ner* (Candle). Clearly, Ihud became largely a moot organization after the founding of the Jewish state of Israel in 1948.

Irgun (Irgun Tzevai Leumi (IZL) — Military National Organization — Founded in 1931 by a group of Haganah (qv) commanders headed by Abraham Tehomi, who disagreed with what they considered to be the Haganah policy of restraint (Havlagah) towards the Palestinian-Arab opposition to Zionist colonization in Palestine Eretz Israel. In 1937 the Irgun split and about half if its membership returned to the Haganah. After the split, the Irgun formally affiliated to the right-wing Zionist Revisionist Party (see Herut (qv)) and Ze'ev Jabotinsky became its chief commander. The Irgun focussed its terror operation against the Arab population and the British Mandatory administration. With the outbreak of World War II, it declared a truce in its struggle against the British, and consequently underwent another split (1940). The seceding group, headed by Abrahaim (Yair) Stern, established the Lehi (qv), which, as one of its strategies, entered into initial negotiations with the Nazi delegation in Beirut to investigate the possibilities of cooperation in the struggle against the British.

The Irgun participated in the Jewish Brigade (qv) (see also Haganah) and established close cooperation with British secret operations in the Middle East. Its commander, David Raziel, was killed in Iraq in 1941 in a British-sponsored underground operation against the pro-Nazi regime of Rashid Ali. Next to assume command was Jacob Meridor, now Israel's largest shipping and oil-container magnate (co-owner of the multinational Maritime Fruit Carriers Co.). He was replaced in 1943 by Menahem Begin (see Herut).

The Irgun terminated its truce in 1944. The Haganah responded by joining with the British in an all-out hunt for the Irgun command and rank and file (the sezon — hunting season) which resulted in the exile of 251 Irgun commanders and members to Eritrea. This did not prevent the establishment, immediately after World War II, of the united front — the Hebrew Revolt Movement (1945-46) (see Haganah).

After the establishment of the state in 1948, both the Irgun and Lehi were disbanded and incorporated into the Israeli state army. These two groups were responsible and proud of the full-scale terror attack on Jaffa, which left the city nearly empty of its Palestinian-Arab population (April 1948) and the murderous attack on Deir Yasin (Also April 1948), massacring approximately 200 people, over half women and children, and marching the blood-stained survivors in a victory parade through the streets of Jerusalem.

Israeli Black Panther Organization — Emerged on the political scene in summer 1971, initially making liberal demands. Rooted in the Israeli-Jewish community of Asian and African origin (approximately 60% of the total Israeli-Jewish population), it is primarily located in those communities populating the heavy metropolitan slum belts around all major Israeli cities. The original leadership is from Jerusalem. Some members have a history of crime. The increasing Russian immigration helped to trigger off the Panthers' emergence.

The Asian and African Jewish communities were brought into Israel mainly between 1949 and 1956. They were designated to replace about one million dispossessed Arab peasants, who were relegated to refugee camps outside the borders of the newly established exclusively Jewish state after the 1949 cease-fire agreements at Rhodes. Asian and African Jews sometimes spent years in provisional housing of tarpaulin, tin, or asbestos (ma'abarot). Many were transfered into impoverished moshavim (qv) and development cities on the outskirts of the large metropolitan areas. Many drifted into the expanding manual wage labour markets in the cities and the metropolitan slum belts.

After 1967 the very limited number of apartments originally designated for Oriental Jewish slum renewal projects in Jerusalem and elsehere were overnight handed over to the new Ashkenazi Yiddish (Jewish) — speaking Russian immigrants. Also, the increase of Russians was clamorously welcomed as the *true* Jewish immigration. Finally, care was taken to provide them with decent housing and a variety of privileges, job opportunities, tax exemptions, etc., while the Oriental-Jewish communities were left in abject misery. These developments triggered off the Panthers, whose initial demands were moderate: equal access to decent housing, job opportunities, army commissions (the overwhelming majority of the army officers are of white Ashkenazi (European) origin). However, the brutal police attack on their first demonstration quickly radicalized the group. With the radicalization, the organization split into the Israeli Black Panther Organization and the Panthers-Blue and White (the Israeli national colours). The former became increasingly radical and critical of Zionism, while the latter insisted on conducting the struggle within a Zionist framework.

The Israeli divisions by poverty, ethnicity, and politics are co-extensive. Jews of Asian and African origin are effectively excluded from equal participation in the Israeli body-politics. They tend to populate the metropolitan slums and constitute the overwhelming majority of the population under the poverty line. The following article may serve as a concrete indication:

'Approximately 80 per cent of the children in material and mental distress are children of wage-earning families. Their number approaches 180,000, 92 per cent of which are children of families of Asian and African origins. The report of the Premier's Committee on Children and Youth in Distress was officially published yesterday. It stated the criteria for determining youth distress:
1. Minimal income of 75 Israeli pounds (approximately US 20) per month per person;
2. Housing density of three persons or more per room;
3. Low level of parent education.' (5)

The Israeli Black Panther Organization has recently merged with the Israeli Democrats Party headed by Shalom Cohen (see Ha-Olam ha-Zeh). The joint slate of candidates, however, failed to obtain seats in Parliament at the 1973 elections.

Jewish National Fund (JNF) — Keren Kayemet le-Israel — The land acquisition and development arm of the Zionist movement, founded at the fifth Zionist Congress (December 1901) and mandated to be 'the eternal possession of the Jewish people; its funds shall not be used except for purchase of lands in Palestine and Syria.' Most of the Zionist Movement's urban and rural holdings until 1948 were purchased through the JNF. By 1947 the land holdings under its possession totalled 936,000 dunams (234,000 acres), approximately 4% of the total area, and over half of the Jewish holdings in Mandatory Palestine. In face of the mounting native opposition to the Zionist colonization endeavour, much of the land could only be purchased by way of making deals with the large, often absentee, landlords: 'In our office in Haifa,' writes Musa Goldenberg, 'we worked in "full steam". One of the methods was registration of the lands I purchased in the name of some Arabs, who had guaranteed in advance, by way of complicated legal procedures, that the land would be transferred to us through the court execution office or through certain nominees.' (6)

After the conclusion of the 1949 armistice agreements, the newly established state of Israel gained control over vast tracts of dispossessed Palestinian-Arab lands (see moshav). The 1953 Land Acquisition Act legalized the robbery of huge amounts of land from Palestinian-Arab refugees and 'present-absentees', the latter being voting citizens of the new state, whose urban and rural land holdings were declared null and void. Reasonable estimates of land thus acquired amount to three and a half million dunams (one dunam equals approximately one quarter of an acre).

It is in this context that the JNF was given a concession by the Israeli provisional government over more than 5,000,000 dunams (125,000 acres) in 1948. Its total holdings in 1967 amounted to 2,549,000 dunams (637,000 acres). Between 1967 and 1971 the JNF further acquired 33,000 dunams (8,250 acres) in the post-1967 occupied territories, above and beyond the massive government confiscation of lands in the post-1967 territories as part of its colonization projects.

The Jewish National Fund operates in close coordination with the Israeli government. An indication of the nature and the subject matter of this close cooperation can be gotten from such reports as the one cited below.

> The Department for Settlement of the Jewish Agency has submitted a proposal to the coordinating committee for settlement . . . (concerning) new settlements to be established in the next four years (1974-1978). According to the proposal (which has not yet been finally approved . . .), 36 new settlements will be established in 11 different regions in Israel. The distribution of these settlements is as follows: 10 are to be established within the (pre-1967) borders of the Green Line . . . The rest will be established in the Golan Heights,(6) in the Jordan Valley (7), in the Gush Etzion area (1), in the Rafiah Approaches (6), in the Gaza Strip (3), and in the Gulf of Suez (3). (7)

Since 1961 the JNF has operated in terms of a contractual agreement with the Israeli government. As to the legal partnership between the Israeli government and the Jewish National Fund, one must examine the details of the JNF Constitution on the one hand and the Covenant signed in 1961 between the JNF and the Israeli government on the other. According to the JNF Constitution, the JNF is 'a company under Jewish control engaged in the settlement of Jews and in promoting such settlement'. 'Lands owned by the JNF are exclusively for Jewish use, in perpetuity. These lands shall not be transferred either by sale or in any other manner.' Furthermore, non-Jewish labour cannot be employed on these lands. The JNF was established for the purpose of settling Jews on such lands and was required to make any donation 'likely to promote the interests of Jews, and to use funds in ways which shall in the opinion of the

Association be directly or indirectly beneficial to persons of Jewish religion, race or origin.' The JNF is now 'a public institution recognized by the government of Israel and the World Zionist Organization as the exclusive instrument for the development of Israel lands'.

As to the Covenant signed between the State of Israel and the JNF, the JNF has undertaken under the terms of this Covenant to establish a Land Development Administration and to appoint a director 'who shall be subordinate to the JNF'. This development Administration is responsible for the 'scheme for the development and afforestation of Israel lands as the agent of the registered owners'. 'The Board for Land Reclamation and Development attached to the Keren Kayemet le-Israel (JNF) shall lay down the development policy in accordance with the agricultural development scheme of the Minister of Agriculture'. It must be noted that the term Israel lands refers to state owned lands. 75% of pre-1967 Israel is owned by the state. Of the remainder 14% is directly owned by the JNF and 11% is under private ownership. In other words, close to 90% of the land of pre-1967 Israel is under the control of a Company which is constitutionally committed to act exclusively in ways that are beneficial to persons of Jewish religion, race or origin.

Kufr Qasim Massacre — Just before the 1956 War, a battalion commanded by Brigadier Yisaskhar Shadmi was posted to the Jordanian border, re-inforced with a Border Police Unit (Green Berets) under Major Shmuel Melinsky. On 29 October, the first day of the war Major General Zvi Tzur (later Israel's 6th Chief of Staff) briefed Shadmi with other battalion commanders on policy of treatment of the Arab population during the emergency. Shadmi requested and obtained authority to impose a curfew. On the same day, Brigadier Shadmi summoned Major Melinsky to his headquarters and instructed him on his duties. These included the impo-sition of curfew in the villages of Kufr Qasim, Kufr Bara, Jaljuliya, Tira, Tayyiba, Qalasawa, Bir al-Sikka and Ibthan to be imposed between 17.00 p.m. to 06.00 a.m. According to official court records the instruc-tions given by Brigadier Shadmi to Major Melinsky explicity said that it would not be enough to arrest those who broke the curfew — they must be shot. He further added that a dead man (or according to other evidence 'a few dead men') is better than the complications of detentions. When Major Melinsky asked what was to happen to a man returning from his work outside the village unaware of the curfew, who might well, on return, meet the Border Police cordon at the entrance of the village, Brigadier Shadmi replied: 'I do not want any sentimentality and that is just too bad for him.'

Major Melinsky in turn, briefed his Border Police officers accordingly. He informed them that the war had begun and that they are now under the command of Brigadier Shadmi, of the Central Command; that they were to impose curfew over the Arab villages in the area; that it was forbidden to harm any inhabitants staying in their homes, but anyone found outside his home (or according to other witnesses, anyone leaving his home or anyone breaking the curfew) was to be shot dead. He added that there were to be no arrests, and that if a number of people were killed that night (according to other witnesses: it was desirable that a number of people should be killed) this would facilitate the imposition of the curfew during succeeding nights.

The curfew was imposed on schedule. The Mukhtar (Chief) of Kufr Qasim was informed of the curfew at 4.30 p.m. — just half an hour before its coming into force. The Mukhtar warned the Border Police unit that there were 400 villagers working outside the village to whom it was not possible to announce the curfew in time. He was promised that all villagers returning from work would be allowed into the village. This, however, was not to be the case. 49 villagers, men, women and children were murdered by the Border Police on their return to the village from work between 17.00 — 18.00 p.m. Of the 49 killed during this hour, 43 were killed at the western entrance to the village. These included seven boys and girls and nine women of all ages — one 66 years old. The people were taken off bicycles, carts and lorries, lined up and shot at close range. When reports of the killing of the first 15 villagers reached Major Melinsky he gave orders for the shooting to stop and for more moderate procedure to be adopted. By the time the order reached his men at the checkposts 47 people were already dead.

For a number of weeks the government kept the Kufr Qasim massacre under official secrecy, imposing censorship. Information, however, began to filter through the press, after the *Democratic Paper* and *Ha-Olam ha-Zeh* qv) published the full facts in defiance of the Censor. The scandal forced the government to bring Major Shmuel Melinsky and ten others to trial. Brigadier Shadmi was tried separately before a specially appointed military tribunal. Major Melinsky was sentenced to 17 years in jail. Lieutenant Dahan and Sergeant Ofer were sentenced to 15 years each, Corporal Olial and the Privates Hreish, Abraham, Fahimi and Nahmani were sentenced to 7 years each. Corporal Abd al-Rahman, Private Zakariya and Private Semnitz were acquitted. On appeal, however, the sentences were reduced. Then the President followed suit and granted the convicted partial pardon. The prison authorities exercised their power of discretion and further reduced the sentences by one third. By 1960 — three and a half years after the massacre — the last was released from jail. Brigadier Shadmi was tried separately by a specially appointed Military Tribunal. The Court found him guilty of a 'merely technical error' and he was fined one and a half Israeli Piasters. The final touch of irony and mockery was added, however, by the Ramleh Municipality which appointed Lieutenant Dahan after his release from jail as its officer for Arab Affairs.

Law of Return — The Israeli Law of Return (1950) guarantees every Jew

immigrating to Israel immediate citizenship. In 1952 it was incorporated
into the Israel Nationality Law. The Law of Return was modified in 1971
so as to enable the Israeli Minister of Interior to grant Israeli citizenship to
Jews in the Diaspora even prior to their actual immigration to Israel.
The Law of Return states:

1.   Every Jew has the right to immigrate to the country.

2.(a) Immigration shall be on the basis of immigration visas.

  (b) Immigrant visas shall be issued to any Jew expressing a desire to
settle in Israel except if the Minister of Immigration is satisfied that the
applicant:

      (i)   acts against the Jewish nation; or

      (ii)   may threaten the public health or State security.

3.(a) A Jew who comes to Israel and after his arrival expresses a desire to
settle there may, while in Israel, obtain an immigrant certificate.

  (b) The exceptions listed in Article 2(b) shall apply also with respect
to the issue of an immigrant certificate, but a person shall not be regarded
as a threat to public health as a result of an illness that he contracts after
his arrival in Israel.

4.   Every Jew who migrated to the country before this law goes into
effect, and every Jew who was born in the country either before or after
the law is effective enjoys the same status as any person who migrated
on the basis of this law.

5.   The Minister of Immigration is delegated to enforce this law and he
may enact regulations in connection with its implementation and for the
issue of immigrant visas and immigrant certificates. (9)

Lehi — Lohamei Herut Israel — Israel Freedom Fighters — The Stern Gang
— Founded by a 1940 Irgun (qv) splinter, under the leadership of Abraham
Stern (Yair) (1907-1942). Split from the Irgun over its decision to declare
a truce in underground armed resistance against the British Mandatory
administration during World War II. Lehi insisted on continued underground struggle against the British, opposed Jewish participation in the
British Army Jewish Brigade (qv) and attempted to establish contacts
with the Axis representatives towards a possible anti-British alliance. The
British Mandate authorities, in collaboration with the Haganah (qv)
responded by launching an all-out hunt for Lehi people. Stern was uncov-
ered and assassinated in his Tel Aviv hideout and many of the hard-core
members were placed under administrative detention in Palestine (Mazra's,
Latrun, Jerusalem, Acre, Atlit) and abroad (Eritrea, Sudan, Kenya).

With the escape of some of the Lehi detainees, the organization regroup-
ed in 1944 under the leadership of Nathan Yalin-Mor (Friedman), Yitzhak
Shamir, and Israel Eldad-Sheib, resuming its terror operations, which
included the assassination of the British Minister of State, Lord Moyne,
in Cairo (November 1944). The 1944 sezon (see Haganah and Irgun) did
not prevent the establishment of the Hebrew Rebellion Movement

(1945-46) by which the Haganah, Irgun, and Lehi coordinated massive
terror operations and military attacks against the Arab regular armies,
Arab civilian population, and British installations in the country. With the
collapse of the front, coordination between the groups did not cease,
though the Lehi and Irgun acted independently e.g., the Deir Yasin
Massacre (see Irgun) and mailing letter bombs to British statesmen.

Though officially disbanded after the declaration of Israeli independence, both Lehi and the Irgun endured. The Lehi was finally disbanded
after the murder of the United Nations Middle East mediator Count Folke
Bernadotte (Jerusalem, September 1948), which has been attributed to
the Lehi. Its leadership was placed under administrative detention by the
newly established Israeli Provisional Government. Before the first parliamentary elections (1949), Lehi veterans formed the Fighters List and ran
Nathan Yalin-Mor, still in adminstrative detention, first on the list. The
list won one seat in parliament, which forced Yalin-Mor's release.

The Lehi is quite commonly thought to have been the most consistent
anti-imperialist Zionist organization, often implying that the Zionist
movement, at least at the time, was, in part, a truly socialist revolutionary
force in the area. A few of Abraham Stern's *Eighteen Principles of
Liberation* are rather revealing in this context:

'1. *The People:* The Jewish people is the chosen people, which gave
birth to monotheism, to the ethics of the prophets and the culture
of the world; it excels in tradition and devotion, its will to live, its
endurance and its confidence in the coming liberation.
2. *The homeland:* The homeland is the home of Israel within the
boundaries defined by the Bible (Gen. 9,18). This is the land of life,
where the entire Jewish people will dwell in saftey.
3. *The people and its homeland:* The land of Israel has been conquered by the Jewish people by the sword. Here they fought and
here they will rise again to life. Therefore, Israel, and Israel alone,
has the right of possession of the land of Israel. This right is absolute.
It has never expired and can never expire.
4. *The mission:* a) Redemption of the land; b) revival of sovereignty;
c) rebirth of the people. There cannot be revival of sovereignty
without the redemption of the land, and there cannot be rebirth
of the people without revival of sovereignty. *These are the tasks of
the organization in the period of war and conquest.*
6. *Unity:* The whole people must be united under the banner of the
movement for Jewish freedom. The genius, position, and force of
individuals, the energy, devotion and revolutionary enthusiasm of
the masses must be directed to the struggle for liberation.
7. *Alliances:* Alliances should be made with anybody interested in
the fight of the organization and ready to assist it.
10. *Conquest:* Conquest of the homeland from the hands of the
non-Jews by force, so that it should become ours forever.
14. *The problem of the non-Jews* (living in Palestine): This must be
solved by exchange of population.
16. *Government:* The Jewish people must become a military, political, and cultural factor of the first order in the eastern part of the
Mediterranean.' (10)

Magnes, Judah L. (1877-1948) — American Rabbi, communal leader; Chancellor and first President of the Hebrew University in Jerusalem. A Zionist disciple of Ahad ha-Am (qv), served as secretary of the American Zionist Federation (1905-1908) and became one of the more important pre-World War I leaders of the American Jewish community and the Zionist movement. However, his opposition, out of pacifist commitments, to the United States entry into World War I (1917) and his activity in the peace movement during the war undermined his leadership of a Jewish community firmly committed to the war and concerned over possible charges of disloyalty. Magnes's brilliant Jewish communal career came to an abrupt end. In 1922 he immigrated to Palestine. He became Chancellor of the Hebrew University in Jerusalem in 1925 and its first President in 1935, a post he held until his death (1948).

Magnes was an active vocal supporter of a Zionist bi-nationalism and strongly opposed partition. Until 1942 the contradictions of the Zionist situation were of such a nature that it was possible for the architect of Zionist colonization, Arthur Rupin, to be one of the founders of Berit Shalom (qv) (Covenant of Peace) together with Magnes, who, in his opening speech of the Hebrew University academic year 1929-30 could state that one of the greatest cultural duties of the Jewish people is the attempt to enter the promised land not by means of conquest like Joshua, but through peaceful and cultural means, through hard work, sacrifice and love, and with resolve not to do anything which cannot be justified before the conscience of the world.

Mapai — Mifleget Poalei Eretz Israel — The Eretz Israel Workers' Party — Established in 1930 by merger of Ahdut ha-Avodah (qv) and Ha-Poel ha-Tzair (qv) as the ruling political elite of the Zionist movement and the state of Israel. In spite of transformations, splits, and regroupings its hard core remains intact and constitutes the power elite of the ruling Israel Labour Party.

Mapam — Mifleget ha-Poalim ha-Me'uhedet — The United Workers' Party — Established in 1948 by a merger of Ha-Shomer ha-Tzair (qv) and Ahdut ha-Avodah (qv) under the banner: For Zionism, Socialism, and Brotherhood Among Nations. Since 1955, except for the period 1961-1965, it has been a member of all Israeli coalition governments, and since 1969 in alignment with the ruling Labour Party.

It was within Mapam that the debate over the incompatibility of Zionism and socialism survived longest, generating guilt, bad faith and contradictory ideologies on the Palestinian-Arab question. In practice, the party has hardly wavered, and played a prominent role in the Zionist colonization.

Poalei Zion — The Workers of Zion — Founded in 1907 in the Hague as the

World Socialist Union of Jewish Workers — Poalei Zion. In 1919 merged with a minority from Ha-Poel ha-Tzair (qv) and independents to form Ahdut ha-Avodah (qv), retaining, however, an independent Poalei Zion entity in the World Zionist Organization. In 1920 split into Poalei Zion-Left and Poalei Zion-Right. In 1930 Ahdut ha-Avodah merged with Ha-Poel ha-Tzair to form the Eretz Israel Workers Party — Mapai (qv).

Ha-Poal ha-Tzair — The Young Worker — Founded by members of the second Aliyah (qv) at Petah Tikvah in 1905; the motto: 'An indispensable condition for the realization of Zionism is the conquest (sic) of all branches of labour in Eretz Israel by the Jews.'

Rakah — Reshimah Komunistit Hadashah — The New Communist List — The Israeli Communist Party split in 1965. The smaller faction, Maki (Miflagah Komunistit Israelit) — Israel Communist Party — under the leadership of the late Dr. Moshe Sneh, has retained (until the 1973 elections) one seat in Parliament. It has almost exclusively Jewish membership and took a 180 degree turnabout to Zionism. The larger faction, Rakah, under the leadership of Meir Vilner, has had (until the 1973 elections) three seats in Parliament. It has also faithfully retained the Israeli Communist Party's pro-Moscow line. Its membership is approximately two thirds Arab and one third Jewish. It officially supports the resolution of the Middle East conflict in terms of the United Nations Resolution 242 (qv). Despite its ideological conservatism, Rakah has admirably maintained the struggle against violation of human and political rights of the Palestinian-Arab population under Israeli rule. Towards the 1973 elections Maki merged with Siah (Tel Aviv Branch) (qv) and formed Moked, which gained one seat in Parliament. Moked's Member of Parliament is General (Reserve) Meir Pail. Maki leadership is no longer represented in Parliament and the party can hardly be said to exist any more as independent political organization. Rakah, on the other hand, has increased its strength and gained four seats in the 1973 elections. There is every indication that its strength not only among the Arab population, but also among the Israeli Jewish population, is rapidly increasing.

Ha-Shomer ha-Tzair — The Young Guards — Full title: Ha-Kibbutz ha-Artzi/Ha-Shomer ha-Tzair — The National Kibbutz/The Young Guards. Established by a merger of the Ha-Shomer ha-Tzair Zionist Movement with the Ha-Kibbutz ha-Artzi Federation in 1927. In 1948 the Ha-Shomer ha-Tzair merged with the Ahdut ha-Avodah to form the socialist-Zionist United Workers Party — Mapam (qv). Since 1955, Mapam has been a traditional member of all (except one) Israeli government coalitions and since 1969 has been in alignment with the ruling Labour Party (see Mapai).

Siah — Smol Israeli Hadash — The New Israeli Left — Established shortly before the 1969 elections by dissident splinters from Maki (see Rakah) and Mapam (qv). Ideologically Siah is split on the question of Zionism. Whereas most of its founding membership of Mapam origin are explicitly Zionist (Siah Tel Aviv Branch), and insist on identifying Siah as a Zionist organization, the minority of its founding membership, the hard core of which is of Communist Party origin, (Siah Jerusalem Branch) would like to see Siah either not commit itself ideologically on the question of Zionism or, alternatively, identify as non-Zionist. In its 1972 national convention the majority (Zionist) position was institutionalized into Siah's platform.

Siah is a direct-action oriented group with most of the initiative sustained by its Jerusalem branch, focused against Israeli post-1967 occupation and colonization policies. Siah members have been arrested repeatedly for protesting against the Jewish colonization of Hebron, the defoliation of the fields of the West Bank village of Aqraba and the establishment on the defoliated land of the Israeli-Jewish collective settlement Gitit, etc.

Zionist Congresses — The first Zionist Congress (1897), fully aware of the reality of its limited power-political position, adopted the Basle Programme, and thereby toned down the original vision as articulated in Herzl's (qv) *Der Judenstaat.* The basic demands of the Basle Programme were:

Zionism seeks to establish for the Jewish people a home in Palestine, secured under public law. The Congress contemplates the following means to the attainment of this end:

1.   The promotion by appropriate means the settlement in Palestine of Jewish farmers, artisans and manufacturers.

2.   The organization and uniting of the whole of Jewry by means of appropriate institutions, both local and international, in accordance with the laws of each country.

3.   The strengthening and fostering of Jewish national settlement and national consciousness.

4.   Preparatory steps towards obtaining the consent of governments, where necessary, in order to reach the goal of Zionism.

Notwithstanding the tremendous effort invested by Herzl and others in obtaining a Charter from the imperial powers involved in the area (Ottoman Empire, Czarist Russia, Austro-Hungarian Empire, and the British) the Zionist movement failed to obtain the consent necessary to achieve the goals of Zionism from governments or one single government. The efforts to obtain an imperial Charter, were, however, finally crowned with success in the 1917 declaration of the British Foreign Secretary, Lord Arthur James Balfour, submitted as a letter to the British banking magnate Lord Lionel Walter Rothschild. It read:

Foreign Office
November 2, 1917

Dear Lord Rothschild,

I have much pleasure in conveying to you on behalf of His Majesty's Government, the following declaration of sympathy with the Jewish Zionist aspirations, which has been submitted to, and approved by the Cabinet.

'His Majesty's Government view with favour the establishment in Palestine of a national home for the Jewish people, and will use their best endeavours to facilitate the achievement of this object, it being clearly understood that nothing shall be done which may prejudice the civil and religious rights of existing non-Jewish communities in Palestine or the rights and political status enjoyed by Jews in any other country.'

I should be grateful if you would bring this declaration to the knowledge of the Zionist Federation.

Yours,
Arthur James Balfour

With the consolidation of the Zionist endeavour in Palestine and of the World Zionist Organization, the Zionist programme further developed. At the extra-ordinary session of the Zionist Conference initiated by the American Zionist Federation at the Biltmore Hotel in New York City in May 1942, the Biltmore Programme, later officially adopted by the World Zionist movement, demanded that Palestine be established as a Jewish Commonwealth and that the Jewish Agency (qv), rather than the British Mandatory administration, be authorized to develop the country:

The Conference urges that the gates of Palestine be opened; that the Jewish Agency be vested with control of immigration into Palestine and with the necessary authority for upbuilding the country, including the development of its unoccupied and uncultivated lands; and that Palestine be established as a Jewish Commonwealth integrated in the structure of the new democratic world.

The lack of specific borders for the proposed Jewish Commonwealth is conspicuous. In 1951 the 23rd Zionist Congress convening in Jerusalem felt the need to reformulate the Basle Programme in much more explicit terms. Ultimately, the text of the Basle Programme was left unchanged, but an addendum titled 'The Task of Zionism' (better known as the Jerusalem Programme) was added and incorporated into the new constitution of the World Zionist Organization (1960).

'The task of Zionism' — it says — 'is the consolidation of the State of Israel, the ingathering of the exiles in Eretz Israel and the fostering of the unity of the Jewish people.'

This statement was again reformulated by the 27th Zionist Congress convening in Jerusalem in 1968 in response to the consolidation of post-1967 Greater Israel. The revised version of the Jerusalem Programme officially adopted reads as follows:

The aims of Zionism are:

The unity of the Jewish people and the centrality of Israel in Jewish life;
The ingathering of the Jewish people in its historic homeland Eretz Israel through Aliyah (qv) from all countries;
The strengthening of the state of Israel, which is based on the prophetic vision of justice and peace;
The preservation of the identity of the Jewish people through the fostering of Jewish and Hebrew education and of Jewish spiritual and cultural values;
The protection of Jewish rights everywhere.

There was quite strong resistance to the varied Jerusalem Programme. Membership in the World Zionist Organization is now conditional on its endorsement.

APPENDICES

Corporation	Owner
1. Adler Israel	Adler
2. Adrat	No information
3. Africa-Israel Investments	Jewish Agency through Registration Company of Bank Leumi
4. Alliance	Histadrut and private foreign interests
5. Alubin	Privately owned
6. Amgat	Privately owned by Ampa and the Taicher and Geler families
7. Amkor	Histadrut, through Ha'argaz and Workers' Bank, and Ampa, a privately owned co-pany of five partners, including Elman
8. Ampal — American Israel Corporation	see above p.78.
9. Argaman	Privately owned. Major shareholders are Klir family, Recanati through Bank Dis-count, Klal and Bank Leumi
10. Argat	Government
11. Ashdod Company	Government and private investors, headed by Ben-Ami
12. Asia	Privately owned. Biggest single shareholder is Central Trade and Investment Corpor-ation
13. Askar	Hashomer Hatzair, in conjunction with Hevrat Ovdim (who have a founding share) and the affiliated kibbutzim, through Techen Works and the Hashomer Hatzair Fund
14. Ata	Biggest Israeli shareholder is Registration Company of Bank Leumi, which owns the majority of all shares except for 'A' shares, which are owned by the Ata Trust in Lichtenstein
15. Autocars	Majority privately owned. Four shareholders are Shubinsky, Leyland of England, the

Corporation	Owner
	Central Trade and Investment Corporation and Koor; Histadrut through Workers' Company
16. Avik	Hapoel Hamizrahi through Meshhav
17. Bank Discount	Recanati family
18. Bank Leumi of Israel	Jewish Agency
19. Barzalit	Lichtenstein family
20. Berkshav	Privately owned. No clear majority to any single shareholder
21. Binyamini Building Company	No information
22. Caesaria Textile Enterprises	Jewish Agency through G.A.S. Rassco, and Shapira and Hoger
23. Chemicals and Phosphates	Government
24. Construction Agr. Corp.	No information
25. Dan	Histadrut cooperative
26. Dan Hotels	Privately owned. No clear majority to any single individual. Major shareholders include Israel-American Enterprises; Panama Company; a N.Y. company; Government; and Federman family
27. Dead Sea Works	Government (45%)
28. Deco	Kibbutz Bror-Hayil; a Genevan, Wolfgang Messer; Uviko; a Zurich company; and others
29. Dubek	Privately owned. No clear majority to any single shareholder
30. Egged	Histadrut cooperative
31. El-Al	Government
32. Elbar	Recanati family through Registration Company of Bank Discount
33. Electra	Jewish Agency through Rassco and a number of families through G.H.R.D.
34. Electric Corporation	Government
35. Eled	Zentur, Bloch, Millar and Goldberg families
36. Elite	Privately owned. Biggest single shareholder is Parmetzenko family. Others include Moshvitz and Kopilov families among others
37. Etzion	Etzion
38. Friedman	Friedman family
39. Gad Goldstein	Goldstein brothers

Corporation	Owner
40. Gal'am	Hashomer Hatzair through Techen Works and the Soomer Hatzair Fund
41. Gan	Grossman family
42. Gavish	Cooperative of Gavish Workers
43. Gazit	Diksel and Netzer
44. Gershon Navon	Navon family
45. Globus	Dreizman family and M.D.M., a company owned by the Megido, Magrizo and Cohen families
46. Ha'argaz	Histadrut through Trustee Company of Workers' Bank and the Ha.Argaz Workers' Cooperative
47. Ha'aretz Printing House	Privately owned by Shocken family
48. Haifa Oil Refineries	Government
49. Ha-Kibbutz Ha-artzi Building Company	Hashomer Hatzair through its Fund
50. Ha-Kibbutz Hameuhad Building Company	Kibbutz Hameuchad. Hevrat Ovdim has special share
51. Ha-Kibbutz ha-Meuhad Fund	The Ha-Kibbutz ha-Meuhad Federation
52. Hamashbir Hamerkazi	Histadrut cooperative
53. Hamashbir Latzarkhan	Histadrut cooperative
54. Hamegaper	Hevrat Ovdim through Hamashbir Hamerkazi and the special share of Hevrat Ovdim
55. Harsit and Hol Zach Banegev	Government
56. Hashahar	General Zionist Federation
57. Ha-Shomer ha-Tzair Fund	Ha-Kibbutz ha-Artzi Federation
58. Hasneh	Histadrut
59. Hatzatz Israel-American	Histadrut through Solel Boneh and private shareholders
60. Hishulei Hacarmel	Koor and S.A.L.G.P. (Luxembourg) through Soltam
61. Hula Textile	Government, through Argat Investment Company and Histadrut, through Hevrat Ovdim — both of whom own it through Teus Azorei Pituah, which owns the majority shares in Hula Textile; Molar Textile is a minority partner
62. Huton	Privately owned. No clear majority to any single shareholder. Biggest is Saharov family through Sahar Investment Company

Corporation	Owner
63. Ihud ha-Kevutzot ve-ha-Kibbutzim Fund	The Ihud ha-Kevutzot ve-ha-Kibbutzim Federation
64. Ilan Gat	Gat and Ilan
65. Industrial Development Bank	Government
66. Investment Company of Bank Leumi	Jewish Agency through Bank Leumi
67. Investment Fund of Hevrat Ovdim	Histadrut through Hevrat Ovdim
68. Israel Ceramic Enterprises 'Harsah'	Koor; Hevrat Ovdim has a special share
69. Israel Cigarette Company	Foreign-owned by British and Foreign Tobacco Company Ltd., Wicks and Block families
70. Israel Enterprises of Scientific Translations	Government, through Maniv Investment Company
71. Israel Mineral Industries — Institute for Research and Development	Government
72. Israel Rope Enterprises	Privately owned. No clear majority to any single shareholder
73. Israel Shipyards	Government
74. Israel Steel Works	Koor
75. Israel Sugar Enterprises	Histadrut, through Tnuva and Trustee Company of Hevrat Ovdim. Government is a minority shareholder through Agricultural Investment Company
76. Jerusalem Fibres	Privately owned. Biggest single shareholder is International Yarn Investment Trust, Vaduz, Lichtenstein
77. Jerusalem Shoes	Cooperative Fund
78. Kabir	Levi, Mirzkendof, Goodman, Bar Natan and Shohan families and Carmel Trust Lichtenstein, all through Mevashelet Shachar Leumit Ltd.
79. Kaiser-Ilin	Ilin
80. Kaufman and Tovilski	Privately owned by the Kaufman and Tovilski families, and Klal
81. Kerah	No information
82. Kiron Investments	Privately owned by Swiss-Israel Bank and Klal
83. Kitan Dimona	Privately owned. Three biggest shareholders are The Central Trade and Investment Corporation, Keren Kad (majority private-

Corporation	Owner
	ly owned) and the Investment Company of the Industrial Development Bank
84. Klal	Jewish Agency through Bank Leumi; Government through Industrial Development Bank and other banks; Histadrut through Workers' Bank, Koor, Sollel Boneh; private companies, including the Central Trade and Investment Corporation, Bank for Foreign Trade and others
85. Klil	Recanati through Bank Discount and a group of American investors
86. Koor	Histadrut through Workers' Company
87. Lapid Eshet	Lish and Herman
88. Legin	American Can Company. Minority partner is Kibbutz Yagur
89. Lena Knitting Enterprises	Cohen family
90. Levidei Ashkelon	Histadrut, through Koor
91. Levitt, Y and Sons	Levitt family
92. Leyland	Leyland Motor Company, England
93. Lumir	Lustig, Reviv, Milstein, Levinton, Katz and Schlesinger
94. Lodzia	Stern Anstelt, Vaduz, Lichtenstein
95. Lustig Brothers	Lustig family
96. Ma'ariv Printing House	Oved Ben-Ami and Disenchik. (The latter by virtue of his position as editor-in chief.)
97. Machteshi, Chemical Works	Koor; Hevrat Ovdim has a special share
98. Maonot Amamiyim	Progressive Party through the Progressive Party Enterprises
99. Marino	Privately owned. No clear majority to any single shareholder
100. Mechanical Equipment Mekorot	Government through Mekorot
101. Meir Investment Company	Meir family
102. Mekorot	Government
103. Merkavim	Histadrut through Koor; Hevrat Ovdim has a special share
104. Meshhav	Hapoel Hamizrahi
105. MGM	Privately owned. No clear majority to any single shareholder
106. Migdal-Binyan	Jewish Agency through Bank Leumi through Africa-Israel Investments
107. Migdalei Pri-Ze	Frank family

Corporation	Owner
108. Mivnei Taasiya	Government
109. Modiin Publishing House	Ben-Ami and Disenchik
110. Molar Textile	Elern family; Registration Company of Bank Leumi; Investment Company of Industrial Development Bank
111. Moshe Shaked and Sons	Shaked family
112. Nakid	Privately owned by seven families through Essem Investments
113. National Oil Company	Government
114. Na'aman	Hashomer Hatzair, through Hashomer Hatzair Fund and Techen Enterprises
115. Nefta	Government
116. Nehushtan	Mosberg
117. New Printing Company	Hashomer Hatzair through Techen Enterprises
118. Nur	Sweish and English Companies
119. Ogen	Histadrut through Solel Boneh and Zim. Government and Jewish Agency are minority owners, through the latter
120. Oil Services	Government
121. Op-Er	Yaakovovitz, and Zilberstein families and Margot Bik, who are chief shareholders in Keshet, which owns Arigim which owns Op-Er
122. Otzar Letaasiyah	Government
123. Pan-Lon	Leon family and Pan-American Investment and Real Estate Company
124. Petrochemical Industries (Protrum)	Privately owned. Foreign shareholders own the majority shares. Among local shareholders, the largest are Delek, the Registration Company of Bank Leumi, the American-Israeli Gas Corporation, Ronnie Ltd., PEC, the Investment Company of the Foreign Trade Bank, Klal and Bank Discount
125. Phoenicia	Histadrut through Koor
126. Polgat	Panama Company
127. Pri-Sucar	Privately owned, mainly by Parmtzenko, Moshvitz and Kepilov families
128. Ramin	Privately owned; single largest shareholder is Denski family
129. Rassco	Jewish Agency
130. Registration Company of Bank Discount	Recanati family through Bank Discount

Corporation	Owner
131. Remet	Alperin
132. Remet-Siv	Rozov family
133. Reviv Brothers	Reviv family
134. Rogozin Enterprises	Government
135. Rubenstein and Partners	Rubinstein family
136. Sefen	Histadrut through kibbutzim and Ampal
137. Sela	No information
138. Shalom Tower Building	Wolfson, Chlore and Meir
139. Sharfon	PEC
140. Sharon	Privately owned. No clear majority to any single shareholder
141. Shemen	Histadrut through Trustee Company of Workers' Bank
142. Shikun Errahi	General Zionists, through their Fund for Constructive Enterprises
143. Shikun Ovdim	Histadrut through Hevrat Ovdim, Sollel Boneh and Neve Oved
144. Shimshon	Privately owned. Major shareholders are Bank Discount, the Central Trade and Investment Corporation, PEC, Ampa and the Shalom family
145. Sivei Dimona	Privately owned. Majority shareholder (Type 'A') is Neufina A.G., Zurich
146. Slilim	Histadrut through Hevrat Ovdim and Hamashbir Hamerkazi
147. Sollel Boneh	Histadrut through Hevrat Ovdim
148. Soltam	Koor and S.A.L.G.D. (Luxembourg)
149. Sugat	Mexican Company
150. Supersol	Private Canadian Company
151. Ta'al	Chief shareholders include the Fund of the Ichud Hakvutzot Vehakibbutzim and the Saharov family
152. Ta'asiyot Blamim	Eliahu Gelerstein and Eretz family
153. Ta'asiyot Ereg Israeliot	Privately owned by Leon Trading Trust, Lichtenstein. Minority partners include Weiz and Lenk
154. Ta'asiyot Even va-Sid	Sollel Boneh
155. Ta'asiyot Matechect Veamail	Investment Company of the Industrial Development Bank
156. Tera — A Joint Agricultural Productive Union in Nahalat Yitzhak	Private cooperative
157. Tet-Bet	Privately owned. Two biggest shareholders are Trubovitz and Berger families

Corporation	*Owner*
158. Te'us Development Area	Histadrut through Workers' Company
159. The Company for Cables and Electric Wires in Israel	Privately owned. Biggest single shareholder is Recanati family through the Registration Company of Bank Discount. Others include the Lichtenstein family and the Registration Company of Bank Leumi
160. Timna Copper Mines	Government
161. Tnuvah	Histadrut cooperative
162. Tovala Enterprises	Government
163. Tozereth Mazon Israelit	R.F.T. Ltd., London
164. Trustee Company of Workers' Bank	Histadrut through Workers' Bank
165. Trustee Company of Workers' Company	Histadrut through Workers' Company
166. Tvi — Jerusalem Yarns	Politi family
167. Tzitor	Privately owned. Biggest single shareholder is Swiss-Israel Trade Bank
168. Uniko	Sabat
169. Union of Cooperative Vineyards of the Wine-Growers of Rishon LeZion and Zichron Yaakov	Private Cooperative
170. United Company for Publicity Services	Privately owned by five different companies, one of which (Dahat) has a partnership with Mapai kibbutzim
171. United Dairies	Rassco through Otzar Investment Company
172. United Textiles of Y Tchorli	Tchorli family
173. Vita	Plutkin family
174. Vitelgo	Vitela family
175. Voldmann Schlesinger	Voldmann, Schlesinger and Israel-Swiss Trade Bank through Kidum Ta'asiya in Israel
176. Voltex Industries	Klir, Mochomovski, Weiz and Leon Trading Trust through Zemron
177. Workers' Bank	Histadrut (see above p.
178. Yaf-Ora	Jewish Agency through Bank Leumi through Eframan Trustees Ltd.
179. Yakhin	Cooperative, in conjunction with Histadrut and Jewish Agency
180. Yakhin-Hakal	Histadrut, through Yahin, and Jewish Agency

Corporation	*Owners*
181. Yitzhar	No information
182. Zeksonia	Privately owned; no clear majority to any single shareholder
183. Zemron	Privately owned by Weiz, Nochomovski and Klir and by Leon Trading Trust, Vaduz, Lichtenstein
184. Zim	Government through State and Jewish Agency; Histadrut through Hevrat Ovdim has minority interest
185. Zion-Jeudah	Taiber family
186. Stone and Lime Company	Histadrut through Workers' Company

Corporation	Owner
1. Alliance	Histadrut and private foreign interests
2. Amkor	Histadrut, through Ha'argaz and Workers' Bank, and Ampa, a privately owned company of five partners, including Elman
3. Ampal — American Israel Corporation	see above p.78.
4. Askar	Hashomer Hatzair, in conjunction with Hevrat Ovdim (who have a founding share) and the affiliated kibbutzim, through Techen Works and the Hashomer Hatzair Fund
5. Autocars	Histadrut through Workers' Company and private investors
6. Dan	Histadrut cooperative
7. Deco	Kibbutz Bror-Hayil; A Genevan, Wolfgang Messer; Uviko; a Zurich company; and others
8. Egged	Histadrut cooperative
9. Gal'am	Hashomer Hatzair through Techen Works and the Soomer Hatzair Fund
10. Gavish	Cooperative of Gavish Workers
11. Ha'argaz	Histadrut, through Trustee Company of Workers' Bank and the Ha'Argaz Workers' Cooperative
12. Ha-Kibbutz Ha'artzi Building Company	Hashomer Hatzair through its Fund
13. Ha-Kibbutz Hameuhad Building Company	Kibbutz Hameuchad. Hevrat Ovdim has special share
14. Ha-Kibbutz ha-Meuhad Fund	The ha-Kibbutz ha-Meuhad Federation
15. Hamashbir Hamerkazi	Histadrut cooperative
16. Hamashbir Latzarkhan	Histadrut cooperative
17. Hamegaper	Hevrat Ovdim through Hamashbir Hamerkazi and the special share of Hevrat Ovdim

Corporation	Owner
18. Hasneh	Histadrut
19. Ha-Shomer ha-Tzair Fund	Ha-Kibbutz ha-Artzi Federation
20. Hatzatz Israel-American	Histadrut through Sollel Boneh and private shareholders
21. Hishulei Hacarmel	Koor and S.A.L.G.P. (Luxembourg) through Soltam
22. Hula Textile	Government, through Argat Investment Company and Histadrut, through Hevrat Ovdim — both of whom own it through Teus Azorei Pituah, which owns the majority shares in Hula Textile; Molar Textile is a minority partner
23. Ihud ha-Kevutzot ve-ha-Kibbutzim Fund	The Ihud ha-Kevutzot ve-ha-Kibbutzim Federation
24. Investment Fund of Hevrat Ovdim	Histadrut through Hevrat Ovdim
25. Israel Ceramic Enterprises 'Harsah'	Koor; Hevrat Ovdim has a special share
26. Israel Steel Works	Koor
27. Israel Sugar Enterprises	Histadrut, through Tnuva and Trustee Company of Hevrat Ovdim. Government is a minority shareholder through Agricultural Investment Company
28. Jerusalem Shoes	Cooperative Fund
29. Koor	Histadrut through Workers' Company
30. Legin	American Can Company. Minority partner is Kibbutz Yagur
31. Levidei Ashkelon	Histadrut, through Koor
32. Machteshim, Chemical Works	Koor; Hevrat Ovdim has a special share
33. Merkavim	Histadrut through Koor; Hevrat Ovdim has a special share
34. Na'aman	Hashomer Hatzair, through Hashomer Hatzair Fund and Techen Enterprises
35. New Printing Company	Hashomer Hatzair through Techen Enterprises
36. Ogen	Histadrut through Sollel Boneh and Zim. Government and Jewish Agency are minority owners, through the latter
37. Phoenicia	Histadrut through Koor
38. Sefen	Histadrut through kibbutzim and Ampal
39. Shemen	Histadrut through Trustee Company of Workers' Bank

Corporation	Owner
40. Shikun Ovdim	Histadrut through Hevrat Ovdim, Sollel Boneh and Neve Oved
41. Slilim	Histadrut through Hevrat Ovdim and Hamashbir Hamerkazi
42. Sollel Boneh	Histadrut through Hevrat Ovdim
43. Soltam	Koor and S.A.L.G.D. (Luxembourg)
44. Ta'al	Chief shareholders include the Fund of the Ichud Hakvutzot Vehakibbutzim and the Saharov family
45. Ta'asiyot Even va-Sid	Sollel Boneh
46. Te'us Development Areas	Histadrut through Workers' Company
47. Trustee Company of Workers' Bank	Histadrut through Workers' Bank
48. Trustee Company of the Workers' Company	Histadrut through Workers' Company
49. United Company for Publicity	Privately owned by five different companies one of which (Dahat) has a partnership with Mapai kibbutzim
50. Workers' Bank	Histadrut (see above p.
51. Yakhin	Cooperative, in conjunction with Histadrut and Jewish Agency
52. Yakhin-Hakal	Histadrut, through Yahin, and Jewish Agency
53. Zim	Government through State and Jewish Agency; Histadrut through Hevrat Ovdim has minority interest
54. Stone and Lime Company	Histadrut through Workers' Company
55. Tnuvah, A Cooperative Cenre for Marketing Agricultural Produce in Israel Ltd.	Histadrut through Workers' Company

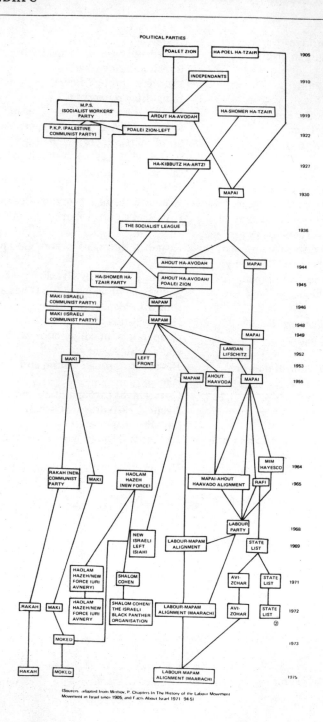

POLITICAL PARTIES

(Sources: adapted from Merhov, P. Chapters In The History of the Labour Movement
Movement in Israel since 1905, and Facts About Israel 1971, 94-5)

REFERENCES

Introduction

1. R. Rosenzweig and G. Tamarin, 'Israel's Power Elite', *Transaction*, no. 7, (July, 1970).

The Moral Dilemma

1. A. Amad, (ed.), *The Israeli League for Human and Civil Rights (The Shakak Papers)*, MEEBI, (Beirut, 1973).
2. T. Herzl, *The Jewish State*, Newman, (Tel Aviv, 1956).
3. A. Ruppin, *Three Decades of Palestine*, Schocken, (Jerusalem, 1936).
4. *Ha-aretz*, 18/4/1972.
5. E. Childers, reprinted in W. Laqueur, *A History of Zionism*, Weidenfeld and Nicholson, (London, 1972), p.181.

The Origins of Zionism

1. cf Lacqueur, (ibid) and B. Halperin, *The Idea of the Jewish State*, Harvard University Press (Harvard, 1969).
2. J. Klatzkin, in B. Matovu, 'The Zionist Wish and the Nazi Deed', *Issue*, Winter 1966-67.
3. J. Prinz, *Wir Juden*, (Berlin, 1934), p.150-151 and 155-156.
4. U. Harari, 'Our Responsibility towards the Jews in the Arab Countries', *Yediot Aharonot*, 9/2/1969.
5. cf. I. Abrahams, *Jewish Life in the Middle Ages*, (London, 1932), S. Diamond, 'Kibbutz and Shtetle', *Social Problems*, 5.2., (1957), A. Leon, *A Jewish Question: A Marxist Interpretation*, Pathfinder, (New York, 1970), M. Samuel, *The World of Sholom Aleichem*, Valentine Mitchell, (London, 1973).

Colonisation

1. H. Enosh, 'The Second Aliyah Viewed Today', *Ba-Mahareh*, (Official Israeli Army Weekly) 25/4/1973.
2. C. Sykes, *Crossroads to Israel*, Midland Books, (London, 1967), p.200.
3. *Ot*, (Organ of the Youth Cadre of the Israeli Labour Party) no. 2, (Winter, 1967).
4. Y. Greenbaum, *Bi-Mei Hurban ve Sho'ah*, Haverim, (Tel Aviv, 1946), pp. 68,69.
5. *Encyclopaedia Judaica*, 'Kibbutz', Keter, (Jerusalem, 1971).
6. Y. Amir, 'Bnei Kibbutzim he-Zehal', *Megamot* 15. 2-3. (August, 1967).

7. D. Leon, *The Kibbutz: A New Way of Life*, Pergammon, (London, 1969).

8. B. Bettelheim, *Children of the Dream*, Macmillan, (New York, 1969), M.E. Spiro, *Kibbutz, Venture in Utopia*, Shocken, (New York, 1963), Y. Talman, *Family and Community in the Kibbutz*, Harvard University Press, (Harvard, 1972).

9. S. Diamond, 'Kibbutz and Shtetle', *Social Problems*, 5.2. (1957).

10. Y. Kutler, 'The Kibbutz in the Age of Affluence', *Ha-aretz*, 19/11/1971.

11. A. Bein, *The Return to the Soil, A History of the Jewish Settlement in Israel*, The Youth and Hechalntz Department of the Zionist Organization, (Jerusalem, 1952).

12. S. Jiryis, *The Arabs in Israel*, Institute for Palestine Studies, (Beirut, 1968).

13. *Census*, no. 8, Israel Central Bureau of Statistics, (1961), Table 3.

14. A. Bein, ibid.

15. A. Weingrod, 'Administered Communities, Some Characteristics of New Immigrant Villages in Israel, *Economic Development and Cultural Change*, no.11, (1962).

16. *Census*, ibid, p.22.

17. *Census*, no.7, (1961), Table 4.

18. *Census*, no.8, (1961), p.22.

The Oriental Jews

1. A. Mack, 'Oriental Jews, Class, Ethnicity and Ideology', in U. Davis, A. Mack and N. Yuval Davis, (Eds.), *Israel and the Palestinians*, Ithaca, (London, 1975).

2. K. Shemesh, 'This Is My Opinion', in U. Davis and N. Mezvinsky, *Documents from Israel*, Ithaca, (London, 1975).

3. A. Bein, ibid.

4. A. Bein, ibid.

5. N. Cohen, cited in T. Maroz, *Ha-aretz Weekend Supplement*, 30/1/1976.

6. B. Nadel, *Yediot Aharonot*, 23/7/1976.

7. B. Nadel, ibid.

8. S. Smooha and Y. Peres, *The Ethnic Gap in Israel*, mimeo, (Tel Aviv, 1972).

9. *Ha-aretz*, 31/10/1975.

10. *Yedio Aharonot*, 13/2/1976.

11. S. Smooha, 'Black Panthers, the Ethnic Dilemma', *Society*, 9.7., (May, 1972).

12. S. Smooha, ibid.

Kinship as History

1. A. Rupin, cited in *Jerusalem Post Weekly*, 30/9/1968.
2. H. Enosh, ibid.
3. V. Auneri, *Israel without Zionism*, Macmillan, (London, 1976)

Israeli Socialism: Utopia Incorporated

1. *Who's Who in Israel 1973-74*, Bronfmonond Cohen, (Tel Aviv, 1973).
2. *Ha-aretz*, 25/11/1976.
3. M. Buber, *Paths in Utopia*, Beacon Press, (New York, 1958), p.14.
4. M. Buber, ibid, p.140.
5. M. Buber, ibid, p.148-149.
6. S. Levitan, *Quest for a Federal Manpower Policy*, Harvard University Press, (Harvard, 1975).
7. *Ha-aretz*, 14/9/1976.
8. *Maariv*, 14/2/1971.
9. *Ha-aretz*, 27/10/1975.
10. *Ha-olam-ha-zeh*, 10/12/1974.
11. *Yediot Aharonot*, 30/5/1976.
12. *Maariv*, 9/12/1976.
13. *Yediot Aharonot*, 12/10/1976.
14. S.B. Schecter, *Israeli Political and Economic Elites and Some Aspects of their Relations*, Ph.D. dissertation, (London School of Economics, 1972).

Israel and the US

1. *Yediot Aharonot*, 5/3/1976.
2. *Journal of Economic Literature*, (December, 1969), p.1177.
3. cf U. Davis and N. Merzvinsky, (Eds.), *Documents from Israel*, Ithaca, (London, 1975) for an analysis of the official use of these funds in Israel and the post '67 occupied territories.
4. *Ha-aretz*, 30/9/1951.
5. *Ha-aretz*, 16/12/1976.
6. *Maariv*, 11/2/1977.
7. A. Emmanuel, 'White Settler Colonialism and the Myth of Investment Imperialism', *New Left Review*, no.73, (May-June, 1972).
8. R. Storrs, *Orientations*, Nicholson and Watson, Definitive edition, (London, 1943).
9. *Ha-aretz*, 25/3/1975.
10. *Boston Globe*, 24/2/1977. cf also the Africa Research Group's *David and Goliath Collaborate in Africa*, (1969), Z.Y. Herischag, *Israel*

Africa Cooperation Research Project, (Tel Aviv, 1970), and Leopold Laufer's report to the US Agency for International Development, *Israel and the Developing Nations,* (1967).

The Future

1. T. Shanin, *The Awkward Class,* Oxford University Press, (Oxford, 1972).
2. H. Hanegbi, M. Machover and A. Orr, 'The Class Nature of Israel', *New Left Review,* no.65, (January-February, 1971).
3. *Maariv,* 12/10/1975.
4. *Yediot Aharonot,* 17/5/1976.
5. *Maariv,* 4/5/1976.
6. *Yediot Aharonot,* 28/5/1976.
7. *Yediot Aharonot,* 3/5/1976.
8. *Yediot Aharonot,* 6/6/1976.
9. *Ha-aretz,* 12/1/1975.
10. *Ha-aretz,* 7/5/1976.
11. *Yediot Aharonot,* 13/5/1976.
12. *Ha-aretz,* 6/6/1976.

Glossary

1. A. ha-Am, *Truth from Eretz-Israel,* (1891) Complete Works, Devir and the Hebrew Publishing House, (Tel Aviv, 1965), 8th ed., p.23.
2. *Jerusalem Post Weekly Magazine,* 30/9/1968.
3. Statement made before the Convention of the Lawyer's Association, see *ha-Praklit,* (The Lawyer), (February, 1946).
4. *Palestine Gazette,* no. 1442, Supplement no. 2, 27/9/1945.
5. *Maariv,* 28/6/1973.
6. M. Goldberg, *And the Fund is Still Alive,* Sifriyat Poalim, (Tel Aviv, 1965), p.162.
7. *Ha-aretz,* 24/8/1973.
8. *Report on the Legal Structure, Activities, Assets, Income and Liabilities of the Keren Kaymet le-Israel,* (Jerusalem, 1973), pp. 18,86.
9. Walter Laqueur (ed.), *The Israeli-Arab Reader,* Penguin, (1970), pp. 162-3.
10. *Pi ha-Aton,* 24/2/1971.

BIBLIOGRAPHY

J. S. Abarbanel, *The Cooperative Farmer and the Welfare State: Economic Change in an Israeli Moshav*, Manchester University Press, (1974).

I. Abrahams, *Jewish Life in the Middle Ages*, (London, 1932).

Action Society Trust, *Management Success*, Acton Society Trust, (London 1956).

Y. Allon, *The Making of Israel's Army*, Vallentine Mitchell, (London,1971).

A. Amad, (ed.), *The Israeli League for Human and Civil Rights (The Shahak Papers)*, Near East Ecumenical Bureau for Information and Interpretation (MEEBII), Beirut, (1973).

H. Arendt, *Eichmann in Jerusalem*, Faber & Faber, (London, 1963).

H. Arendt, "Antisemitism', *The Origins of Totalitarianism*, Meridan Books, (New York, 1958).

John A. Armstrong, *The Soviet Bureaucratic Elite: A Case Study of the Ukranian Apparatus*, Stevens & Sons, (London, 1959).

Y. Amir, *Bnei Kibbutzim be-Zahal*, (Heb.) (Sons of Kibbutzim in the Israeli Army, *Megamot*, Vo. 15, Nos.2-3, August 1967.

R. Aron, 'Social Structure and The Ruling Class', *British Journal of Sociology*, Vol. 1, No.1, March 1950, pp.1-16 and Vol. 1, No. 2, June 1950, pp.126-143.

T. Asad, (ed.), *Anthropology and the Colonial Encounter*, Ithaca Press, (London, 1973).

Fouzi el-Asmar, *To Be An Arab in Israel*, Frances Pinter, (London, 1975).

W.H. Auden, 'Archaeology', *Thank You Fog*, Faber & Faber, (London, 1974).

U. Avnery, *Israel Without Zionism*, Collier, Macmillan, (London, 1971).

J.J. Bachofen, *Myth, Religion and Mother Right*, trans. Ralph Manheim, Routledge and Kegan Paul, (London, 1967).

E. Digby Baltzell, *An American Business Aristocracy*, Collier Books, (New York, 1962), (originally published as *Philadelphia Gentlemen: The Making of a National Class*, 1958).

P. Baratz, and M. Bachrach, "Two Faces of Power", *The American Political Science Review*, December 1962.

H.B. Barnett, *Anthropology in Administration*, Evanston, ICC. Rwo Peterson & Co., (1956).

Barrington-Moore Jr., *Social Origins of Dictatorship and Democracy*, Deacon Press, (Boston, 1965).

Charles A. Beard, *An Economic Interpretation of the Constitution of the United State*, Macmillan, (New York, 1962 (1913)).

Charles A. Beard, *Economic Origins of Jeffersonian Democracy*, Macmillan, (New York, 1952 (1915)).

Charles A. Beard, *The Economic Basis of Politics*, George Allen & Unwin, (London, 1934 (1922)).

I. Beer, *Israel's Security: Yesterday, Today and Tomorrow* (Heb.), Amikam,

(Tel Aviv, 1966).

A. Bein, *The Return To The Soil: A History of The Jewish Settlement in Israel.* The Youth and Hechalntz Department of the Zionist Organization, (Jerusalem, 1952).

R. Bendix, *Higher Civil Servants in American Society*, Boulder, University of Colorado Press, (1949).

M. Bentwich, *Fulfilment in The Promised Land (1917-1937)*, (London, 1938).

A.A. Berle and G.C. Means, The Modern Corporation and Private Property, Macmillan, (New York, 1933).

M. Bloch, *Feudal Society*, Routledge & Kegan Paul, (London, 1961).

B. Bettleheim, *Children of The Dream*, Macmillan, (New York, 1969).

M. Blatt, U. Davis and P. Keinbaum (eds.), *Dissent and Ideology In Israel: Resistance to the Draft 1948-1973*, Ithaca Press, (London, 1975).

T.B. Bottomore, *Elites and Society*, Penguin, (1964).

M. Caldwell,'Aseanization', *Journal of Contemporary Asia*, Vol.2, No. 2 (1973).

P. Cardan, *Modern Capitalism and Revolution*, Solidarity, (London, 1974).

G.V. Childe, *The Dawn of European Civilization*, Knopf, (New York, 1958).

G.V. Childe, *New Light On the Most Ancient East*, Praegner, (New York, 1953).

A. Cohen, *Arab Border Villages*, Manchester University Press, (1965).

A. Cohen, *Israel and the Arab World*, (Heb.), Sifriyat Poalim, (Tel Aviv, 1964).

G.H. Copeman, *Leaders of British Industry: A Study of the Careers of More Than a Thousand Public Company Directors*, Gee & Co., (London, 1955).

P. Dagan, *Pillars of Israel Economy*, Lipschitz, (Tel Aviv, 1955).

R. Dahl, 'A Critique of the Ruling Elite Model', *American Political Science Review*, March, 1968.

U. Davis, 'Palestine Into Israel', *Journal of Palestine Studies*, Vol. 3, No. 1, Autumn 1973.

U. Davis, A. Mack and Yuval-Davis, N. (eds.), *Israel and the Palestinians*, Ithaca Press, (London, 1975).

U. Davis and N. Mezvinsky, (eds.), *Documents from Israel: Readings for a Critique of Zionism*, Ithaca Press, (London, 1975).

S. Diamond, 'The Rule of Law Versus the Order of Custom', *Critical Anthropology*, Vol.2, No.1, pp.2-23, Spring 1971.

S. Diamond, 'The Search for the Primitive', in Goldston, I. (ed.), *Man's Image in Medicure and Anthropology*, Monography IV, Institute of Social and Historical Medicine, The New York Academy of Medicine, International Universities Press Inc., pp. 62-115, (New York, 1963).

S. Diamond, 'Anthropology: A Revolutionary Discipline', *Current Anthropology*, Vol. 5, (1964).

S. Diamond, 'The Uses of the Primitive' in S. Diamond (ed.), *Primitive Views of the World: Essays from Culture in History*, Columbia University Press, (New York, 1969).

S. Diamond, 'Kibbutz and Shtetle', *Social Problems*, Vol. 5, No.2. (1957).

W. Domhoff, *Who Rules America?* Prentice-Hall, (New Jersey, 1967).

Y. Elam, *An Introduction to Another Zionist History*, (Heb.), Levy-Epstein, (1972).

A. Emmanuel, *Unequal Exchange*, Monthly Review Press, (New York, 1972).

F. Engels, 'Socialism: Utopian and Scientific', in Arthur P. Mendel (ed.), *Essential Works of Marxism*, Bantham Books, (New York, 1971 (1880)).

H. Enosh, 'The Second Aliyah Viewed Today', (Heb.), *Ba-Mahaneh* (In The Camp), The Official Weekly of the Israeli Army, April 25, 1973.

E.E. Evans-Pritchard, *Social Anthropology and Other Essays*, Free Press, (New York, 1962).

R. Firth, *Elements of Social Organization*, Watts & Co., (London, 1956).

M.M. Fried, (ed.), *Readings in Anthropology*, Thomas Y. Crowell Co., (New York, 1968).

J. Galtung, 'A Structural Theory of Aggression', *Journal of Peace Research*, No. 2, 1964.

M. Goldenberg, *And the Fund is Still Alive*, (Heb.), Sifriyat Poalim (1965).

Henry George, *Progress and Poverty*, Robert Schalkenback Foundation, (New York, 1971).

J.M. Goode, *World Revolution and Family Patterns*, Free Press, (New York, 1963).

J. Goody, (ed.), *Kinship*, Penguin, (1971).

K. Gough, 'Anthropology: Child of Imperialism', *Monthly Review*, April 1968.

T. Guzansky, *Economic Independence — How? Summary of the Economic Development of Israel: 1948-1968*, (Heb.), Iyyon, (Tel Aviv, 1969).

T. Guzansky, 'Trends in Israel's Economic Development', (Heb.), *Arakhim*, The Bulletin of the Israeli Communist Party on Questions of Theory and Practice, No.1 (13), February 1971.

Y. Greenbaum, *Bi-Mei Hurban ve-Sho'ah*, (Heb.), (In Days of Destruction and Disaster), Haverim Publishing House, (Tel Aviv, 1946).

J.J. Gumperz and D. Hymes, (ed.), *Directions in Sociolinguistics*, Holt, Reinhart & Winston, (New York, 1972.).

W.L. Guttsman, *The British Political Elite*, MacGibbon & Kee, (London, 1963).

B. Halperin, *The Idea of the Jewish State*, Harvard University Press, (1969).

H. Hanegbi, M. Machover & A. Orr, 'The Class Nature of Israel', *New Left Review*, No. 65, January-February 1971.

M.J. Herskovits, *Acculturation*, (New York, 1938).

T. Hezl, *The Jewish State*, Newman Publishing House, English Ed., (Tel Aviv, 1956 (1896)).

A. Hertzberg, (ed.), *The Zionist Idea*, Doubleday & Herzl Press, (1959).

E.J. Hobsbaum, *Primitive Rebels: Studies in Archaic Forms of Social Movements in the 19th and 20th Centuries*, Praeger, (New York, 1963).

D. Horowitz, *My Yesterday*, (Heb.), Schocken, (Tel Aviv, 1970).

D. Hymes, (ed.), *Language, Culture and Society*, Harper and Row, (New York, 1964).

Ibn Khaldun, *Prolegomena*, Ed. by Charles Issawi, Selections from the Prolegomena of Ibn Kahldun of Tunis (1332-1406), John Murray, (London, 1950 (1379)).

Israel Central Bureau of Statistics, *Population and Housing Census*, Jerusalem, (1961).

G. Jabbour, *Settler Colonialism in Southern Africa and the Middle East*, Palestine Books No. 30, University of Khartoum and PLO Research Centre, (Beirut, 1970).

S. Jiryis, *The Arabs in Israel*, Institute for Palestine Studies, (Beirut, 1968).

E. Kanovsky, *The Economy of the Israeli Kibbutz*, Harvard Middle East Monograph Series, No. 13, Harvard University Press, (1966).

B. Kimmerling, *The Struggle Over the Land: A Chapter in the Sociology of Jewish-Arab Conflict*, (Heb.), Papers in Sociology, The Hebrew University of Jerusalem, (1973).

B.A. Kean, *The Agricultural Development of the Middle East*, (London, 1946).

J. Klatzkin, in B. Matovu, 'The Zionist Wish and the Nazi Deed', *Issue*, Winter 1966-7.

L. Krader, *Formations of the State*, Foundations of Modern Anthropology Series, Prentice-Hall, (New York, 1968).

P. Kropotkin, *The State: Its Historic Role*, Freedom Press, (London, 1969 (1897)).

Y. Kutler, 'The Kibbutz in the Age of Affluence: The Member Mortgages Himself' (Part 4), *Ha-aretz*, November 19, 1971.

W. Laqueur, *A History of Zionism*, Weidenfeld and Nicolson, (London, 1972).

F. Langer, *With My Own Eyes*, Ithaca Press, (London, 1975).

H. D. Lasswell, D. Lerner and C.E. Rothwell, *The Comparative Study of Elites*, Hoover Institute Studies, Series B: Elites, No. 1,(Standford, 1952).

H.D. Laswell, *Politics: Who Gets What, When, How?*, McGraw Hill, (New York, 1936).

E.E. LeClair and H.N. Schneider, (eds.), *Economic Anthropology*, Holt Rinehart & Winston, (New York, 1968).

D. Lee, *Freedom and Culture*, Prentice-Hall. A Spectrum Book, (1959).

A. Leon, *The Jewish Question: A Marxist Interpretation*, Pathfinder, (New York, 1970).

D. Leon, *The Kibbutz: A New Way of Life*, Pergamon Press, (London, 1969).

Levi-Strauss, C., *Structural Anthropology*, Doubleday Anchor Books,

New York, 1967).

C. Levi-Strauss, *The Elementary Structures of Kinship*, Revised Ed. by Rodney Needham, trans. by J.H. Bell, J.R. von Strumer and R. Needham, Beacon Press, (Boston, 1969).

C. Levi-Strauss, *The Raw and the Cooked*, Harper Torchbooks, (New York, 1969).

C. Levi-Strauss, *Tristes Tropiques*, Atheneum, (New York, 1971).

G. Lichtheim, *Marxism: An Historical and Critical Study*, Routledge, (London, 1964).

T. Lupton and C.S. Wilson, 'The Social Background and Connections of "Top Decision Makers" ', *The Manchester School of Economics and Social Studies*, Vol. 27, No.1, January 1959.

C.A. McCoy and J. Playford, (eds.), *Apolitical Politics*, Cromwell, (New York, 1967).

H. Maine, *Ancient Law*, Murray, (London, 19   (1861))).

B. Malinowski, *A Diary in the Strictest Sense of the Term*, Harcourt and World, (New York, 1967).

K. Manheim, *Ideology and Utopia*, Kegan Paul, (London, 1936).

K. Manheim, *Man and Society in an Age of Reconstruction*, Kegan Paul, (London, 1940).

K. Manheim, *Essays on the Sociology of Culture*, Routledge & Kegan Paul, (London, 1956).

O. Mannoni, *Prospero and Cabilan: The Psychology of Colonization*, Praeger, (New York, 1964).

Dwaine Marvick, (ed.), *Political Decision Makers*, (Glencoe, The Free Press) (The Introduction provides a survey of current research). (1961).

D.R. Matthews, *The Social Background of Political Decision-Makers*, Doubleday, (New York, 1954).

C. Wright Mills, *The Power Elite*, Oxford University Press, (New York, 1956).

C. Wright Mills, *The Sociological Imagination*, Oxford University Press, (1959).

S.F. Nadel, *A Black Byzantium*, Oxford University Press, (1946).

F. Oppenheimer, *The State*, Arno Press & New York Times, (New York, 1972 (1926)).

Ot, (Heb.), *The Organ of the Youth Cadre of the Israeli (Ruling) Labour Party*, No. 2, Winter 1967.

R. Owen, *Cotton and the Egyptian Economy: 1820-1914*, Oxford University Press, (1968).

A. Perlmuter, *Military and Politics in Israel*, Praeger, (1969).

Sir Alan Pim, *Colonial Agriculture Production*, Oxford University Press, (1946).

K. Polanyi, C.M. Arenbsberg and H.W. Pearson (eds.), *Trade and Markets in Early Empires*, The Free Press, (Glencoe, Ill., 1957).

K. Polanyi, 'Anthropology and Economic Theory', in M.M. Fried, (ed.)

Readings in Anthropology, Vol. 2, Chapter 14, Thomas Y. Cromwell Co., (New York, 1968).

H. Powdermaker, *Stranger and Friend*, Norton & Co., (New York, 1967).

P. Radin, *The World of Primitive Man*, Schuman, (New York, 1953).

R. Redfield, *Peasant Society and Culture: An Anthropological Approach to Civilization*, Chicago University Press, (1956).

R. Redfield, 'The Folk Society' in M.M. Fried, *Readings In Anthropology*, Thomas Y. Crowell Co., NY, Vol. 2, pp.497-517, (1968).

C. Reining, 'The Lost Period in Anthropology', *American Anthropologist*, Vol. 5, (1962).

M. Rodinson, *Israel: A Colonial Settler State?*, Pathfinder, (New York, 1973).

M. Rodinson, *Israel and the Arabs*, Penguin, (1968).

H. Rosenfeld, *The Were Peasants*, (Heb.), Ha-kibbutz ha-Meuchad Publishing House, (Tel Aviv, 1964).

R. Rosenzweig and G. Tamarin, 'Israel's Power Elite', *Trans-action*, Vol. 7, July 1970.

A. Ruppin, *Three Decades of Palestine*, Schocken, (Jerusalem, 1936).

E. Salpeter and Y. Elitzur, *Who Runs Israel* (Heb.), Levi-Epstein (1973), (English Ed. available by Harper & Row, 1974).

M. Samuel, *The World of Sholom Aleichem*, Vallentine Mitchell, (London, 1973).

J.P. Sartre, *The Problem of Method*, Methuen & Co. Ltd., (London, 1963).

J.P. Sartre, *Anti-Semite and Jew*, Schocken Books, (New York, 1948).

J.A. Schumpeter, *Capitalism, Socialism and Democracy*, Allen & Unwin, (london, 1943).

M. Shalev and M. Portugali, *The System*, (Heb.), Alon, (Tel Aviv, 1972).

H. Schmid, 'Peace Research as Pacification Research', *IPRA*, Third World General Conference, Karlovy Vary, Czechoslovakia, September 20-23, 1969.

I. Shahak, *For a Judaism of Truth and Justice: Against the Treatment of Non-Jews in Judaism*, (Heb.), Private edition, (1966).

T. Shanin (ed.), *Peasants and Peasant Studies*, Penguin, (1971).

J. Shim'oni, *The Arabs and Eretz Israel*, (Heb.), Am-Oved, (Tel Aviv, 1947).

M. Smilansky, *Collected Works*, Massada, (Tel Aviv, 1953-4.

M.E. Spiro, *Kibbutz: Venture in Utopia*, Schocken Books, (New York, 1963).

M. Stavsky, *The Arab Village*, (Heb.), Am Oved Publishing House, (Tel Aviv, 1946).

J. Strachey, *Contemporary Capitalism*, Gollancz, (London, 1956).

C. Sykes, *Crossroads to Israel*, (London, 1967).

Y. Telmon, *Family and Community in the Kibbutz*, Harvard University Press, (1972).

G. Tamarin, *The Israeli Dilemma: Essays on a Warfare State*, Rotterdam University Press, (1973).

F. Turki, *The Disinherited, Monthly Review Press*, (New York, 1972).

Lloyd W. Warner and James C. Abbegglen, *Big Business Leaders in America*, Harper, (New York, 1955).

S. Weiss, *Politicians in Israel*, (Heb.), Achiasaf Publishing House, (Tel Aviv, 1973).

J. Weitz, 'A Solution to the Refugee Problem: The State of Israel with a Small Arab Minority', *Davar*, 29.9.1967. Translated from the Hebrew by U. Davis and N. Mezvinsky, (eds.), *Documents from Israel: Readings for a Critique of Zionism*, Ithaca Press, (London, 1975).

Godrey and Monica Wilson, *Analysis of Social Change*, Cambridge, (London, 1945).

E.C. Wolf, *Peasant Wars in the Twentieth Century*, Faber and Faber, (London, 1971).

ZED PRESS

ZED is a new socialist publishing house dedicated to creating an international forum on Third World issues. Our books fill critical gaps in the information available on five main areas: Imperialism and Revolution, Women in the Third World, the Middle East, Africa, and Asia. If you wish to be kept informed of forthcoming titles, please write to:

ZED PRESS
57 Caledonian Road, London, N.1.

MALCOLM CALDWELL — THE WEALTH OF SOME NATIONS

A provocative introductory text, the first to relate the Third World food shortage to the Western energy crisis. Caldwell explains the equations which underly 'protein imperialism' and examines the extent of the Western lifestyle's dependence on cheap raw materials imported from the Third World. He traces this exploitative relationship historically and out-lines its implications: for the West, overdevelopment, parasitism, excess tertiarisation; for the Third World, underdevelopment, corruption and malnutrition.

The author details the agricultural, ecological and industrial policies of the revolutionary Third World governments. He argues that as more and more countries work towards self-reliance and seize control of their own resources, the West will be forced to drastically restructure its economy. The return to the land, de-industrialisation and care of the environment will become the pre-requisites of survival.

This book, covering both the scientific and the political aspects of food and energy production, is an ideal introduction to the subject for first year students in several disciplines.

Please order direct from: ZED PRESS
57 Caledonian Road,
London, N.1.

Price: Hb £5.00   US $10.00
      Pb £3.00   US $ 6.00

DAN NABUDERE
— THE POLITICAL ECONOMY OF IMPERIALISM

This book is a major contribution to the body of political theory from
Africa. The author, a Ugandan professor at the University of Dar-es-Salam,
has produced a complete history of Western economic power. Nabudere's
detailed coverage of the growth of capitalism, from the mediaeval mercantile system through the industrial revolution to the present hegemony of
finance capital, makes this work an ideal textbook and a vital introduction
to the dialectics of world domination. Basing himself rigourously on Marx
and Lenin, he shows how the characteristics of the external expansion
of the main capitalist powers have changed with the evolution of their
internal contradictions. His analysis follows the repercussions of these
changes in the rest of the world.

With startling clarity Professor Nabudere exposes the process whereby
the economies of colonies and neo-colonies were first destroyed, then
re-structured to boost Western profits. Throughout the author stresses
that Imperialism is a necessary feature of Capitalism's struggle to contain
its own crisis. *The Political Economy of Imperialism* is not a book which
explains only how the modern world economic system came into being;
the author's elaborate survey of contemporary financial institutions,
economic theories and power politics gives it the added quality of
offering a firm basis for understanding the future.

Please order direct from: ZED PRESS
                                  57 Caledonian Road,
                                  London, N.1.

Price: Hb £7.75
      US $15.00   Publ. October 1977

NZULA — A PEOPLE'S HISTORY OF AFRICA IN THE 1920's

This is the history of Africa as seen by a black African intellectual of the 1920's. Nzula, one of the first black revolutionary leaders, was forced to leave South Africa, and was brought to Moscow by the Comintern. There he established the African Studies Institute and campaigned on behalf of his people.

His book, written in exile, documents the consistent and direct oppression of Africans by their colonisers, the forcible exploitation of land and people in Western, Central and Southern Africa. Nzula has a unique knowledge of his people's aspirations: he deals extensively with the growth of the rural opposition, the rise of the peasant movements and the rebellions of early trade unionists.

This is one of the earliest heroes writing on Africa's long struggle for political and economic independence. His work provides us with a remarkable interpretation of the process of colonisation, from someone who lived through it.

Pre-publication orders direct to: ZED PRESS
            57 Caledonian Road,
            London, N.1.

Expected price: Hb £6.00 US $12.00
       Pb Africa only $6.00

BELINDA PROBERT — THE NORTHERN IRELAND CRISIS

The complexity of the Northern Ireland question is notorious. It is, therefore, a joy to read a study which brings a remarkable clarity to bear on the baffling confusion of forces behind recent events. Belinda Probert has focused on the core of the problem, the failure of Irish capital to develop autonomously. Around this issue she has gathered the ideological and political factors which divide Irish society and propel it into violent conflict.

Her book traces the breakdown of the old alliance between the Orange orders and the Unionist party and shows it as the collapse of a system of patronage established in the course of a previous penetration of the Irish economy by foreign capital.

Ireland's tragedy is the tragedy of a working class searching for its real enemies. Its political evolution can only be understood in the light of Irish underdevelopment and the changing role of British Imperialism. Ms. Probert's book allows us to grasp the nub of a conflict which will remain at the forefront of British politics.

Pre-publication orders direct to: ZED PRESS
                                 57 Caledonian Road,
                                 London, N.1.

Expected price: Hb £6.00 US $12.00
               Pb £3.00 US $ 6.00

VICTOR KIERNAN — AMERICA THE IMPERIAL RECORD

The imperial expansion of the United States has a long history, most of it shrouded in ideology. The nation that set itself up by proclaiming liberty and free trade in 1789 has in fact consistently resorted to imperialist tactics to secure its own economic well-being.

Victor Kiernan's book follows American foreign policy from the independence of the original thirteen colonies to the Vietnam war, and carefully demolishes the myths that have disguised the imperial progress. The author shows how the early white settlers colonised the North American continent, destroyed the native Indian population and fought a civil war to unite the nation under the hegemony of industrial interests. He outlines the United States' challenge to Britain and Europe in Japan and China in the middle of the 19th century, the war with Spain and the penetration of Latin America. Kiernan reveals the intensification of America's imperial projects in the 20th century and the bid for world domination which underlay the US's role as financer of the two World Wars. His book is a unique account of the rise of an empire which has always presented a particularly hypocritical view of itself to the world.

Pre-publication orders direct to: ZED PRESS
                                      57 Caledonian Road,
                                      London, N.1.

Expected price: Hb £6.00 US $12.00
                    Pb £3.00 US $ 6.00

CLAUDE AKE — REVOLUTIONARY PRESSURES IN AFRICA

Ake deals with those internal conflicts and contradictions within African societies which are today leading rapidly towards revolution. He argues that the necessity and possibility of revolution stem from:
— The material base of the societies and their inadequate economic growth.
— The dominance of the single party state subject to recurrent military coups.
— The class structure of societies politically dominated by a ruling comprador class.

This is an important work of theory which complements Nabudere's work: *Political Economy of Imperialism*. While Nabudere focuses on the growth of external imperialist pressures, Ake is concerned with domestic structures which make revolution inevitable.

Pre-publication orders direct to: ZED PRESS,
57 Caledonian Road,
London, N.1.

Expected price: Hb £6.00 US $12.00
Pb Africa only $6.00

DAVE ELLIOTT — IMPERIALISM AND UNDERDEVELOP-MENT: ORIGINS OF MILITARY RULE IN THAILAND

The author sets out to describe in Marxist terms a country and a mode of production very different to the classical Western models on which Marxist political economy was based.

After an introduction to the Marxist approach, Dave Elliott succintly picks out the key factors of Thai economic and social organisation, factors which are typical of the Asiatic mode of production. In clear sequence he isolates the most important aspects of pre-capitalist economic life in the East: the role of the state, the nature and division of property and resources, the importance of irrigation and its relationship to class formation, and the stable produce which holds the structure together, rice.

Dave Elliott's book follows the Thai transition from pre-capitalist modes of production to underdeveloped forms of Capitalistm into the present day. The second half describes the historical evolution of Thai society exposed to the onslaughts of foreign capitalist. The growth of modern Thailand, (one of the few countries of Asia and Africa not directly colonised by the Western powers), is mapped out. The reorganisation of the state and its adaptation to Western influence is closely followed, providing a full account of the political figures, parties and forces which have shaped it. The central issues of contemporary Thai society emerge very naturally from Elliott's account; the divisions within the bourgeoisie, the economic positions of the proletariat and the peasantry, and the role of the despotic ruling class fall neatly into place.

The book closes with an analysis of new social and economic forces and a description of the events and figures which dominate Thailand today.

Pre-publication orders from: ZED PRESS,
57 Caledonian Road,
London, N.1.

Expected price: Hb £7.75 US $15.50
Pb US only $6.00